RACE ON THE MOVE

Stanford Studies in

COMPARATIVE RACE AND ETHNICITY

RACE ON THE MOVE

Brazilian Migrants and the

Global Reconstruction of Race

Tiffany D. Joseph

Stanford University Press
Stanford, California

Stanford University Press
Stanford, California

Printed in the United States of America on acid-free, archival-quality paper

Library of Congress Cataloging-in-Publication Data

Joseph, Tiffany D., author.
   Race on the move : Brazilian migrants and the global reconstruction of race /
Tiffany D. Joseph.
      pages cm. — (Stanford studies in comparative race and ethnicity)
   Includes bibliographical references and index.
   ISBN 978-0-8047-9220-2 (cloth : alk. paper)
   ISBN 978-0-8047-9435-0 (pbk. : alk. paper)
   1. Brazilians—Race identity—United States. 2. Return migrants—Brazil—
Governador Valadares—Attitudes. 3. Race—Cross-cultural studies. 4. Ethnicity—
Cross-cultural studies. 5. Brazil—Race relations. 6. United States—Race relations.
7. Brazil—Emigration and immigration—Social aspects. 8. United States—
Emigration and immigration—Social aspects. I. Title. II. Series: Stanford studies
in comparative race and ethnicity.
E184.B68J67 2015
305.800981—dc23
                                                                    2014030848

ISBN 978-0-8047-9439-8 (electronic)

To the Valadarenses, who are making Brazil and America every day

In loving memory of Zondra Joseph and James Rogers, whose joyous and enduring spirit in the face of adversity continues to inspire me every day

CONTENTS

MAP, FIGURES, TABLES, AND PHOTOS

PHOTOS

ACKNOWLEDGMENTS

There is an African proverb that says it takes a village to raise a child; the same could be said for becoming a scholar. Throughout my personal and professional life, I have been incredibly fortunate to encounter people who have encouraged me on my journey. An international, multilingual project of this scope would not have been possible without a village of supporters, rallying behind me every step of the way—from my first conception of this study to the finished product. Immense gratitude goes to my primary mentors at the University of Michigan (UM), Sarah Burgard, James House, James Jackson, and Alford Young Jr., for their tireless patience, constant support, and ample feedback at every stage. Thank you so much for pushing me to go deeper analytically and believing that I could accomplish this huge scholarly endeavor. I admire and look to you as role models for the type of scholar, teacher, and mentor I want to be. Other UM faculty, staff, and administrators I wish to acknowledge for their assistance and having an open door for me over the years are: Elizabeth Armstrong, Phil Bowman, Sueann Caulfield, Mark Chesler, Douglas Keasel, Karyn Lacy, Jeannie Loughry, Karin Martin, Debby Mitchell, Silvia Pedraza, Patricia Preston, and Karen Spirl. I offer special thanks as well to my former UM colleagues, with whom I shared many triumphs and challenges on our way to becoming independent researchers: Rosalyn Campbell, Amy Cooter, A. Kilolo Harris Evans, David Flores, Kristie Ford, Ivy Forsythe-Brown, Marco Garrido, Lloyd Grieger, Angel Harris, Laura Hirshfield, Kristen Hopewell, Maria Johnson, Zakiya Luna, Kristine Molina, Stephanie Osbakken, Rachel Quinn, Latasha Robinson, Grace Saunders, Jessi Streib, and Jeannie Thrall.

During my time at Harvard University as a Robert Wood Johnson Foundation (RWJF) Health Policy Scholar, various faculty in Boston took time to read and comment extensively on earlier versions of this work. I am very grateful to: Margarita Alegría, Larry Bobo, Susan Eckstein, Jennifer Hochschild, James Ito-Adler, and Peggy Levitt. Peggy merits additional recognition for being an exceptional mentor to me over the years; she saw this project come full circle, even Skyping with me while I was conducting the research in Governador Valadares (GV). I also thank other Boston faculty who met with me to discuss the project at various stages: Silvia Dominguez, Mary-Jo Good, Michèle Lamont, Rosalyn Negrón, Mary Ruggie, Saher Selod, Eduardo Siqueira, Jocelyn Viterna, Mary Waters, and David Williams. My participation in Harvard's Transnational Studies Initiative and the Sociology Department's workshops offered additional opportunities to present my research and to meet former and current graduate students who helped me learn the lay of the land: Asad Asad, Monica Bell, Deirdre Bloom, Kreg Steven Brown, Anthony Jack, Jeremy Levine, Sanjay Pinto, Cassi Pittman, Tracey Shollenberger, Chana Teeger, and Jessica Tollette.

My new extended scholarly family, gained through RWJF, deserves special mention for engaging me in conversations about this project while I began a new project on health care access for Brazilian immigrants in Boston: Christopher Bail, Wendy Cadge, Alan Cohen, Cybelle Fox, Daniel Gillion, Alice Goffman, Benjamin Hertzberg, Sage Kochavi, Laura López-Sanders, Neale Mahoney, Jamila Michener, Francisco Pedraza, David Pellow, Dianne Pinderhughes, Rashawn Ray, Rubén Rumbaut, Michael Sauder, Katherine Swartz, Van Tran, Robert Vargas, and Celeste Watkins-Hayes. Christopher Bonastia gets extra special thanks for his willingness to learn more about Brazil by reviewing early drafts of the manuscript.

I must also thank my current colleagues in the Sociology Department at Stony Brook University: Rebekah Burroway, Kathleen Fallon, Kenneth Feldman, Crystal Fleming, Norman Goodman, Michael Kimmel, Daniel Levy, Catherine Marrone, Timothy Moran, Oyeronke Oyewumi, Ian Roxborough,

Michael Schwartz, Carrie Shandra, John Shandra, and Arnout van de Rijt. Your enthusiasm about this book gave me the last wind I needed to get it done! Patricia Bremer, Wanda Vega, and Sharon Worksman, thanks for your smiles and enduring patience whenever I had administrative questions; the department would not work without you. Other Stony Brook faculty and staff also deserve special mention for ensuring that I took writing breaks by inviting me to social events: Abena Absare, Nerissa Balce, Lena Burgos-LaFuente, Lisa Diedrich, Victoria Hesford, Rachel Kidman, Tia Palermo, Joseph Pierce, Javier Uriarte, and Gilda Zwerman.

Conducting research in GV would not have been possible without the support of numerous Brazilian scholars and institutions. I thank Letícia Marteleto and Solange Simões, native Mineiros, for introducing me to GV early in my academic career. Our discussions of my scholarly interest in comparatively exploring race in Brazil and the United States planted the seeds that became the basis for this book. They also provided essential research connections at the Federal University of Minas Gerais (UFMG) and the University of Rio Doce, including Sueli Siqueira, Neuza Aguilar, Antonio Augusto Prates, Otavio Dulci, and Weber Soares. Without Sueli's assistance, my first month in GV would have been extremely difficult. I am grateful to her for welcoming me into her home and family and for introducing me to invaluable research contacts and to my transcriptionists, Sandra Nicoli, Neuza Santos, and Simone de Oliveira. The staff at the Centro de Informação Apoio e Amparo á Família e ao Trabalhador no Exterior (CIAAT) and Consagrarte were also gracious and receptive as I learned more about GV's multifaceted ties to the United States. I feel especially blessed to have made wonderful lifelong friends in GV, including Sandra Ferreira de Araujo and Sandra Nicoli, who made GV a home away from home for me. I am especially appreciative to the Valadarenses who were willing to be interviewed for the project and to share their migration stories with me. I am humbled by your resilience, and I have been changed for the better by your presence in my life. To my fellow 2007–2008 Fulbrighters and other foreign friends I made in Brazil, our *bate papos* about the vast differences between the United States and Brazil helped me better contextualize my surroundings in light of this project. Thanks to Erika Edwards, Shayna Harris, Kelly Richardson, Gaye Russell, Noé de la Sancha, Sara Tartof, and the Sparks family for your curiosity and for listening.

There were also numerous U.S. scholars who provided guidance, reviewed drafts of my work, and met with me at conferences regarding this project. I am very thankful for their time: Elijah Anderson, Stanley Bailey, H. Russell Bernard, Eduardo Bonilla-Silva, Letícia Braga, Giovanni Burgos, Erika Busse, Ginetta Candelario, G. Reginald Daniel, Tyrone Forman, Tanya Golash-Boza, Antonio Guimarães, Nadia Kim, Mary Clare Lennon, Alan Marcus, Maxine Margolis, Helen Marrow, Judith McDonnell, Graziella Morães da Silva, Aldon Morris, Kerry Ann Rockquemore, Wendy Roth, Sandra Susan Smith, Edward Telles, Vilna Bashi Treitler, and Frederick Wherry. To Helen, Nadia, Tanya, and Wendy, thanks for sharing your insights on the book publication process and academia, and for being accessible and excellent scholars that I truly admire. I am also thankful to fellow junior scholars Orly Clergé, Juanita Garcia, Mosi Ifatunji, Elizabeth Hordge-Freeman, Onoso Imoagene, Jennifer Jones, Chinyere Osuji, Tianna Paschel, and Silvia Zamora, whose work on race and migration in the Americas inspires me. I have gained so much from our conversations over the years and look forward to many more in the future.

This project would not have been possible without funding from many sources: the Department of State/Institute of International Education (IIE) Fulbright Program, the Ford Foundation Predoctoral Fellowship Program, the Mellon Mays Undergraduate Fellowship Program, the National Science Foundation, the Sociologists without Borders-Brazil Summer Fellowship, the Woodrow Wilson Foundation, and the University of Michigan. Over the years, I have presented this work domestically and internationally at many professional meetings and academic institutions: the American Sociological Association, the Association of Black Sociologists, the Eastern Sociological Association, the International Sociological Association, the Latin American Studies Association, Brown University, Harvard University, PUC-Minas Gerais, Stanford University, Stony Brook University, the University of Michigan, the University of Texas-Austin, Universidade Federal do Rio de Janeiro, Universidade Vale do Rio Doce-Governador Valadares, Wellesley College, Winston Salem State University, and Phillips Academy-Andover. The insightful comments I received helped me to better articulate the relevance of this research. Special thanks also goes to Tony Claudino and his IIE colleagues for helping me fully recognize the value of international cultural exchange, which this project epitomizes. I truly appreciate the work you all do to make the Fulbright program a success.

To Kate Wahl, Tim Roberts, Janet Mowery, and other staff at Stanford University Press, thank you for making this process as seamless as possible. Kate, you are a legend, and I am so honored to have worked with you on this book! So many scholars that I admire sang your praises, and I can now sing them too. I also have to thank the reviewers, whose comments helped me transform the original manuscript into this polished book. To my Stony Brook undergraduate research assistants, Ligaya Rebolos and Shannon Sunny, I appreciate your dedication and patience in helping me prepare the final product. To James Massol and Satya Stainton, your close review of earlier drafts allowed me to further refine my ideas; thank you so much.

More personally, I first thank God for giving me the courage, strength, and energy to make it through this and other endeavors throughout my life. Next, I thank my parents, N. L. and Sarah Joseph, for their unconditional love, nurturing, and support, which allowed me to believe that anything is possible. Thanks for cultivating my intellectual curiosity from a young age and for being brave enough to let me fully pursue my ambition wherever it has taken me: from Memphis to Andover to Providence to Ann Arbor to Brazil and everywhere else I have been. Just as I am fortunate to have the encouragement of my parents, this journey would have not possible without my extended family—the Josephs and Cashs—and dear family friends such as the Griffin, Harris, Matthews, and Turner families; I am thankful for your prayers, phone calls, emails, and cards over the years. Special thanks goes to the Sherman and Copeland families, relatives who made Michigan feel like home during my time in Ann Arbor. Along the way, I have also had transformational teachers in and out of the classroom who pushed me further intellectually than I sometimes thought I could go. I would not be where I am today without them: Lou Bernieri, James Campbell, Anani Dzidzienyo, Bobby Edwards, Gregory Elliott, Joyce Foster, Linda Griffith, José Itzigsohn, Joy James, Mary Jane Lewis, Suzanne Oboler, Temba and Vuyelwa Maqubela, James Rogers (RIP), Christopher Shaw, Shirley Shipp, Hilary Silver, Ruth Simmons, Susan Smulyan, Becky Sykes, and Valerie Wilson. The examples you have set inspired me to become a scholar who uses research and education to create the positive social change I would like to see in the world. I hope I can make a lifelong impression on my students just as you have on me. I am also grateful for faithful and incredible friends whom I consider family: the Bourne family, the Flores family, the Garrido family, the

Harris Evans family, the Yannello family, Brookes Brown, Sandra Cruz, Tom Cruz, Rosedel Davies-Adewebi, Michelle Glasgow, Anna Hidalgo, Jennifer Jackson, Tammy Kotniansky, Amy Krentzman, Eduardo Piña, Nancy Sankaran, Gita Sjahrir, Tulani Thaw, and Mary Ziegler. No matter what was going on in their lives, they asked me how this project was going and motivated me. I also thank countless others who have supported me in this endeavor.

RACE ON THE MOVE

INTRODUCTION

Migration and Racial Movement across Borders

> I had the following thinking: that we are all equal, for me, when
> I left [Brazil], we are all equal. And arriving there [in the U.S.], I
> saw that it's completely different. I had situations that to me were
> racism. And I got confused. The black neighborhood, the white
> neighborhood, this division; I couldn't believe I saw this. It was the
> same in my neighborhood, which was the Latino neighborhood,
> on the other side of the black neighborhood, and the other side of
> the white neighborhood. So, I had never dealt with this. I never
> imagined the U.S. would have this division, everyone together
> without mixing.
>
> Fernanda, age 30[1]

With light-brown skin, brown eyes, and long, slightly curly, dyed-blonde hair, Fernanda thought of herself as black. In her native Brazil, however, her fellow Brazilians racially classified her as white or sometimes as a light *morena*, a term generally ascribed to individuals with a racially mixed phenotype.[2] In the United States, others believed her to be Latino or Hispanic. Fernanda had migrated to the United States for one year, and during that time she quickly had to make sense of U.S. race relations. She was shocked and confused to observe racially segregated neighborhoods, overt discrimination, and general social division based on race in the United States.[3] Her experiences were not unique, and many migrants to the United States find the hyper-significance of race to be perplexing.[4] Fernanda is different from those who migrate permanently to the United States in that she eventually returned to Brazil. And as a consequence of living in the United States, she subconsciously acquired U.S. racial ideals and brought them back with her.[5]

Our increasingly connected world has altered contemporary migration, and advanced technology makes it easier for immigrants to lead transnational lives.[6] Today, immigrants can live both "here" in their host country and "there" in their country of origin. They can communicate with family and friends via phone and the Internet, send financial remittances, and travel back and forth if they are documented. As a result, transnational migration has significantly influenced culture, gender dynamics, and political practices in both immigrant-receiving and -sending communities.[7] Migration, and return migration in particular, also allows individuals to keep a racial foot in their host and home societies, providing a useful perspective for understanding how race in various countries is transformed via migrants on the move.[8] Through their movement across national borders, migrants come to view and interpret race differently, in turn reconstructing and giving new meaning to race. The social meanings attached to skin color, hair texture, and other physical features can vary dramatically from one country to the next. Migrants first negotiate race transnationally by relying on racial ideals from their country of origin to understand and interpret race in their host society as immigrants.[9] After their *return* migration, however, they draw on racial ideals acquired abroad to readapt to race at home.

I explore how this process unfolds by focusing on the experiences of return migrants from Governador Valadares (GV), which is a small Brazilian city in the state of Minas Gerais.[10] I examine how these migrants negotiated racial classification, stratification, and discrimination primarily as undocumented immigrants of color in the United States.[11] I then consider how their experiences abroad changed their assessment of broader racial dynamics in Brazil after returning. GV has been Brazil's largest immigrant-sending city to the United States for the past 60 years and is a "transnational social field," where people, culture, goods, and money flow continuously between there and Brazilian immigrant enclaves in the United States.[12] Nearly every resident has migrated or has relatives who have migrated to the United States, and many of these immigrants eventually return to GV after living and working abroad for many years.[13] This movement across national borders has dramatically altered the economy, culture, and social life of the city, so much so that some Brazilians call GV "Governador Vala-Dolares," a reference to U.S. dollars.[14]

RACIAL CONVERGENCE

Both the 2000 and 2010 United States censuses indicate that the Latino and multiracial populations are growing and that the percentage of non-Hispanic whites as a proportion of the entire population is decreasing.[15] Some U.S. scholars of race argue that the conventional black-white racial binary will shift in the wake of such changes.[16] Sociologist Eduardo Bonilla-Silva has posited that the United States will undergo a "Latin Americanization" of its race relations; an "honorary white" group of multiracial individuals will serve as a buffer between blacks and whites, which is a racial pattern more typical in Latin American countries.[17] In Brazil, by contrast, new racial quotas in universities that were implemented to increase Afro-Brazilian enrollment have made it necessary to specify who is black and would therefore benefit from the new policy.[18] Sociologist and journalist Ali Kamel argues that the quotas are an American import that will transform Brazil's black-*pardo*-white society into a black-white binary.[19] For many Brazilian and U.S. scholars, these demographic changes have produced shifts in racial discourse, signaling that the approach to race in both countries is starting to converge.[20]

Brazil and the United States have been the focus of numerous comparative and scholarly studies about race.[21] Both countries are former European colonies, had sizable Indigenous populations, and were the largest slaveholding societies in the Americas until the mid to late 1800s.[22] However, both Brazil and the United States took divergent paths incorporating the descendants of African slaves and other racial minority groups into their post-abolition societies. Brazil earned a global reputation as a racial paradise due to its fluid racial boundaries, absence of overtly racist legislation, and social acceptance of interracial (sexual and marital) relationships. Conversely, the United States developed rigidly defined racial categories and extensive *de jure* and *de facto* racist policies aimed at separating racial groups and emphasizing (white) racial purity.[23] Brazilian scholars have used the "racist" United States as a point of comparison for interpreting the seemingly more cordial relations between Brazilians of different skin tones.[24] Similarly, U.S. scholars have looked to Brazil to solve "the racial problem," presuming that fluid racial boundaries and friendly interracial relations meant that racism was non-existent.[25]

Thus, Brazil and the United States have been each other's "backyard social laboratories," using the other country as a benchmark for assessing race relations, inequality, and democracy in their respective societies. Much historical and contemporary research has revealed extensive differences in the construction of racial categories and interracial relations alongside the persistence of inequality between whites and nonwhites in both countries.[26] However, most of those studies have relied on survey data or qualitative accounts conducted among Brazilians located in Brazil or among Americans situated in the United States. Few studies of Brazilian immigrants in the United States or return migrants to Brazil have directly examined how race influences the migration experiences of Brazilians, or the racial impact of such movement in Brazilian cities like GV, which have significant U.S.-Brazil migration.

Incorporating migration as an analytical tool to compare race in the United States and Brazil is relevant because migration has influenced the development of race in each nation. The United States has always been a nation of immigrants, and its race relations and racial categories have shifted over time to accommodate various ethnic groups.[27] There were times in U.S. history when Irish, Italian, and Jewish immigrants were not socially white; U.S. blacks could classify as negro, mulatto, or quadroon; and Mexicans and South Asians were legally white.[28] In Brazil, the influx of immigrants was dominated by Portuguese colonizers and the importation of African slaves in the seventeenth to nineteenth centuries. Between World Wars I and II, immigrants arrived in large numbers from Italy, Spain, and Portugal since Brazil's migration policy favored "white" immigrants.[29] The Japanese also began migrating to Brazil for work during that same period, and currently Brazil has the largest Japanese-descended population outside of Japan.[30] Most recently, as Brazil has emerged as a global power, migration from neighboring Latin American countries has increased.[31] As in the United States, these waves of migration have influenced how ethnic groups are racialized relative to white, black, brown, and Indigenous Brazilians.

Migration has also informed various scholars' interpretation of U.S. race relations. Swedish social scientist Gunnar Myrdal spent significant time in the United States observing race relations before writing *The American Dilemma: The Negro Problem and American Democracy* in 1944.[32] In it, he argued that Jim Crow segregation and the discriminatory treatment of people of color was in direct contradiction to the nation's democratic principles. Renowned U.S. sociologist W. E. B. Du Bois, an African American who experienced significant racial discrimination in the United States, studied abroad in Germany from 1892 to 1894, where:

His skin color was no hindrance in his relations with Europeans, either strangers or those he came to know personally . . . Du Bois's studies in Germany were a profound influence on the course of his life's work. When he returned to the United States in 1894 he had been inspired by his academic and social experiences abroad . . . He brought some of this inspiration to the study of the black community.[33]

Du Bois's experiences abroad played a crucial role in his scholarship on U.S. race relations, which influenced his political views about black social advancement and resulted in *The Philadelphia Negro* in 1899 and *The Souls of Black Folk* in 1903.[34]

Given my comparative focus on Brazil, it is important to note the work of the distinguished Brazilian anthropologist Gilberto Freyre. As an undergraduate student at Baylor University in Waco, Texas, and then a graduate student of the anthropologist Franz Boas at Columbia University from 1917 to 1921, Freyre spent time in the American South, where he witnessed the systematic oppression of black Americans at the height of the eugenics movement. Upon completing his studies, Freyre returned to Brazil. He immediately noticed that relations between Brazilians of different colors were more cordial than those in the American South, and there was an absence of overtly racist legislation. He conceptualized the ideology of racial democracy (*Democracia racial*), theorizing that Brazilians could not be separated into distinct groups because of their racially mixed phenotypes.[35] For this reason, Freyre believed Brazilians could not be targets or perpetrators of the de jure and de facto racism he observed in the United States. He argued that racism and an explicit emphasis on having separate racial groups were antithetical to racial democracy, an ideology that became the basis for Brazilian national identity.[36] Freyre's U.S. migration significantly influenced his perception of Brazil as a racial utopia upon his return.

Though U.S. race relations have improved considerably since Freyre's time abroad, contemporary Brazilian immigrants still find race to be more socially divisive in the United States than in Brazil.[37] As natives of the only Portuguese colony in predominantly Spanish Latin America, Brazilians challenge existing U.S. ethno-racial categories.[38] Unlike Mexicans, Puerto Ricans, and Dominicans, who are the focus of most immigration and race studies, Brazilians are not Hispanic; they see themselves as culturally and socially distinct from Latinos in the United States and from other Latin Americans. Their unique social position complicates how scholars and the general population understand the relationship between skin color, race, ethnicity, and nationality in the changing ethno-racial landscape of the United States. In comparison with other Latin American immigrants, Brazilians have a more recent migration history, are more likely to be undocumented, have a higher level of education, and are much further geographically from their homeland, which means they need more resources to migrate and maintain transnational ties.[39] The rise of Brazil as a global market at the beginning of the twenty-first century has drawn more attention to issues of social inequality and poverty with regard to race, skin color, and class in the country.[40] Thus, exploring the migratory movement of people and racial ideals between both countries is timely, and it bridges various gaps between previous studies of Brazilian migrants, migration in general, and comparative studies of race in global contexts.

THE TRANSNATIONAL RACIAL OPTIC

The all-consuming importance of race in the United States has often confused immigrants as they construct new lives here. Racial assimilation is intrinsically a transnational process: migrants bring racial conceptions from their home country and use them to make sense of how race works in the United States. Furthermore, technology has enhanced their transnational ties, allowing continued contact with non-migrant relatives and temporary visits, which keep migrants racially connected to home. Exposure to U.S. racial ideals and sustaining transnational ties yield a merging of race "here" and "there" in migrants' minds, which influences how they *see* race as they go about their daily lives. The longer these immigrants remain in the United States, the more likely they are to become inculcated with and eventually acquire U.S. racial ideals, either consciously or subconsciously. For the returnees examined in this book, the United States became a new reference point for assessing Brazilian race relations post-migration. They used the racial ideals they were introduced to abroad to recalibrate their understanding of racial categories and inequality in Brazil. Emigration *and* return migration transformed how they viewed race abroad and at home, influencing their racial (re)adaptation in each society. This "transnational racial optic" is a lens through which migrants observe, negotiate, and interpret race by drawing simultaneously on transnationally formed racial conceptions from the host and home societies.[41]

The transnational racial optic is social-psychological and influenced by various factors that in turn shape migrants' racial conceptions. Among the returnees I interviewed in GV, I found that five factors shaped their perceptions of race in the United States during their migration and in Brazil after their return.[42] First, migrants received their initial racial socialization in Brazil that provided the foundation from which they would interpret broader social relations based on race and influenced their self-classifications, identity development, interpersonal relationships, and observations of inequality.[43] Their subsequent movement from Brazil to the United States required a racial resocialization that allowed them to adapt temporarily to race in their new society. But even as this movement and resocialization occurred, Brazil remained a racial reference point for them while they were in the United States.

Second, the differences in the social construction of race in the host and home countries had a profound impact on returnees' interpretation of race in each country. In the United States, migrants confronted the social construction of race as they searched for work and housing and adjusted to living in the country. The historical importance of race in the United States yielded experiences of overt discrimination that many returnees had not encountered in Brazil, causing them to reflect on differences between the significance of phenotype and ancestry in shaping social outcomes in the two countries.

Third, transnational ties between the host and home countries influenced migrants' knowledge about race at each stage of their migration. In GV, where people have been migrating to and from the United States for decades, potential migrants learn about racial issues in the United States from family and friends. This information helps prepare them for what they will likely encounter. Similarly, while living in the United States, migrants communicate additional information to non-migrant family and friends in GV, and non-migrants continue to transmit Brazilian racial ideals to migrants abroad. These exchanges create a cycle in which racial ideals from each country are simultaneously shared and merged, altering returnees' and non-migrants' views of race in each society.

Fourth, migrants' ethno-racial backgrounds—being or looking white, brown, or black—likely influence their experiences with racial classification and discrimination in both countries before, during, and after migration. While self-classification is important in shaping migrants' experiences and observations, how Americans and other Brazilians racialize these migrants, based on the racial classification norms of each society, demands consideration.[44] The consistency, or lack thereof, between self-classification and perceived external classification influences social treatment and outcomes.[45] Among Brazilian returnees, looking white, brown, or black—and the different standards for each in Brazil and the United States—was equally important for their interpretation of race in the two societies.

Finally, returning to the home country, either temporarily or permanently, increases the influence of the transnational racial optic on migrants' racial conceptions. The process of returning home re-exposes migrants to the norms of race relations in the place where they were initially socialized. Their exposure to race abroad, though, contributes to reshaping how migrants interpret the norms of their home country. Of course, a migrant's legal status in the host country affects his ability to return. A migrant with legal permanent residency (a "green card") or dual citizenship can travel more easily than the undocumented, who must usually return home permanently. The return migration can be viewed as a quintessential transnational tie that more explicitly connects the two countries. Sociologist Nancy Foner maintains that such individuals "truly have their feet in two societies . . . and [their] plans to return entail a continuing commitment to the norms, values, and aspirations of the home society."[46] Through their return, these migrants contribute to the cycle of transmitting U.S. racial ideals by sharing their experiences and observations with non-migrants, some of whom may later make the migration, thereby continuing the cycle and further shaping the transnational racial optic for others.

My expansion of the transnational optic to encompass race is grounded in a social psychological framework in which I highlight the role of the pre-migration context in shaping migrants' racial conceptions in the host country. That context lays the foundation for navigating the social world both at home and abroad. Furthermore, the other factors account more explicitly for how the social construction of race in a country, one's position within that racial hierarchy, and migration between countries form individuals' racial views.

Since the late 1990s, scholars have argued for a cognitive approach to study how individuals use perception, judgment, and memory to understand race and identity, and in particular how migration can yield transformations of these concepts.[47] Answering that call, sociologist Wendy Roth developed the concept of racial schemas, which she defines as "racial categories and the set of rules for what they mean, how they are ordered, and how to apply them to oneself and others."[48] She examines how migration influences the racial schemas of Dominican and Puerto Rican migrants in New York and demonstrates that these schemas travel across borders back to the Dominican Republic and Puerto Rico, where non-migrants use them to understand racial classification in those contexts.[49] Taking the racial schemas concept one step further, she suggests that individuals have schemas filed away in a mental "portfolio," where they can draw on them in different contexts, switching between the schemas they associate with different locales.

Roth's cognitive racial schemas are useful for understanding how individuals negotiate racial categories across national borders. The relevance of ethno-racial categories—particularly for government classification purposes—requires immigrants to determine what those categories mean, to whom they apply, and where immigrants fit within them in the United States. However, the racial schemas concept is narrow in two ways: first through its primary emphasis on racial classification, and second through Roth's implication that the racial schemas are separate. Although racial categories are crucial for understanding how individuals use physical characteristics to classify themselves and others, alone they do not explain how people make sense of the broader impacts of those categories—interpersonal relationships, experiences of discrimination, and segregation—in a society. In the context of transnational migration, it is likely that migrants hybridize racial schemas by combining elements from the host and home countries in their own minds. The transnational racial optic accounts for how this hybridization can occur.

The cognitive approach, as exemplified in Roth's work, provides a nuanced way to examine how individuals navigate race and ethnicity in multiple contexts. But it also focuses on how an individual's present setting shapes her views at one moment in time. Little attention has been devoted to how an individual's pre-migration socialization and positionality in the racial hierarchy shape her later cognitive negotiation of race. Before individuals can cognitively act on racial or other schemas, they must first recognize those schemas. The transnational racial optic allows individuals to see race broadly before they cognitively sort people into groups based on physical appearance or understand how groups are racially stratified in a society.

Finally, my goal in focusing on the transnational racial optic among return migrants is to elucidate our understanding of how racial ideals cross borders and potentially change a country's racial dynamics. Other scholars have explored the influence of migration on individuals' racial conceptions among immigrants in the United States and non-migrants in other countries.[50] Sociologists Nadia Kim and Sylvia Zamora demonstrate how the transnational flow of U.S. racial ideals through migrants, the media, U.S. policy, and U.S. military intervention can influence immigrants' (in receiving societies) and non-migrants' (in sending societies) understanding of U.S. racial categories and relations.[51] Although these studies are innovative in their exploration of non-migrants' exposure to U.S. racial ideals in the home country, their primary frame of reference is migrants who live and remain in the United States.

Few studies have analyzed the experiences of return migrants in migration studies, let alone studies that focus on race. Because migration to the United States has an enormous impact on the immigrants themselves, their return migration presents a unique set of challenges. Return migrants to the Caribbean, Brazil, and Asia experience disillusionment and a sense of "in-betweenness," as both the migrants and their home communities have changed while the migrants were away.[52] Discord in personal relationships between returnees and non-migrants may influence their interpretation of cultural and political practices. Similarly, this discord can affect returnees' perceptions of race, skin color, and the inequality and discrimination associated with the two.[53] Racial discord is evidence of the transnational racial optic at work, reshaping how migrants see race and interpret broader racial dynamics.

RESEARCHING RACE AND MIGRATION
IN GOVERNADOR VALADARES

To conduct this study, I lived in GV from September 2007 to October 2008. I am an African American woman with light-brown skin and extremely curly dark hair. Because I was not white and spoke proficient Portuguese, Brazilians rarely believed I was American and usually assumed I was parda or morena. My ability to pass for a Brazilian, and my position as a temporary migrant, although under very different circumstances, gave me significant pseudo-insider status and allowed me to establish community rapport. I attended church services, volunteered with emigrant service organizations, and frequented social events. I was also invited to do local television and newspaper interviews when Valadarenses learned more about my project.

I used a combination of purposive snowball and quota sampling to recruit people to interview. The personal relationships I developed with Valadarenses facilitated their willingness to participate and to introduce me to others. Also, I asked respondents at the end of each interview if they knew other returnees who would like to participate. I asked returnees if they had a non-migrant sibling or cousin I could also interview. To be eligible for the study, returnees had to be at least 18 years old, they must have lived in the United States for at least one year, and they must have returned from the United States within the past twenty years. I sought to interview an equal number of men and women, since men and women can experience race differently. I accounted for the different racial perceptions and experiences potential respondents, especially returnees, might have had in each country, based on their skin color, hair texture, and other physical features, by recruiting a phenotypically diverse sample.[54] I aimed to interview a relatively equal number of returnees who appeared to be white, pardo, or black by Brazilian standards.[55] To elicit a broad variety of views and experiences, I took all of these factors into consideration, as well as gender, age, and length of time in the United States.

I interviewed 73 Valadarenses—49 migrants and 24 non-migrants—in Brazilian Portuguese. The 49 returnees were on average 40 years old and had lived primarily in the northeastern United States for an average of eight years. Most had a high school education and came from working- and middle-class backgrounds before migrating. While living in the United States, most resided in Brazilian immigrant enclaves in Massachusetts, Connecticut, and New Jersey. They typically worked as housecleaners, dishwashers, and babysitters, or in construction, and had limited English proficiency. Though the majority arrived legally with tourist visas, most migrants became undocumented by overstaying their visas.[56] Men and women were equally represented, and most returned to GV between 2000 and early 2008. Before leaving GV, the majority (80 percent) intended to return. Half of the returnees migrated only once, in order to work or be reunited with family members in the United States.

To comparatively assess how U.S. migration influenced the returnees' racial conceptions, I also interviewed 24 non-migrants who were relatives of 24 returnees.[57] Within the non-migrant sample, there were 14 women and 10 men with an average age of 39. The majority had completed at least high school and worked in sales and business occupations, either as employees or as small-business owners. By interviewing the relatives of migrants, I was able to increase the demographic similarities between the return migrant and non-migrant samples such that the primary difference between the two groups was that one relative migrated and the other did not.

Since it was not possible to follow each returnee through his or her individual migration experience, I asked return migrants to reconstruct their perceptions of their lives before, during, and after migration.[58] For some, many years had passed since their return, and their probable inability to accurately recall all aspects of their migration experience is a limitation of this study. But because U.S. migration had had such a profound impact on returnees' lives, most were able to paint very clear and detailed pictures of their lives as migrants.[59] Having the comparison sample of 24 non-migrant relatives was also useful in validating the returnees' experiences.

In analyzing the interviews and my fieldnotes, I allowed respondents' racial conceptions to guide the process in order to minimize the influence of my U.S.-based and sociologically trained interpretation of the data. Using open-ended and closed-ended questions allowed me to assess consistency, patterns of evidence, and counterevidence in respondents' perceptions and to explore the nuanced ways that respondents negotiated race in Brazilian and U.S. society. Nevertheless, I would be remiss to not acknowledge my own intersecting and at times conflicting social identities as a highly educated, middle-class, and light-skinned African American woman conducting this research.[60] I was concerned about how these identities might influence my entry into the field, my ability to recruit and interview participants, and my evaluation of the data. As a native Southerner, I grew up in an environment where black and white racial and spatial boundaries were clearly defined and where there is a diversity of skin tones and hair textures evident among southern African Americans and among members of my own family. Though I have multiracial ancestry, I have always self-identified as black. Because of my previous travels to Latin America, however, I was aware I might not be considered black in Brazil.

Although my physical characteristics allowed me to pass as Brazilian, I was often reminded of my privileged outsider status when returnees shared graphic accounts of living in fear because of their undocumented status in the United States; some told me they did not like President George W. Bush. Some even treated me more positively and wanted to befriend me after I disclosed my U.S. nationality. Although it is possible my social identities influenced how Valadarenses answered my questions, I believe the respondents were candid and sincere in our interviews. Relative to Americans, I found that Brazilians could be brutally honest when sharing their personal or political opinions, not seeming to worry that they might offend others or not be politically correct. Therefore I do not think respondents were telling me what they thought I wanted to hear.[61]

The time frame in which I conducted this research is relevant for interpreting the findings that I present. I lived in Brazil and conducted interviews during the 2008 U.S. presidential campaign, which was also a period when the debate on racial quotas in Brazil was intensifying. Most Valadarenses were heavily invested in the U.S. candidates' views on immigration policy. Because many returnees had lived in the United States during Bill Clinton's presidency, Valadarenses highly favored Hillary Clinton early in the campaign. But as Barack Obama's candidacy gained momentum, Valadarenses (and Brazilians in general) became fascinated by the fact that he had a good chance of winning and becoming the country's first black president.[62] Although no respondents referred to Obama in their interviews, some Valadarenses initiated informal conversations about him, the campaign, and the upcoming election. Some Valadarenses also made references to the implementation of racial quotas in elite Brazilian federal universities, illustrating how racial discourse in Brazil was changing through the growing importance of racial classification. Respondents discussed media accounts of instances in which white Brazilian applicants felt they were denied admission to universities as a consequence of quota policies, which reserved 20 percent of the spaces for black, pardo, and Indigenous Brazilians. Conducting this study during that unique historical moment allowed me to capture insights into Brazilian and U.S. race relations that might not have been evident a few years earlier or later.

The chapters that follow take readers on a journey from Brazil to the United States and back again in order to explore the transnational racial optic at work among return migrants in GV. Examining the racial influence and consequences of migration in GV is important for understanding how race functions as a social construction at the micro and macro levels in and across countries. At the micro level, migration can alter individuals' perceptions of racial categories, the relationship between skin color and racial classification, and how such categorization can shape interpersonal interactions through stereotyping and discriminatory behavior. This can, in turn, shape macro-level processes, such as racial stratification and the implementation of race-based public policies, as shifts in micro-level perceptions can change racial attitudes and public opinions regarding racial inequality. While the findings of this study should not be considered generalizable beyond this group of individuals, their perceptions shed light on how racial ideals can travel back to immigrant-sending communities through migrants on the move across borders. The same process likely occurs in other cities around the globe as migrants return home. Thus these Valadarenses' perceptions may yield additional theories and insights into how migration can remake race in Brazil, the United States, and beyond.

THE BRAZILIAN TOWN
THAT UNCLE SAM BUILT

> It [migration] has been very good for Valadares [GV]. Excellent for
> two things: the economy and the development of the city, house
> construction. Many people who before [migrating] were poor and
> did not live comfortably. Today they have nice homes. They have
> comfort, they can educate their children. There are many parents
> who work there [in the U.S.] and leave their children behind. The
> person who goes there and returns comes back more sociable, with
> much better manners, [they're] much calmer than the Brazilians who
> stay here and more socially conscious [in recognizing] that what is
> public is for everyone. This they [migrants] learned there [in the
> U.S.]. So I think it improved the economy and social relations a lot.
>
> Lorena, age 40, returnee

Lorena's thoughts about the influence of U.S. migration on GV are pervasive in
the city. Though Lorena's perspective is mostly positive, I could also sense the
tension in her voice when she mentioned that some parents leave their children
behind, implying that migration had negative effects as well. Over the course of
my time in GV, I heard a range of comments about the benefits and disadvantages of migration ties between GV and the United States that indicated just
how intricately connected the two places are.[1] I still remember walking around
downtown GV on a Sunday evening after first settling in and being surprised
by the lack of activity on the streets. Typically, everything shuts down on Sun-

days for the Sabbath, and most evangelical Brazilians go to worship services in the evening. In search of a place to have dinner, I wandered into a small pizzeria—the one place that was open. I was the only customer and greeted the staff of three inside: the server—a short woman with light-brown skin similar to my own and shoulder-length loosely curled black hair; another server—a woman of average height with fairer skin, dark-brown eyes, and long, straight light-brown hair; and the cook—a tall fair-skinned man with hazel eyes and short, slightly curly light-brown hair. After taking my order, the second woman, Carla, engaged me in conversation.[2] Noticing my foreign-accented Portuguese, she asked where I was from. When I replied that I was American, Carla told me that her boss, the pizzeria owner, had lived in the United States for ten years where he worked in an Italian restaurant. When she told the cook—who was also her boyfriend and the owner's nephew—that I was American, he came over to speak with me while my pizza cooked. Ernesto, the cook, told me his uncle had returned to GV many years earlier; with the cooking skills he acquired working in the United States, he opened three pizzerias—the one we were currently in and two others in another part of the city. Each had been relatively successful, and Ernesto showed me framed pictures, newspaper clippings, and plaques on the wall honoring his uncle for his civic contributions. Carla also told me that she had relatives living in New York City and someday hoped to emigrate with Ernesto, if not there, then to Europe. I told them about my research and thanked them for sharing their insights with me. Over the course of my time in GV, I occasionally stopped in to the pizzeria to have a meal and chat with them.[3] It was through informal conversations like these that I began to understand the all-encompassing impact of U.S. migration in the city, which was not obvious at first glance.

Before arriving, I had heard stories about GV through my own transnational network of Brazilian and U.S. scholars. I had heard it was possible to exchange U.S. dollars on the street, that local stores and restaurants had American-English names, and that English was spoken widely in everyday conversation. I expected to see various aspects of "America" around me in GV. What I encountered was a beautiful small city with a distinctly rural aesthetic that was very different from the scenic tropical and beach-filled images of Rio de Janeiro that foreigners typically associate with Brazil. Aside from seeing a few shops with English-language names, I did not hear much English or see any U.S. dollars being exchanged in the streets. Since GV is not a major U.S. tourist destination, I encountered few Americans, and I realized I would have to rely on my Portuguese to better understand how GV became the town that "Tio [Uncle] Sam Built."[4] As I made GV my temporary home, I wondered how this city had become Brazil's largest emigrant-sending city to the United States. I also wanted to learn how the U.S. presence began in GV, how transnational ties had been maintained in both places, and how GV racial demographics differed from those in other parts of Brazil. In this chapter, I examine these themes to shed light on the social context that shaped Valadarenses' racial conceptions before migrating and influenced their development of the transnational racial optic throughout the migration experience.

FROM GOVERNADOR VALADARES TO VALA-DOLARES

Originally incorporated in 1937, GV is a young city with 260,000 residents, and it is located in the southeastern part of Minas Gerais in south central Brazil. Minas Gerais is completely landlocked and one of the largest states in Brazil (see map). Called Minas for short, it is Brazil's leading producer of coffee, milk, beef, and *cachaça*, which is the Brazilian rum used to make the national drink, *caipirinha*. Because of its rugged landscape, cattle farming is important for the state and national economy. The nearby Rio Doce (Sweet River) has reserves of amethyst, topaz, quartz, and mica, which attracted American mining companies in the 1940s. The city is also home to Ibituruna Peak, which has an elevation of 3,700 feet and attracts international visitors every year for its world championship paragliding competition.

Although GV is a city, it has a relaxed ambiance, perhaps due to its somewhat isolated location in the state.[5] The closest major Brazilian cities are the state capital of Belo Horizonte (193 miles to the west) and Rio de Janeiro (360 miles to the south). However, GV is the closest urban center to the smaller 22 Brazilian towns surrounding it.[6] Due to the slower pace of life in GV, I found Valadarenses to be friendlier and more personable than Brazilians I met in more populous parts of the country. This pace of life is also reflected in the *Sertaneja* music that is popular in GV, as well as in the traditional home-cooked food of Minas Gerais, called *comida caseira*, which is delicious but heavy.[7] Similar to the southern United States, the climate in GV is hot and humid, with temper-

Map. Brazil with Governador Valadares inset.

atures exceeding 100 degrees Fahrenheit in the summer and 80 degrees in the winter, which made me wonder why most Valadarenses migrate to the frigid northeastern United States.

Before I arrived, I repeatedly heard two things from non-GV Brazilians: (1) "Governador Valadares is so hot" and (2) "nearly the entire city is in the United States." Because so many Valadarenses have migrated to the United States, the city has become heavily dependent on financial remittances sent from migrants in the United States and elsewhere to sustain its economy; an estimated U.S.$2.4 billion was sent in 2004.[8] Money sent by Valadarenses abroad drives the local economy and is used to support family members, construct homes and other buildings, start businesses, and facilitate post-migration financial security and social mobility.[9] Formally recognizing its importance, the city government erected a plaque in a prominent plaza that pays homage to the sons and daughters of GV who have migrated and worked abroad, usually performing unskilled and low-wage labor in industrialized countries. While walking through this plaza on my way home one day, I stopped to read the plaque's inscription: "A tribute to the emigrants who do justice to dignified labor, they are heroes for their contribution to the development of Governador Valadares."[10] What stood out to me symbolically was that it was dedicated on July 4, 2006. July 4 is, of course, Independence Day in the United States, and in GV it is the annual "Day of the Emigrant," celebrated with a festival in the main city plaza, illustrating the significant tie that bonds GV and the United States.

The economic development spurred by GV-to-United States migration has increased land and property values in the region, leading to real estate and commercial development in the outskirts of the city. Nicolas, a 52-year-old non-migrant, agreed:

Valadares is a city that for many years has generated lots of money, since many of its people are in the U.S. and they send money, especially [for] civil construction. There is much development in this regard including real estate and land, [and] farms . . . have become really expensive because of this. Now that the dollar is lower, people are investing less here [in real estate], but civil construction in Valadares has not fallen as much because Brazil is picking up and there is internal investment. If the dollar gets higher again, then immigrants will send more money and civil construction will be better here than in the rest of the country.

However, one unintended consequence of economic remittances has been a rise in the cost of living for all Valadarenses; the local economy's dependence on the U.S. dollar has inflated prices for basic goods, cars, and homes.[11] Nicolas and other Valadarenses I interviewed made a direct link between GV's economic stability and the value of the U.S. dollar. Consequently, the local GV economy has an inverse relationship to Brazil's national economy: when the Brazilian currency is as strong as the U.S. dollar, GV's economy suffers. The socioeconomic context in which most Valadarenses learn about their city, its position within Brazil, and the larger world are heavily shaped by GV's migration ties to the United States.

Photo 1. House in GV built with U.S. remittances. Source: Author

THE ARRIVAL OF THE *AMERICANOS*

The history of the U.S. presence in GV dates back to the 1940s, when U.S. mining executives arrived to extract mica, a mineral in high demand during World War II for making radios.[12] At that time, the U.S. government also established an anti-malarial public health campaign in GV and the surrounding area.[13] The presence of white Americans and U.S.-funded public health projects were Valadarenses' first and primary exposure to the United States. Many were impressed by the high value of the U.S. dollar, which some Valadarenses received as payment for employment or services from the Americans. The modern appliances and cars that the Americans brought with them also represented the good life in America, which left an indelible mark on many Valadarenses. According to sociologist Sueli Siqueira, "[the U.S. dollar] which had a value much higher than Brazilian money, gave them [Valadarenses] an idea of the opulence and abundance of the place that the Americans came from . . . it gave them the vision of the USA as El Dorado."[14]

Valadarenses' encounters with Americans during the peak of the mining industry had already begun to shape their perceptions of the United States as a land of opportunity. But the lucrative mining industry that brought Americans to GV declined in the 1960s, and nearly all of these visitors eventually returned to the United States. One American family, the Simpsons, remained in GV. They established an English school and started a cultural exchange program that brought a small number of middle- and upper-class Valadarenses to the United States in the 1960s.[15] This initial group of temporary migrants established the social networks that would be influential in the large migration stream from GV that occurred in the 1980s at the onset of a huge Brazilian economic crisis.[16]

Although they left Brazil to pursue new opportunities, many Valadarenses planned to return before they had even left Brazil. Their desire to return home was strong motivation for migrants to remain socially and financially connected to GV during migration. Migrants from GV hoped to work for a few years and save enough money to return and buy a home or a car, or to start a business. This process has been referred to in the scholarship on Brazilian return migration as "*fazer a América*," which translates to "making America."[17] The goal of many Valadarenses has been to "make America" in Brazil after their U.S. migration. Of the returnees I interviewed, 39 of 49 went to the United States with the intent to return.

Photo 2. Former home of the Simpsons, the American family that stayed in GV and created the first U.S. cultural exchanges. This is now a museum. Source: Author

The goal of "making America" was what brought 34-year-old returnee Felipe to Massachusetts in 1999. Unable to get a tourist visa, Felipe traveled from Brazil to Mexico, where he crossed the border illegally:[18]

In Brazil ten years ago, Brazil was very difficult. I had a lot of trouble finding a job and I wanted something better for my family. I wanted to go there for a while, to earn money so I could return . . . I always had the desire to go to the U.S. So, [I went for] two reasons, necessity and also curiosity and desire to be in a different country.

Because Felipe initially left behind his wife and daughter, he sent back money to support them and eventually financed their trip to the United States a few years later. Although Felipe lived in fear of being deported, he felt he accomplished his financial goals. Before migrating, Felipe had worked in construction and at a hardware store, earning about $1,100 a month. When I interviewed him in 2007, Felipe told me his monthly income of about $8,700

Photo 3. Skyline of GV with condominium and apartment buildings constructed with U.S. remittances. Source: Author

(USD) came from owning a store and some rental properties that he acquired with money earned in the United States, where he worked at Dunkin' Donuts and as a carpenter.[19]

Through transnational ties and the accounts of returnees, potential migrants become aware of the challenges they may encounter after migrating. Many returnees described their perception of U.S. migration as a *sonho* (dream) that would make possible a better quality of life in Brazil. This idea was pervasive in GV. Luiz, a 43-year-old returnee who lived in New Jersey for three years, discussed having the *vontade*, or desire, to go to the United States like other Valadarenses:

The dream of every Mineiro and Valadarense is the dream of going to the U.S. Since the '80s and even today every Valadarense has the desire to go to the U.S., and I had the desire to go to the U.S., to learn about the U.S. And also to work and buy a house for my parents . . . So I got a one-year visa and stayed three years and four months and I liked it. America is very good.

The dream of making America in Brazil was evident not only among return-ees, but also among non-migrants. My conversation with Olivia, a 19-year-old non-migrant whose sister, Rafaela, migrated to Georgia, explained how economic factors in GV and Brazil stimulated Valadarenses' eventual decision to migrate:

I think the dream of the majority of people is to go to the U.S. because life here, it's very difficult. You can have a college degree, a high level of education, [but finding] work is difficult here. And there, the doors, even though we know we're immigrants and illegal, the opportunities for Brazilians there are better than here. That's why I think many dream of going there, making a life, buying a house, a car. And when they have accomplished this, which is important for me, they leave. That's what most Brazilians think [about U.S. migration].

Olivia's words demonstrate how deeply entrenched migration is in Valada-renses' psyches and how potential migrants weigh the economic and social costs and benefits of U.S. migration. Given their low wages, it is difficult for most Brazilians to achieve higher social mobility even with post-secondary education, which is a strong motivating factor for migrating.[20] For potential migrants from GV, the pursuit of the American Dream overshadows the immense challenges that being an undocumented and racialized immigrant pose. Valadarenses' portrayals of U.S. migration as a dream can be heard in casual conversations throughout the city. Despite the changing Brazilian and U.S. economies and more stringent immigration policies, migration is still considered a rite of passage that will allow Valadarenses to "make America" back home.[21] From a young age they hear that U.S. migration is the path to social mobility. Thus, transnational ties are only one of many influences on Valadarenses' socializa-tion and the transnational racial optic.

MAINTAINING TRANSNATIONAL LIVES ABROAD

While living in the United States, nearly all the returnees I interviewed com-municated weekly with loved ones about their experiences abroad. Through these conversations, they also kept up with life in GV. Migrants also talked about the difficulties of living undocumented, working long hours in physi-cally taxing jobs, experiencing racial and anti-immigrant discrimination, and saving enough money to achieve their financial goals after returning. Something that was especially difficult for migrants was dealing with the *saudades* (extreme longing for home), particularly for returnees who had left spouses or children behind. I spoke with 12 return migrants who obtained green cards or U.S. citizenship and could periodically visit Brazil while living in the United States to lessen this longing. But even those unable to return regularly communicated with family about their U.S. lives.

Although many returnees told everyone back home that their lives were going well, some admitted that they did not disclose all of their struggles. Because non-migrants sometimes hold high expectations for the quality of life that returnees should be living in GV post-migration, returnees feel pressure to be economically successful in the United States. This was the case for Carolina, who migrated twice with her husband. During their first migration, they left their four-month-old child behind in the care of relatives. The couple briefly returned to GV to get their child and then remigrated. During their second migration, the couple had another child, but their marriage did not last. Carolina recalled:

TJ: So, what did you talk about in your conversations with family back home?

CAROLINA: How much I missed everyone, friends, food, hanging out, the sun, everything.

TJ: And you talked about your life there and the experience of living there?

CAROLINA: For a while no, because I kept a lot from my dad. So I didn't like talking about my problems there, I always said I was [doing] well there. So I missed everything, but even though I said things were good, I preferred to keep my parents from knowing about everything.

TJ: And what types of things did you not want to talk about with your family?

CAROLINA: Me, my personal life, marital problems, problems I was having without my husband. I was alone and they [my parents] didn't know it was just me with the kids. So they thought we were together, and I wasn't with him. I was having financial problems, all kinds of difficulties, and they didn't know, I didn't tell them.

Although migrants tend to withhold the whole story from family back home, the information they do share helps non-migrants learn about some aspects of American life. Similarly, family and friends kept them informed about events at home. This transnational flow of information influences perspectives and social practices in both countries, where intrapersonal identities and interpersonal social relations are altered and reconfigured.[22] It is likely such ties have similarly influenced the racial socialization and pre-migration racial conceptions of Valadarenses.

RACIAL FORMATIONS IN GV AND BRAZIL

As in the United States, race in GV and throughout Brazil is associated with how social meaning is ascribed to individuals' physical features. Sociologists Michael Omi and Howard Winant developed a theory of racial formations to explain how the racial categories that are ascribed to human bodies with different skin tones and hair textures change over time.[23] Omi and Winant suggest that in many societies these racialized bodies have different positions in the social hierarchy. Though they conceptualized this theory of racial formations from a U.S.-oriented perspective, the theory applies in Brazil as well, where physical features also structure social relations and facilitate inequality. While the racial categories used to describe such phenotypes in Brazil are different from those used in the United States, the meanings of those categories have shifted over time and structured Brazilian society along color lines.[24]

Racial formations specific to GV are important to consider, just as the racial conceptions of the Valadarenses I interviewed reflect racial dynamics at national and local levels. While respondents compared racial issues in the United States and Brazil, it was clear that racial demographics and relations in GV shaped their interpretations of each country's national discourse. Various studies have examined national Brazilian racial formations, but none have extensively explored racial formations in GV. In informal conversations, I learned that Mineiros and Brazilians from other states consider Minas Gerais, where GV is located, to be more racially mixed than other states.[25] Generally speaking, Mineiros and Valadarenses have a phenotype that falls in the middle of the black-white continuum and is characteristic of the Brazilian phenotype: light- to medium-brown skin and straight black hair. Data from the 2010 Brazilian census confirm this perception: 56 percent of Valadarenses self-classified as pardo, in comparison with 43 percent of Brazilians nationally.[26] These differences in racial classification parallel the historical distribution of racial "groups" across the country. Northeastern Brazil, for instance, has a large black population owing to the importation of African slaves in the seventeenth century; southern

Brazil has a large white population owing to significant European migration after the two World Wars; and western Brazil is where much of the country's Indigenous population resides.[27] Some of the Valadarenses I interviewed even thought GV was less racist than other parts of the country because of the city's racially mixed population. These individuals believed that people of different "races" generally got along very well. One of them was Vinícius, a 31-year-old returnee who had lived in Florida:

I think that racism here [in GV] at least is more moderate because there are lots of different people here . . . I think that it is very mixed race. So that's why [I don't think] there's as much racism here as in other parts of the world or in Brazil. For example, in southern Brazil, Santa Catarina and places like that have more German influence. So there are many white people. I think there might be a little more racism than here for the fact that there's not much mixture.

Nevertheless, larger Brazilian racial discourse still shapes Valadarenses' racial conceptions. Valadarenses embrace racial democracy and Brazil's heritage as one in which race mixing created a population of individuals with a variety of skin tones that range from white to black and everything in between.[28] This was very different from the United States, where racial mixing was stigmatized and illegal until 1967. In GV and Brazil, having one drop of black blood did not automatically make a person black, unlike in the United States from the antebellum period to the late twentieth century.[29] Brazilians with multiracial ancestry could self-classify or be classified by others as nonblack or even white depending on their phenotype.

Thus, in the present day, racial boundaries are not rigidly defined, and racial classification is usually associated with a Brazilian's skin color rather than with ancestry. Because the population is mixed, most Brazilians see themselves as pardo rather than as black or white. The extent of *mestiçagem* (race mixing) in the country has led Brazilians and people from other countries to believe that Brazil has little racism and to perceive interracial relations as cordial. But while racial group membership is not meaningful for Brazilians, skin color does have social significance. "White" racial features such as fair skin, straight blonde hair, and light-colored eyes are idealized as the standard of beauty and sought after by many Brazilians; black racial features—dark skin and very curly hair—are devalued and negated.[30] Skin color also correlates strongly with social outcomes;

lighter Brazilians are more likely to be middle class, more highly educated, and healthier than darker Brazilians.[31]

Coincidentally, various studies have documented the extreme structural racial inequality between lighter and darker Brazilians in the midst of these supposedly cordial interpersonal relations.[32] Moreover, despite there being higher levels of interracial marriage and lower levels of residential segregation in Brazil than in the United States, anti-black jokes, stereotypes, and discrimination persist in Brazilian society.[33] Sociologist Edward Telles suggests that this seeming contradiction in Brazilian race relations can be explained using his theory of "vertical" and "horizontal" social relations.[34] Horizontal social relations are interpersonal relationships such as friendships, marriage, and residential proximity, while vertical relations refer to economic indicators, such as income, education, and wealth. Telles finds that although Brazil has cordial horizontal interracial relations, its vertical relations are strained: "While Brazil's fluid horizontal relations may be interpreted as signs of a less racist system, they also facilitate vertical racial domination."[35] Similar dynamics exist in GV, although extensive U.S. migration, and the American influence that comes with it, have influenced Valadarenses' racial conceptions in nuanced ways.

TRANSMISSION OF U.S. RACIAL FORMATIONS TO GV

Although Omi and Winant's racial formations theory is useful for understanding how the social construction of race in the United States and Brazil has changed over time, it does not account for how migration and transnational media dissemination can transform racial formations in immigrant- receiving and -sending societies. In GV, the information Valadarenses hear about U.S. race relations from migrants abroad and returnees provides non-migrants with another lens for making sense of race relations at home. This information helps prepare potential migrants for what they might encounter and for how their social positions will change. In general, migrants who are perceived as white and full citizens in Brazil are regarded as undocumented nonwhite immigrants in the United States.

Most Valadarenses told me they had heard things about race in the United States from returnees, immigrants still in the United States, or from the media. This was the case for 30 of the 49 returnees and 17 of the 24 non-migrants I spoke with. Valadarenses learned there was much racial segregation and animosity between black and white Americans, that black Americans lived in separate neighborhoods and had separate institutions by choice, that anti-immigrant sentiment was rampant, and that the United States was a country full of white people.[36] Oddly, almost no returnees or non-migrants had heard anything about Latinos or the Hispanic/Latino label, despite the growth of that group in recent years. Sérgio, a 46-year-old returnee, told me:

Even through the media, cinema, [and] television [in Brazil], we [Brazilians], I saw that skin color in the U.S. is well defined: You are white or black. If you are white, you have access to this area. If you are black, you have access to that area. It works, they [Americans] socialize, but each one [group] has his space.

Sérgio learned about the power of race to determine one's access to social spaces in the United States from the media, before leaving Brazil. My conversation with Camila, a 48-year-old returnee, revealed another common perception:

Before immigrating? We heard, we thought that the American was typically [someone with] white skin, but when we arrive there, it's different. We see that there are people from around the world, there is a big mixture. I always told my friends that the U.S.A. is a country of immigrants, it absorbs immigrants from the whole world. If you walk in the streets, you see an Indian person, a Chinese person, a Japanese person, an African person, a real African . . . you find all races and there is space for everyone. [I learned these things about race in the U.S.] from TV and films. Not only about there, but here too. TV shows only beautiful people, [with] light skin, blue or green eyes, straight hair, blonde [hair] just like here in Brazil. You see successful Americans, but there are Americans who go hungry. So, TV can give the wrong impression of any country.

These perceptions, which Camila acquired before leaving GV, shaped her and other Valadarenses' ideas about the racial dynamics they would encounter abroad. Sérgio and Camila's remarks demonstrate how intensely the media can shape individuals' perceptions of race in society. How Valadarenses interpret and perceive U.S. race relations does not develop in a vacuum; their views are informed by transnational communication and media forms that broadcast U.S. culture, including race relations, to GV.[37]

GV's reputation as the town that Tio Sam built symbolizes its transformation, first by the Americans who arrived in the 1940s and then through the ongoing back-and-forth migration that has occurred for the past 60 years. GV's long-time direct ties to the United States are especially important for assessing how transnational flows of money, culture, and information between the two have influenced the social environment where Valadarenses derive their primary interpretation of the social world, particularly as it relates to race. Together, national-level racial discourses in Brazil, along with the dissemination of U.S. racial ideals through transnational migration, communication, and media, have indelibly shaped Valadarenses' localized racial conceptions. All of these links primed potential migrants for what they would encounter in the United States before they migrated and are important for understanding how the transnational racial optic influenced their racial conceptions after their arrival.

DECIPHERING U.S. RACIAL CATEGORIES

When I arrived in the U.S., I went to get married at the courthouse and a woman [employee] there asked me for my color [racial classification]. I said "I am white." She said "no, you are not white, you are black." I said "then put black." So for me, white, parda, there, there isn't this category. There, you are black or white. I didn't question it because I know that in the U.S. [that's what] they use. Because in Brazil, there's white, there's moreno, you know? So it didn't offend me that much because there are people who would've felt offended [classifying as black]. I made a joke of it later: "for the American, I'm black."

Stephane, morena, age 43[1]

Despite having very light skin, brown eyes, and straight, medium-length dark-brown hair—features that are typically considered white in Brazil—Stephane was explicitly told she was black in the United States. She appeared to take this in stride and was not offended to be considered black because, in that particular moment, she accepted this norm of U.S. racial classification. At the same time, she was aware of the Brazilian racial categories pardo and moreno, which fell between what she perceived as the U.S. black-white binary. Given the different norms of racial classification in each country, Stephane had to renegotiate her interpretation of Brazilian racial categories to figure out her place in the U.S. ethno-racial hierarchy.[2] While migrating was a physically, psychologically, and financially taxing process, deciphering U.S. ethno-racial categories presented an additional challenge for the 49 migrants. They had to learn what these categories meant, how they differed from Brazilian categories, and, most important, which category applied to them. These migrants had traveled thousands of miles from the town that Tio Sam built, where they perceived racial categories to be fluid, to the land of Tio Sam himself, where racial categories were more fixed.

Wendy Roth refers to the racial categories and norms of racial classification in the United States and Latin America as "racial schemas."[3] For simplicity, I refer to the racial classification systems of each country as the U.S. or Brazilian racial schema. While the Brazilian racial schema is characterized by fluid categories and an emphasis on phenotype over ancestry, the U.S. racial schema has historically been based on rigid categories and an emphasis on ancestry and racial purity. I illustrate how Brazilian migrants incorporated aspects of the Brazilian racial schema to situate themselves within the U.S. racial schema. I compare their pre-migration and U.S. racial classifications and examine the factors that influenced those classifications.[4] These migrants' transnational negotiation of U.S. and Brazilian categories is relevant for understanding how ethno-racial boundaries are constructed, maintained, and internalized across borders and how individuals navigate those boundaries.

MIGRANTS' RACIAL CLASSIFICATIONS BEFORE MIGRATION AND IN THE UNITED STATES

Scholars have argued that people use multiple racial classification systems to determine their color category in Brazil.[5] One of those systems is census-based, in which people use government-formulated categories. Another is the "popular" or "open-ended" system, which consists of a range of categories for every imaginable skin color between black and white. Previous studies report that Brazilians use as many as 200 phrases to describe their *classificação racial*.[6] Similar racial classification systems are commonly used in other Latin American countries to represent the extensive mixture of European, African, and Indigenous ancestry in the population.[7] Given the more flexible norms and multiple systems of classification in the Brazilian racial schema, I assessed migrants' classifications in the two countries using both the self-ascribed census categories and the open-ended categories. In short, respondents' pre-migration norms for classification in Brazil were at odds with U.S. categories, particularly the white and black categories, which have different meanings in each country. Those differences had a profound impact on migrants' racial classification choices in Brazil and the United States.

Self-Ascribed Racial Classifications

I asked respondents how they self-classified using categories derived from the 2000 Brazilian and U.S. censuses. Their responses revealed that migrants' perceptions of themselves align with those of official state-designated categories. Various scholars argue that government census categories, which measure population demographics, have institutional power.[8] Political scientist Melissa Nobles argues that census categories structure race relations by creating ethnoracial boundaries between groups and influencing individuals' understanding of race and ethnicity:

Racial census categories are not self-evidently right or natural, because race itself is not . . . Census-taking is one of the institutional mechanisms by which racial boundaries are set . . . racial enumeration itself creates and advances concepts of race, bringing into being the racial reality that census officials presume is already there, waiting to be counted.[9]

In the United States and Brazil, the census has been used to indirectly align racial categories and hierarchies in a particular way, at times for social, economic, and political purposes that have influenced the development of racial schemas in both countries.

The first U.S. census was conducted in 1790 and has been conducted every ten years since that time. The ethno-racial categories have been different on every census to reflect the changing demography and particular discourses around racial classification. Rather than explicitly asking about race, the 1790 census asked about the number of free white males, free white females, other free persons, and slaves in American households. Such "categories" reflected the relevance of the institution of slavery, which had political implications for determining the number of representatives each congressional district could send to the nation's capital.[10] The term "race" would not be introduced until a hundred years later, when the nation was experiencing increased migration from Europe and Asia, and becoming an empire through westward expansion and the acquisition of Puerto Rico, the Philippines, and other territories. The

1890 census included the following racial categories: white, black, mulatto, qua-droon, octoroon, Chinese, Japanese, and Indian. Nearly 30 years after the Civil War, the four categories associated with black ancestry indicated a recognition of the racial mixture among America's African-descended population. Scien-tists seeking to confirm the degeneracy of racially mixed individuals advocated for the inclusion of the black, mulatto, quadroon, and octoroon categories in order to measure their inferior social outcomes as evidence that miscegenation (black-white especially) would be detrimental to the nation's advancement.[11] The growing popularity of the eugenics movement and increased migration from Europe in the early 1900s led to a heightened emphasis on white and par-ticularly Anglo-Saxon racial purity such that an all-inclusive "black" category was introduced in the 1930 census and has remained on the census since then.

Another major change, and perhaps most important for examining Bra-zilians' racial classification, occurred in 1970 when the U.S. Office of Man-agement and Budget introduced the "Hispanic" category in response to the increase in Latin American migration after the 1965 Immigration and Nation-ality Act. Upon its first appearance in the 1970 census, the term "Hispanic" was ascribed to all Spanish-speaking immigrants and individuals with Latin American ancestry, despite their diversity in national origin and racial back-ground.[12] However, many individuals of Latin American ancestry viewed the term as Eurocentric and not inclusive of all Latin Americans.[13] For instance, the Hispanic category does not include Portuguese-speaking Brazilians, who are Latin American but not Spanish-speaking. "Latino" has been the preferred category for most individuals of Latin American descent because it is similar to the term *Latinoamericano*, which is commonly used in Latin America.[14] But Latin American immigrants initially resisted both the Latino and Hispanic labels.[15] And for Brazilians, the Latino label is more appropriate, although they prefer to classify as "Brazilian."[16] Over time, U.S. racial discourse and the government's definitions of the Hispanic category have determined who is a member of this group. The inclusion of distinct racial categories in the census also created identification ambiguity for multiracial individuals until 2000, when they could acknowledge their racially mixed ancestry by self-classifying in more than one category.

Conversely, in Brazil, the pardo category has been used to signify Brazil-ians' racially mixed heritage, and it overlaps with the dissemination of racial democracy ideology. The first Brazilian census, in 1872, collected data based on color rather than race to focus on phenotype rather than racial ancestry.[17] This census also included the pardo category, which has been a part of the country's racial discourse since then. As in the United States, the collection of racial data in Brazil shifted, depending on the demographic and political changes the nation underwent. Like white Americans in the early 1900s, elite white Brazilians followed scientific debates about the degeneracy of mixed-race individuals and were concerned that Brazil's large multiracial population would stall the nation's development.

Rather than viewing racial mixing and intermarriage as a disadvantage, Brazilian elites thought it would lead to a whitening of the Brazilian population. They in fact saw it as the solution through which the superior European genes and phenotypes would dominate the inferior African and Indigenous elements in the population. Around the same time, Brazil received a large number of immigrants from European countries and barred immigration from Africa.[18] Shortly thereafter, Gilberto Freyre would develop the racial democracy ideology, hailing Brazil's mixed population as a new and improved race made better, rather than worse, by race mixing. These ideas would play a significant role in how census enumerators measured the color of the Brazilian population from then to the present.

Through migration, GV migrants encountered both Brazilian and U.S. census categories. Figure 1 shows their categorical classifications before migrating and their U.S. classifications.[19] Migrants could self-classify using one or more of the U.S. categories or as "other" if they believed the existing categories were not suitable.

Respondents' pre-migration and U.S. categorical self-classifications reveal a clear difference in white racial classification. While nearly half of the sample classified themselves as "white" before migrating, considerably fewer did so when they lived in the United States. Also in the United States, more of them classified themselves as "other." Most important, 19 migrants self-classified as "Hispanic/Latino," categories that do not exist in Brazil (see Table 1).[20]

These findings suggest that migrating to the United States and encountering different government-determined ethno-racial categories influenced how migrants viewed themselves. The shift from the white and pardo categories in Brazil to the Hispanic/Latino categories in the United States demonstrates

Panel A. Migrants' Race in Brazil Pre-Migration

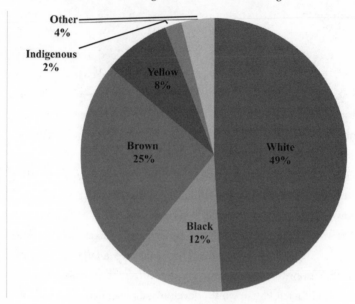

Panel B. Migrants' Race in the U.S.

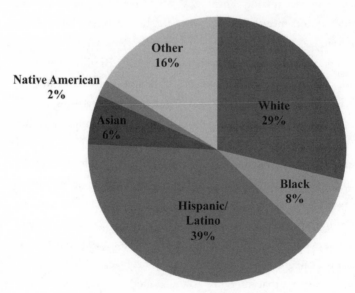

Figure 1. Migrants' Racial Self-Classifications before and during Migration

TABLE 1. MIGRANTS' RACIAL SELF-CLASSIFICATIONS PRE-MIGRATION
AND IN THE UNITED STATES

Race in Brazil before Migrating (Census Categories)	Race in U.S. (Census Categories)				
	White	Black	Hispanic/ Latino	Other*	Total
Branco (white)	11	0	10	3	24
	46%	0%	42%	12%	100%
Preto (black)	1	3	1	1	6
	17%	50%	17%	17%	101%**
Pardo (brown)	2	1	5	4	12
	17%	8%	42%	33%	100%
Outro (other)*	0	0	3	4	7
	0%	0%	43%	57%	100%
Total	14	4	19	12	49
	29%	8%	39%	25%	100%

Note: The dark-gray cells indicate where individuals classified themselves in the same categories in Brazil and the United States; light-gray cells show where migrants moved from one category to another. Perhaps most notably, nearly half of individuals who self-classified as white in Brazil pre-migration shifted to the Hispanic/Latino category in the United States.
*Includes categories such as Asian American (amarelo) and Native American (Indígena).
** Percentages are rounded to nearest integer, so total exceeds 100.

returnees' recognition of the social and cultural meanings attached to specific categories in each country. A few studies have explored categorical classification among Brazilian immigrants and found there is resistance to the Hispanic/ Latino categories.[21] However, most migrants in this study chose to self-classify as Hispanic/Latino despite having the option to classify as "other" or in more than one of the remaining categories (e.g., white and black).

Open-Ended Classifications

In Brazil, it is not uncommon for individuals to self-classify by "writing in" one of the more than 200 categories they feel best describes their color. Scholars of Brazilian race relations evaluate Brazilians' open-ended classifications to see how they align with Brazilian census categories.[22] I did the same for migrants to see if they would classify themselves as Latino or Hispanic in the absence of predetermined categories. Their open-ended classifications (shown in Table 2)

TABLE 2. MIGRANTS' OPEN-ENDED RACIAL SELF-CLASSIFICATIONS
IN THE UNITED STATES

Category	Number	Percent
Mixed/moreno	13	26
White	10	20
Black	5	10
Hispanic	4	8
Latino	2	4
Not white or black	2	4
Did not classify	2	4
White or yellow	1	2
White/Brazilian	1	2
Brazilian	1	2
Brazilian/Latina	1	2
Foreigner	1	2
Yellow	1	2
Lighter	1	2
Mulatta	1	2
Black Hispanic	1	2
Not white or black, foreigner	1	2
Mixed, yellow, white	1	2
Total	49	100

Note: Gray shading indicates migrants who classified themselves as Hispanic or Latino, either solely or in combination with another category.

tell a different story from the categorical classifications shown in Table 1: only 8 of 49 migrants classified themselves as Hispanic or Latino, either solely or in combination with another category.

Respondents' open-ended classifications in Brazil pre-migration also reveal a wide range of categories (see Table 3). Migrants' open-ended self-classifications were more fluid and aligned most closely with the white and

TABLE 3. MIGRANTS' OPEN-ENDED RACIAL SELF-CLASSIFICATIONS
IN BRAZIL PRE-MIGRATION

Category	Number	Percent
White	16	33
Moreno/a	14	29
Black	6	12
Parda	2	4
Mixed/neutral; not white or black	2	4
White/transparent	1	2
White Brazilian, a little darker	1	2
Light morena	1	2
Dark moreno	1	2
Mulatta	1	2
Somewhat yellow	1	2
Portuguese	1	2
Doesn't know how to classify	1	2
Normal: doesn't classify	1	2
Total	49	100

pardo Brazilian census categories. The difference between migrants' open-ended and categorical classifications shows that the words individuals use to classify themselves do not always match official designations, in which case they must figure out for themselves where they belong. This discrepancy explains why respondents did not classify as Latino or Hispanic when given the option to choose their own classification. But once asked to classify themselves using census categories, the majority did so. Most migrants retained their pre-migration open-ended classification but changed their categorical classification.

For Brazilian migrants who are not officially Hispanic but are racialized as Latino, their negotiation of U.S. census categories highlights differences between the Brazilian and U.S. racial schemas. The schemas help explain how phenotypically racially mixed individuals self-classify and are regarded by others in each country. While migrants could classify as pardo, moreno, or mixed in Brazil, in the United States there is no equivalent of the pardo category. Although these migrants could have classified in more than one racial category using U.S. categories, their choice *not to* indicates that they see themselves as racially mixed rather than as members of two different racial groups. This viewpoint overlaps with the Brazilian racial schema through both the legacy of racial democracy and the fluidity of racial boundaries, which makes it difficult for Brazilians to see themselves in mutually exclusive categories. Migration forged the two racial schemas for Brazilian migrants such that the transnational racial optic influenced their negotiation of open-ended and categorical classification in the two countries.

The Role of External Classification

Many migrants told me they negotiated U.S. categories by taking into account how Americans perceived them. Previous studies on identity formation, especially racial and ethnic identity, argue that externally ascribed classifications can shape a person's self-classification and identity claims.[23] Although Brazilian migrants could choose how to classify themselves while living abroad, external social forces such as government institutions and prevailing classification norms influenced their options.[24] Migrants' shifts from the white to the Hispanic/Latino category provide some evidence for this. Given that most migrants were undocumented, did not speak much English, and worked in low-wage jobs, their marginalized social position made it difficult for them to claim a classification that would be socially accepted in the United States. Stephane's earlier comments demonstrate this point. When she asserted to a government official that she was white, that official told her she was black by U.S. standards. The prevailing cultural norms for white classification in Brazil contradicted the criteria for whiteness in the United States.

I asked migrants how they believed Americans classified them while they were living in the United States. The majority (30 of 49) believed they were seen as Hispanic/Latino, with much smaller numbers answering white (8), black (5), and "other" (6). Only 19 migrants (39 percent) self-classified as Hispanic/Latino. Thus the way Americans classified migrants did not always overlap with how the migrants saw themselves. One migrant who said she was externally classified as Hispanic/Latino was Natália, who is very fair skinned and has blue eyes and shoulder-length straight red hair. Though she self-classified as white throughout her migration, she said she was externally perceived as Hispanic/Latino on the basis of the company she kept during her five years in Massachusetts:[25]

NATÁLIA: It was like this because if I was with Hispanics, they [Americans] thought
    I was Brazilian. If it was me and an American, they [Americans] would think I
    was Hispanic . . . When I was with the Portuguese, the Americans thought I was
    Portuguese; only the Portuguese could tell that I was Brazilian. And when I was
    with Brazilians, the Americans many times thought we [Brazilians] were Hispanics.
    So, I think that this irritated me because they [Americans] didn't perceive this
    [me as Brazilian]. It was worse when they sometimes thought I was French; not
    often, but some would ask if I was from some country in Europe, maybe because
    of my skin color [and] hair. My hair was very dark at that time. I remember it
    was very difficult to figure out where I belonged, my goodness!
TJ: Very difficult with the Brazilians, the Hispanics, the Americans, or everyone?
NATÁLIA: It was difficult for me in American society to figure out where I belonged.

Other migrants shared stories like Natália's. Table 4 shows that there was
considerable consistency between self-classification and external classification
for 16 migrants who self-classified as Hispanic/Latino, but less for those who
chose white and "other."

The factors that influenced migrants' open-ended racial classifications in
each country also demonstrate how perceived external classification shaped
their choices. After asking each migrant for his or her open-ended classification, I asked what factors they took into consideration. Respondents
could pick from seven choices: (1) skin color; (2) hair; (3) other physical
characteristics, such as eye color, shape of nose and mouth, etc.; (4) your
family, including parents and grandparents; (5) how other people see you;
(6) none/nothing; and (7) other. Skin color and hair were the most important factors for classification in both countries. However, migrants also reported that perceived external racial classification—how other people saw
them—had a stronger influence on their open-ended classifications in the
United States than it did in Brazil before migrating. This finding suggests
that Americans' perceptions of Brazilians as nonwhite likely influenced
migrants' shift from a white to a nonwhite racial self-classification while
living in the United States.

Vinícius, a 31-year-old migrant with medium-brown skin and short, slightly
curly black hair, was one migrant who felt that how Americans saw him influenced his self-classification. Because of his primarily Portuguese ancestry, Vinícius classified himself as white (categorical) and Portuguese (open-ended) before

TABLE 4. MIGRANTS' SELF- AND EXTERNAL RACIAL CLASSIFICATIONS
IN THE UNITED STATES

| | Perceived External Classification | | | | |
Self- Classification	White	Black	Hispanic/ Latino	Other*	Total
White	4	0	7	3	14
	29%	0%	50%	21%	100%
Black	0	4	0	0	4
	0%	100%	0%	0%	100%
Hispanic/Latino	1	1	16	1	19
	5%	5%	84%	5%	100%
Other	3	0	7	2	12
	25%	0%	58%	17%	100%
Total	8	5	30	6	49
	16%	10%	61%	12%	100%

* Includes Asian American and Native American classifications.
Note: The dark-gray cells indicate where individuals' self- and external racial classifications matched; light-gray cells show inconsistency between the two classifications.

migrating.[26] But his self-classification shifted when he migrated to Florida and realized he was perceived as Hispanic:

TJ: Did you at any time fill out a census or other form in the United States?
VINÍCIUS: I did.
TJ: And did these forms ask for your racial classification?
VINÍCIUS: They did.
TJ: Can you remember how you classified yourself on these forms?
VINÍCIUS: Hispanic.
TJ: What influenced your decision to classify this way?
VINÍCIUS: They [Americans] practically force it on you. They give you the option: there's white, there's black, Hispanic/Latino, [and] there's yellow. If I'm not mistaken, there are only four choices.

Vinícius classified himself as Hispanic because he realized that he was not white by U.S. standards. This was true for most other respondents as well.

Henrique was a migrant who classified as Latino because he thought that Americans might racialize him as Arab. With his light-brown skin, narrow facial features, and slightly curly dark hair, Henrique was afraid Americans would discriminate against him even more because of his appearance:

When I arrived there, I saw that, I was afraid not only because of my color, but I look more Arab, [like] people from the Middle East. And I was mistaken three times for being Moroccan there. My fear was more about looking Arab than anything else. I was fearful because Americans are very afraid of people from the Middle East and I have a more Arab than Brazilian appearance . . . I didn't know much about Moroccan culture. For Brazilians, Moroccans, Arabs, and Muslims are all the same. So I was afraid, three times I was mistaken for a terrorist . . . So I wore Latino clothing, baseball caps [that said] Puerto Rico. I would have my hair cut like Hispanics did . . . I learned Spanish.

Unlike most other Brazilian migrants I interviewed, Henrique wanted to blend in with Latinos so he would not be perceived as a possible terrorist. Though Middle Easterners are considered white by U.S. census enumerators, they are rarely racialized as white in the public consciousness because of national security concerns. Recognizing this, Henrique sought to distance himself from that group. Henrique lived in the United States from 2004 to 2007, during the height of the U.S. "War on Terror" and also when the 2005 London terrorist bombings occurred.[27] Within days of those bombings, a Brazilian immigrant from Minas Gerais, Jean Charles de Menezes, who had lived legally in London for three years was shot and killed by London police in the Stockwell subway station in a case of mistaken identity. The London authorities thought de Menezes was a suspect because of his "Muslim" appearance. Coincidentally, he lived in the same apartment building as one of the suspects. The controversial shooting garnered international media attention, and it is likely that Brazilian immigrants in various countries felt they could similarly be misidentified. These incidents probably influenced Henrique's decision to adopt a Latino identity rather than be mistaken for Middle Eastern in the United States.

Although migrants like Vinícius and Henrique classified predominantly as Hispanic/Latino using United States categories, and most migrants felt Americans perceived them as Hispanic/Latino, it is likely that people's external classifications of them had some influence on their self-classification choices. Although self-classification is important in identity formation, the responses

from my interviews indicate migrants may have self-classified as Hispanic/La-
tino because that is how they were externally perceived, rather than because
they had an attachment to these categories.[28]

The appropriation of ethno-racial categories by minorities in the United
States has been important for developing race and ethnic-based identities and
fostering mobilization around social, economic, and political issues. The Civil
Rights Movement was one response to this mobilization.[29] In the process, minorities created additional symbolic boundaries that determined who was and
was not a member of those groups. Brazilians, who have a shorter migration
history than Mexicans and other Latinos, are still trying to determine their
social positions and categories in the United States, especially with regard to
the Latino and Hispanic categories. Moreover, these labels have important political ramifications. Given the projected growth of the Latino population and
current immigration debates, Brazilians' identification with other Latinos, and
potentially with blacks and whites, may influence their eventual political mobilization and socioeconomic incorporation into U.S. society.

CONFUSION ABOUT U.S. CATEGORIES

Brazilian migrants thought Americans' desire to racially classify other people
reified distinctions between individuals and made them more conscious of
their "racial" group. U.S. ethno-racial categories themselves were also a source
of confusion. Many migrants mentioned being unsure of how to classify
themselves on applications for employment because none of the categories
seemed to apply to them. Trying to figure out which group they belonged to
was not easy given the different meanings of white and black in each country. Furthermore, they were proud of their Brazilian nationality and did not
consider themselves Hispanic.

White and Black in Brazil ≠ White and Black in the United States

Migrants recognized that being white or black in the United States was not the
same as in Brazil. Those who self-classified as white before immigrating felt
they could not automatically do so in this country. In the view of most of my
respondents, white in the United States referred to people with no racially mixed
ancestry who had very pale skin, blue eyes, and straight blonde hair. Although

obviously an oversimplification that would exclude many white Americans, this definition was expressed by many Valadarenses, one of whom was Renata, a 46-year-old migrant with brown skin who lived in New York for 16 years:

TJ: In the U.S., how did you see yourself in terms of skin color?

RENATA: Let me see. When I arrived, I felt that I wasn't as white, you see? I didn't think I was very white, I felt like I [my skin color] was yellow, like I said before. Because I saw that there were white and black people. I saw that the American would not see me as white, you see.

TJ: So, how did you see yourself?

RENATA: Yellow because I was not black. You [referring to me, TJ] to me, here in Brazil, you are mulatta. And you know what mulatta is for us [Brazilians]? It's a fine/thin nose. The black [nose] is bigger, you see. Like in Brooklyn [New York]. You, to us, are mulatta, your skin is light, you are not very black.

In this exchange, Renata clearly states her view of the differences between white and black racial classification in both countries: she defines white and black classification in Brazil based on what they are not in the United States. Because she perceives the white racial category as more exclusive in the United States, she self-classified as yellow when asked for her open-ended classification.[30] Renata believed that yellow was the category that best described her skin tone because she felt it referred to individuals who are not completely white, but have mixed ancestry. Renata used the Brazilian racial schema to figure out her classification in the United States. She used a Brazilian category for her open-ended classification and simultaneously self-classified as Hispanic/Latino when provided with U.S. categories. She used the transnational racial optic to situate herself. Interestingly, earlier in our interview Renata admitted to classifying herself as white on a census when she first arrived in the United States. But she eventually learned that she was not white in this country and adopted a nonwhite classification for the remainder of her stay.

Hardly any of the migrants I interviewed, not even those who classified themselves as white in Brazil, matched Renata's limited description of whiteness in the United States. They recognized that being white in Brazil, where a person can have racially mixed (especially black-white) ancestry and still be white, was not the same as being white in the United States, where similar ancestry has historically excluded an individual from white racial classification.[31]

However, recent research indicates that the white racial category is becoming less rigid owing to projected demographic shifts.[32] Nevertheless, recent immigration debates and the racialization of immigration as a "Latino" issue have emphasized the ethno-racial and national "otherness" of Latinos.[33] Furthermore, since Americans think of Brazil as a nonwhite country, self-classifying "white" Brazilians are not seen as white in the United States after revealing their Brazilian nationality, demonstrating low English proficiency, or speaking English with an accent.[34] Most migrants felt the white racial category did not apply to them during their time in the United States.

Like other migrants, Renata also recognized that the black categories in the United States and Brazil are different. To make her point, she discussed why I am not black in Brazil, even though she and I both recognize that I am considered black in the United States. Applying the Brazilian racial schema, Renata used my skin color and nose shape as physical markers to categorize me as mulatta in Brazil. Because she lived in New York City, she used Brooklyn, a predominantly black borough, as her point of reference for what is black in the United States. Renata did not see me as black in either country, because I do not have dark skin and a broad nose.

Renata was not the only respondent to refer to me when talking about race. Often migrants used my physical features to determine their own classification, to describe their family or friends, or to compare Americans and Brazilians. From their prior exposure to U.S. culture and their experience with the rigidity of U.S. racial classification, the migrants presumed that being American was synonymous with being racially white. For them, real Americans were white, which is another reason why they felt they could not classify themselves as white. Thus migrants' presumptions about the relationship between white racial classification and U.S. nationality influenced their own self-classifications.

Negative Perceptions of Hispanics

Migrants also learned about the social position of Hispanics and Latinos in the United States through the media and their own interactions with these groups.[35] Although the Hispanic category is listed on the U.S. census and on other forms, some Brazilians initially resisted classifying themselves as such because they were reluctant to identify with a group they perceived to be marginalized. This is one reason it has been difficult to get an accurate official count of the Brazilian population in this country.[36] Henrique, the 27-year-old "Arab-looking" migrant, explained the negative stereotypes of Hispanics:

The Latino in the U.S., [people from] other countries in the U.S., they have a lot of problems there. We see that many Americans don't like Mexicans; they [Americans] don't like other types [of nationalities]. So, between us Brazilians, we started, some Brazilians discriminated against Hispanics in the U.S. But on the other hand we knew that this [discrimination] happens to Brazilians there. So at times we were afraid. There was a certain indifference between Brazilians and Hispanics. Sometimes, we discriminated because there were so many Hispanics, and I think that the Hispanic is also responsible for a lot of the crime in the U.S.

Henrique perceived that Americans strongly disliked Hispanics, which was a primary reason migrants did not want to self-classify as Hispanic. Of the 30 migrants who recalled hearing anything about race in the United States before migrating, none recalled hearing anything about Latinos or Hispanics. Henrique and other migrants internalized their pervasive negative stereotypes about Hispanics after arriving.

Migrants also perceived differences in language, physical appearance, culture, and work ethic between themselves and Hispanics. Aside from the obvious difference in language, respondents commented that Hispanics had a different head shape, were lazy, dressed differently, spoke loudly, and liked to accessorize their cars. Juliana, a 41-year-old medium-brown-skinned morena who lived in Massachusetts, discussed the fact that Brazilians noticed Americans' unfavorable perception of Hispanics:

They [Americans] have a way of looking at each other and the Hispanics and we Brazilians recognize this. Because, for example, whoever looks at the Brazilian and at the Hispanic sees the difference in the shape of the head, the way they dress, many things, you understand? They are very different from us, I think they're different. And I felt like this, there are already so many Brazilian immigrants in the U.S., they [Americans have] this classification [Hispanic] there. Why? . . . Because in reality, we are not Hispanic, not because I have anything against them [Hispanics], but we're different to the point that we don't have a place, we are without a place there.

When asked more specifically about whether they would classify themselves as Latino and/or Hispanic, migrants demonstrated less resistance to the Latino category than to Hispanic. They recognized that Brazil is a part of Latin America, and they felt the category was appropriate. But despite being able to see themselves as Latino, they preferred to identify as Brazilian, which allowed them to distinguish themselves from Latinos. Ricardo, a 50-year-old migrant of self-acknowledged Italian ancestry, who has light-brown skin and short salt-and-pepper hair, was especially emphatic about this:

No, I would never classify [myself] in that category [Hispanic], I would always classify myself as Brazilian. [Although] I am classified by others as Latino or Hispanic. (pause) This is my thinking too, maybe as a Brazilian, I am not well informed correctly speaking, I could be Latino. Maybe, but I could be wrong that I can be classified as Latino, but not as Hispanic. I am not Puerto Rican, I am not Dominican, I am not from Costa Rica, I consider myself Brazilian and I will continue to consider myself Brazilian . . . So, will I say I am Hispanic? No, [but] I can be a Latino Brazilian, I am from Latin America, South America. But [I'm] Brazilian because it's the largest country in Latin America if I am not mistaken and the Portuguese language is spoken in various countries . . . So, I consider myself Brazilian, not Latino, that's my opinion.

Ricardo was not the only migrant to express a strong preference for the Latino category or to identify certain nationalities as Latino or Hispanic. Usually when I asked Brazilian migrants about differences between Latinos and Hispanics, respondents said that Mexicans, Puerto Ricans, and Dominicans were Hispanic, and that South Americans, including Argentines and Brazilians, were Latino. Tomás, another migrant, expressed similar sentiments:

TJ: You told me that other people there classified you as Hispanic/Latino. So, what do you think of this category? Would you classify [yourself] in these categories?

TOMÁS: There [the U.S.] has a lot of Hispanics. So, they [Americans] think everyone is an immigrant and Hispanic or Latino. That's what they say.

TJ: So, do you think there's a difference between Hispanics and Latinos? Or are they the same?

TOMÁS: No.

TJ: What's the difference for you?

TOMÁS: Oh, I don't know. I think the Latinos are more serious and work harder than the Hispanics.

TJ: For you, which nationalities represent Latinos and which are Hispanics?

TOMÁS: Hispanics are Mexicans, Hondurans. What else do they have there? Chileans?

TJ: And the Latinos?

TOMÁS: Latinos are Brazilians huh?

TJ: Are there others?

TOMÁS: The Argentines.

Tomás also said he believed that Brazilians, as Latinos, were harder working than Hispanics, invoking the negative stereotype of Hispanics as lazy, and placing Brazilians in a superior social position. Even though most migrants did not encounter many Mexicans, Brazilians recognized Mexicans as the quintessential Hispanic group that was the most marginalized in U.S. society.

This study is the first to show that Brazilian immigrants use a hierarchy of Latin American nationalities to determine which ones are Latino or Hispanic. Other studies of Brazilian immigrants have noted that they resist the Hispanic/Latino categories, yet do not suggest that their resistance is based on a rank-ordering of Latin American nationalities. My respondents classified perceived nonwhite Latin American ethnicities in the United States as Hispanic (e.g., Mexicans, Dominicans) and classified Latin American nationalities that are historically considered to be white as Latino (e.g., Argentines).[37] Brazilians ascribed the more favorable label to "white" Latinos and themselves (who are perceptibly white in comparison with nonwhite Latin American nationalities) and the less desirable label "Hispanic" to "nonwhites." It is possible that this racialized hierarchy of Latin American nationalities also influenced Brazilian migrants' perception of their own positionality while living in the United States.[38]

Brazilian Exceptionalism

In my interviews and informal conversations with Valadarenses and other Brazilians, I detected a strong sense of "Brazilian exceptionalism," which some Brazilians used to distinguish their country from Spanish Latin America.[39] There was a common perception that Brazil dominates Latin America, which may be because Brazil has the largest economy there, its currency is nearly as strong as the U.S. dollar, and it has undergone immense growth and poverty reduction in the last decade.[40] In addition, Brazil was not hit as severely as other countries by the 2008 global recession.[41] I often heard Brazilians make statements about how the Portuguese culture and language make Brazil unique in Latin America. This sense of exceptionalism has likely grown stronger since my time there, as Brazil hosted the 2014 FIFA World Cup and will host the 2016 Olympic Games, the first to be held in Latin America.

Many migrants also made distinctions between Brazilians and other Latinos/Hispanics in the United States that drew on the idea of Brazilian exceptionalism. Brazil's increasing global prominence may continue to heighten this notion of superiority among Brazilians as they compare themselves to other Latin Americans in the United States and Latin America. Anthropologist Maxine Margolis suggested that migrating Brazilians bring an attitude of superiority to the United States, "where feelings of cultural pride, of the uniqueness of the Brazilian 'race' are pronounced."[42] Lucas, a 43-year-old black migrant who lived in the United States for 10 years, spoke about this:

So, it's like this: I see that all the Brazilians in the U.S., they have a position that's somewhat arrogant in relation to our brothers from Latin America. I see [hear] racial expressions like this, some [Brazilians] saying "that Hispanic" as if the Hispanic is inferior to the Brazilian. I think that inside this arrogance, there's an identity maybe that's cultivated because we are the only country in Latin America [that] speaks Portuguese. So we maybe create this sensation of superiority in relation to other people. I see in a manner, generally speaking, there exists a racism and racial discrimination on the part of the Brazilian with the Hispanic or Hispanics.

Living in the United States among stigmatized Hispanics led migrants to put even more emphasis on their Brazilian nationality.[43] Well aware of Brazil's improving socioeconomic position around the world, some migrants believed they could receive better treatment from Americans if they identified themselves as Brazilian, even if they had been externally classified as Hispanic. This was true for Carolina, a 44-year-old morena:

I worked in a factory in Elizabeth [New Jersey] . . . , even though he [my co-worker] was American, he was of Hungarian descent. He was white, with really blonde hair and light eyes, and he never talked to me because he thought I was Hispanic. And he ignored me until he discovered that I was Brazilian. One day, I told him "I am not Hispanic." He asked if I was Colombian and I said "I am not Hispanic, I am Brazilian." That completely changed everything for me. He doesn't like, he did not like Hispanics. So, he came and showed me some photos of Rio de Janeiro, lots of things, and became my friend.

Because of her medium-brown skin and shoulder-length straight black hair, Carolina's co-worker assumed she was Colombian. Carolina not only said that she was Brazilian, she explicitly rejected the Hispanic label. Since her co-worker admitted to not liking Hispanics, Carolina probably used this social distancing from Hispanics to minimize her marginalization. This example demonstrates that some Americans might hold better views of Brazilians than of "other" Hispanics. Observing this behavior, Brazilian migrants internalized American ethnic stereotypes and hierarchies to "give themselves a leg up on the ethnic ladder."[44] Some migrants also expressed concern that negative perceptions of Hispanics would adversely influence Americans' treatment of Brazilians. These findings are consistent with other studies that examine Brazilian immigrants' assessment of the Hispanic/Latino categories.[45]

Although migrants learned about the Latino and Hispanic labels in the United States, the notion of Brazilian exceptionalism reflects their use of the transnational racial optic. Many Brazilians came to the United States with strong national pride and a deeply held belief that Brazil was distinct from the rest of Latin America. Moreover, recognition of the marginalized social position of Hispanics in the United States made these migrants more cognizant of their Brazilian identity, which they increasingly relied on to distance themselves from marginalized groups. Half of the migrants I interviewed rated "being Brazilian" as their most important social identity while living in the United States.[46] These individuals transnationally juxtaposed their privileged positionality as Brazilians in Latin America with the marginality of Hispanics in the United States to situate themselves above both the Latino and Hispanic categories while living in this country.

THE AMERICAN OBSESSION WITH RACIAL CLASSIFICATION

Many migrants puzzled over what they thought was Americans' obsession with racial classification and their desire to place people in distinct racial groups. Thiago, a 49-year-old very light skinned migrant, could have been perceived as white and classified that way. It was very clear to Thiago that there were distinct ethno-racial groups in the United States. He considered racial classification to be an American "thing," expressing astonishment at the importance of racial classification in the United States:

I think this [issue] of racial classification exists more in the U.S. I think it is theirs. Here in Brazil, we don't have this type of thing like in other countries. But there, they insist you're Latino, you're white, you're Hispanic. I don't understand this type of classification; it's one of their things.

For Luana, a 45-year-old migrant with light-brown skin and shoulder-length, slightly curly, dyed-blonde hair, living in the United States made her more cognizant of her racial classification:

Because of the importance they [Americans] give [to racial classification], you begin at times to question your race. Near where I lived, there was a weekly drawing to give away a breakfast. So, you fill out a form and it had name, birthdate, address, telephone, race, I don't know why. What I felt was that there [in the U.S.] race was more important than here in Brazil. That's why I gave more importance to race there, because I had to respond all the time to what race I was.

Luana was one of the few migrants to classify herself as white throughout her stay in the United States, although a librarian in North Carolina told her that she was Latino and not white. As one of the few respondents to live in the South, Luana had to renegotiate her classification in a context where the racial demographics were primarily white, black, and Latino (primarily Mexican).[47] Thus the Brazilian versus Mexican/Latino dynamic was even more relevant for Luana. Her experiences suggest a perception that migrants felt pressure from Americans to self-classify in one ethno-racial category, usually as nonwhite. The American obsession with racial classification made Luana more aware of racial distinctions. Luana and Thiago's comments provide clear examples of how these individuals developed an understanding that U.S. racial classification mattered more than it did in Brazil.

When asked about the importance of their own racial classifications in the United States, 17 migrants responded that their racial classification was important.[48] However, in comparison with the importance of their pre-migration racial classifications, only eight responded that their classification was important or very important; 41 said that it was not important. That nine participants reported their classification as not important in Brazil and then as important or very important in the United States suggests that being in the United States made these individuals more cognizant of the issue.

An overwhelming majority of migrants told me their racial classifications were not important to them in either country. However, cross-tabulations between their categorical racial classification and the importance they ascribed to racial classification tell a slightly different story. Four migrants who classified themselves as black before and after migration reported those classifications as important. For black migrants, awareness of their darker skin and experiences of discrimination in both countries shaped the importance of their racial classification in each place. Fernando, a 42-year-old black migrant with medium-brown skin who returned to GV in 2006 after being deported, said:

It [my racial classification] was important to me. Wherever I go, my [skin] color is important to me . . . I have to go where I can enter without problems. So, it [my classification] will be important all of my life.

Conversely, migrants who did not classify themselves as black in either country usually did not perceive their racial classifications as important. Their advantaged social positions—relative to black Brazilians—likely did not result in racial discrimination or mistreatment in Brazil before migrating. Classifying and being perceived as white or pardo made these classifications less important—that is, until these migrants arrived in the United States and were externally classified as nonwhite and Hispanic.

Brazilian migrants relied on the norms they learned in Brazil before migrating to decipher the racial classification system in the United States. Through migration, the transnational racial optic allowed them to juxtapose the U.S. and Brazilian racial schemas to develop an understanding of U.S. racial categories and discern which individuals were placed in those categories. Exposure to race in the United States presented a conflict for these individuals as they attempted to navigate life among the black, white, and Hispanic/Latino divide. Migrants were surprised to encounter the American obsession with racial classification, which highlighted for them the insignificance of Brazilian racial categories. However, while the majority of these migrants did not personally perceive their own racial classification to be important in the United States, the same was not true for others they encountered in their daily lives. Being racialized as Hispanic had a significant impact on these migrants, shaping their interactions with Americans in their communities and influencing their broader perceptions of U.S. race relations through the transnational racial optic.

CHAPTER 3

NAVIGATING THE U.S. RACIAL DIVIDE

> A black friend of mine in the U.S. told me this, I don't know if it's true because I didn't experience this, but he said, "A redneck, blue-eyed American is like a snake." He doesn't like anything that's different from him. He doesn't like blacks. He doesn't like Hispanics, He doesn't like anyone.
>
> Felipe, "white but not 100% white," age 34

Though migrants had a difficult time negotiating U.S. categories, making sense of the racial divide that structured the relationships between different ethno-racial groups was also a challenge. For Felipe, this divide was pervasive and profoundly affected his experiences as an immigrant. Felipe believed he experienced discrimination because of his undocumented status and appearance. Racialized as Hispanic, he told me earlier in the interview about an altercation he had with a white co-worker, who called him a "fucking Brazilian midget." According to Felipe, this co-worker was unhappy that so many Brazilian immigrants were working at his restaurant. My exploration of migrants' perceptions of U.S. race relations in this chapter sheds light on how migrants used the transnational racial optic to interpret broader racial dynamics, which is relevant for understanding how migrants interpret the U.S. ethno-racial hierarchy.

"SHARP AND VISIBLE" SOCIAL SEGREGATION

Migrants readily observed a lack of social harmony among Americans of different *colors*, which they felt contrasted sharply with life in Brazil, where residential segregation rates are lower and interracial marriage is more common.[1] Twenty-nine migrants explicitly mentioned being shocked by the extensive social segregation they observed in U.S. neighborhoods and between Americans, which Brazilian migrants themselves also experienced. Despite sometimes working alongside Latino immigrants, whites, and blacks, they interacted primarily with other Brazilians. Respondents felt that black-white segregation was the most visible; 32 perceived that black and white Americans did not like or marry each other and lived in separate communities.[2] While migrants recognized there were other groups besides blacks and whites in this country, the lack of black-white interracial relations was most noticeable. This was true for Eduardo, a 45-year-old white migrant with fair skin, dark-brown eyes, and short (balding), straight, dark-brown hair:

I think that in the U.S. there exists a very sharp and visible racial separation, as I've already said before . . . For example, this separation that exists, the black community there, I don't know if it's like this everywhere, but at least where I was, and the white community, they didn't mix. And here [in Brazil], no, here my neighbor is black. For me, it's great and there [in the U.S.], I think it's somewhat difficult to mix.

Eduardo's reference to accepting his black neighbor is indicative of his personal racial attitudes and the larger Brazilian discourse of being racially tolerant. In this example, the transnational racial optic facilitates Eduardo's perception that residential segregation in the United States is at odds with the greater social acceptance present in Brazilian race relations. Eduardo and other migrants also commented on interracial relationships and white Americans' general dislike of nonwhites.

Interracial Friendships and Marriage

Coming from GV, which they thought was more socially mixed than their U.S. communities, many migrants noticed a clear separation between black and white Americans. Juliana, a 41-year-old morena with light-brown skin and long straight black hair, said:

This is something I mentioned before, that I see there, a separation that we don't have a lot of here. You don't see many whites with black friends in the United States. It seems, there are exceptions, but generally, the [racial] groups are more separate.

Juliana felt that this separation made it difficult for her to develop friendly relationships with non-Brazilians where she lived in Massachusetts. Other migrants also reported that race affected their social interactions with Americans. Luana, a 45-year-old white migrant with olive skin and shoulder-length, wavy, dyed-blonde hair, reported similar difficulties living in North Carolina and Virginia with her white American boyfriend, whom she had met in GV a few years earlier.[3] Because her boyfriend interacted primarily with other white Americans, Luana and her boyfriend's social network included other whites, but excluded people of color:

LUANA: I used to spend time with a small group that I knew for certain I would not have, had I not been white. So even though I liked spending time with them, I thought that my race was important for them.

TJ: And why did you feel this way?

LUANA: Because it was expressed transparently: "I don't want a person of this color in my house, I won't accept a person of this color in my family, I would not date a person of this color, I wouldn't let my child marry someone of this color."

TJ: And generally what color?

LUANA: Generally black.

TJ: Were these people white?

LUANA: The group was.

TJ: And how did you feel when this happened, when they said these things?

LUANA: In the beginning, I tried protesting, but in time I decided not to make any more comments because I realized I could not change their opinions.

Because of Luana's appearance and her relationship with a white American, she was accepted by this group that openly opposed socializing with blacks. Their comments reflect the racist behavior that can occur in same-race interactions when other ethno-racial groups are not present.

Research on contemporary racial attitudes suggests that most white Americans do not express overtly racist opinions in multiracial settings.[4] Given that the United States has elected and reelected its first black (biracial) president, other studies suggest that many Americans now believe racism is less prevalent, though not nonexistent. Some also assume that race is no longer a barrier to success for people of color (especially blacks) and that the United States is now a color-blind or post-racial society.[5] However, in Luana's particular experience, it was clear that overtly racist attitudes may still be expressed in whites-only settings.

Eduardo, a white migrant, also discussed how being of a different racial group affected his friendships with black Americans in Florida and Connecticut:

It's very visible, the separation of communities, it's very clear. Even though I hung out with lots of blacks, I had [black] friends from [my] construction [job] . . . I went to visit them. And the first time I went, they said "no, don't come here, something could happen." I was like "what?" And I went one or two more times after that, and they really didn't want me to come again because it could be dangerous.

Although Eduardo did not say that he felt unsafe when visiting his black friends, he sensed that they did not want him in their community. Eduardo believed that his being white was the reason for his friends' ambivalence, since they were accustomed to black-white social segregation. Such segregation was not the norm for Eduardo before migrating. Thus he did not know what to make of his black friends' reluctance to see him, and it made him question their friendship.

The majority of migrants also believed that interracial romantic and marital relationships were less socially acceptable in the United States than in Brazil. Fernanda, a 30-year-old migrant, was one of the few who recalled not hearing anything about U.S. race relations before immigrating. She expressed shock upon seeing hardly any interracial couples during her time in Florida:

The most interesting thing here in Brazil [is that] a black marries a white. I did not see this at all in the United States. So this intrigued me a lot. Not one day did I see a black with a white person there. I didn't see it, I'm telling you like this, a normal person like us [Brazilians] walking in the street, a black and a white, I didn't see it.

Despite having light-brown skin and straight, dyed-blonde hair, Fernanda classified herself as black. She was the product of a black-white interracial marriage, and her immediate and extended family was racially mixed, with a variety of phenotypes. She likely drew on her familial experiences and belief that interracial marriage occurs frequently in Brazil to interpret black-white interracial relationships as happening less frequently in the United States.

Among Fernanda and other respondents, the lack of black-white relationships was more noticeable in this country, which is why respondents discussed them more explicitly. Although in the United States there are higher numbers of interracial relationships between whites and Asians and between whites and Latinos than between whites and blacks, migrants rarely mentioned observing those other interracial relationships.[6] The small Asian-descended population relative to other groups in both countries may have been another reason migrants overlooked Asian-white interracial relationships in the United States. The (presumed) prevalence of black-white relationships in Brazil before migrating was a barometer for assessing the lack of black-white relationships they saw while living in the United States.

Most were quick to say that Brazilian society was more socially integrated than the United States; 13 migrants mentioned believing there was extensive intermarriage between Brazilians of all colors, which they felt indicated social integration. This perception is widespread in Brazil.[7] Though black-white interracial marriage rates are higher in Brazil than in the United States, they are not as high as would be expected given Brazil's large African-descended population. Research has found that marriage between blacks and whites is less common than assumed, as browns (morenos/pardos) serve as a buffer group and marry blacks and whites.[8] Studies on Brazilians' partner preferences have also found that whites are the most desired marital partners, while black women are the least desired.[9] As socioeconomic status (SES) increases for blacks and browns, the likelihood that they will marry whites also increases.[10] Such trends demonstrate the contradiction between Brazilians' perceptions of black-white interracial marriage in Brazil and reality. The opinion of Stephane, the 43-year-old morena I introduced in Chapter 2, reflects this contradiction. Comparing interracial relationships in both countries, she said:

Look, we saw on the TV, in movies, newspapers, you have an idea, you know [about Brazilian race relations in the past]? That it was black and white. I thought like this, in that period, it was more conservative, black was only with black, white with white. They didn't mix, and with the passage of time, there was a change. I think that here in Brazil, clearly every place has prejudiced people, my dad for instance. My dad didn't like blacks. But he gave it a chance because at one time my sister married a black man. My dad almost died [over] this, but he had to suck it up. And my sister is extremely light [white]. So, you had that contrast with today, it's a super natural [very natural] thing. Like in the U.S., they didn't mix. Today this doesn't exist [in Brazil]. You see an artist or musician, a black man with a white woman, a player [athlete] with a white woman and vice versa. And that's everywhere. But in the U.S., I thought it was more prejudiced in this regard.

Stephane suggested that Brazilian attitudes on interracial marriage have shifted to be more positive because she now sees it "everywhere," which is a contrast from her younger years. Stephane talks about Brazilian race relations at a time (in the 1960s and 1970s) when the racial democracy ideology was supposedly more prevalent and popular in Brazilian racial discourse. Her perception is that, despite the prevalence of racial democracy, there was not as much racial mixing in Brazil, or at least not in Stephane's immediate social environment. The examples she gives of interracial marriage happening "everywhere" include black athletes and musicians who marry white women, suggesting that nonwhite Brazilians from a higher social status usually "marry up" racially. This practice overlaps with interracial marriage trends in the United States, where minorities in interracial marriages with whites tend to have a higher SES than minorities on average.[11] Overall, Stephane and other migrants sensed that race was a barrier to having interracial friendships or romantic relationships in the United States. Through the transnational racial optic, these migrants interpreted the frequency of those relationships in the United States using viewpoints that had been shaped by memories of their pre-migration lives in Brazil.

Racially Segregated Communities

Migrants also observed that a person's race or ethnicity influenced where they lived. Racial residential segregation has been extensive and enduring throughout U.S. history, and much research suggests that where one lives affects various social outcomes, including the quality of education and health, as well as wealth accumulation.[12] As mostly undocumented and racialized immigrants of color, migrants themselves experienced residential segregation and lived primarily in lower-income neighborhoods with other Brazilians and/or Latinos.[13] This experience was pivotal for Fernanda, who was appalled by the use of race to separate people:

So, I found this difference from there [U.S.] through [via] Brazil. It was the most difficult for me, I didn't agree with that [racial separation] and I still don't agree with that because this doesn't exist. For me, everyone, if I get cut and you get cut, we are the same [we all bleed]. It's just that there, I didn't see this [sameness], it's different. Everyone has his space. So, this was the most difficult part for me, this prejudice, the fact of having [separate] neighborhoods. This didn't exist for me [in Brazil], I never thought I'd see this. And in addition to the black race and white race there, there was also the Latino . . . The immigrant also, there was a form of racism because it determined [your] neighborhood [such that] a person would not rent a house to you because you're Latino. You don't have papers, so that's a form of prejudice too, not just because of [skin] color, ethnicity, or your race, [but] also being an illegal Brazilian in the country.

Fernanda spoke at length about her experience with residential segregation in the United States because she felt it "did not exist" for her in Brazil. Other migrants similarly reflected on residential segregation, mentioning that whites and blacks lived in separate neighborhoods of different qualities. Sérgio, a 46-year-old moreno, discussed his observations of white and black neighborhoods:

I observed this too, in Danbury [Connecticut], for example, there's an area that is predominantly white with the immigrants that mix the colors [races] there, but there's a part of the city dedicated [delegated] to the blacks. And these blacks that live in this area, they live off the government [welfare], they don't do much [work]. However, there are blacks that look for [a higher] quality of life, that try to study, that produce [contribute to society] who live in the white community like others without a problem. But the great majority of those blacks live in that ghetto. I had a brother that worked as a mechanic in that area. There were constant assault victims, confusion, and the police. So, it was very marginalized.

Sérgio lived for three years in Danbury, which has one of the largest Brazilian immigrant communities in the country. Though Danbury is predominantly white and has a small black population, Sérgio noticed that social class shaped blacks' residential options in the city. Migrants primarily discussed residential segregation as race-based, rather than class-based, indicating that race was more relevant than social class in neighborhood divisions.[14]

Migrants noticed that differences in the quality of white and black communities were indicative of racial residential segregation. They also compared these hyper-segregated neighborhoods to GV and Brazil, where they felt similar race-based segregation did not exist. The few studies exploring racial residential segregation in Brazil have found that it is significantly lower than in the United States, but that the intersection of social class and race does influence Brazilians' residential choices.[15] Since middle-class Brazilians are predominantly white, they tend to live in middle-class communities in the city center where there is more infrastructure (e.g., reliable electricity service, running water, sewage, public transportation); most of their neighbors resemble them, although there are also a smaller number of middle-class, nonwhite Brazilians residing in those neighborhoods. Nonwhites are much more likely than whites to reside outside the city center, many of them in poverty.[16] These characteristics of residential segregation were not mentioned by most migrants, and certainly not in Fernanda's comments. However, these respondents did observe that Brazilian neighborhoods were segregated by social class and noted that Brazilians of any color could live in middle- or upper-class neighborhoods if they had the money.

In GV, there has been no study of racial residential segregation. When I lived there I noticed that lighter Brazilians lived closer to the more expensive city center, while darker Brazilians lived in the poorer areas surrounding the city. Because my monthly living stipend was six times the Brazilian minimum wage, I lived in a nice apartment building close to the city center. All of my neighbors were white by Brazilian standards, yet the *empregada* (domestic helper) who cleaned and the security guard who monitored my building were black by U.S. and Brazilian standards. By virtue of being a U.S. researcher, most of my social connections were middle/upper class and white, while the *empregadas* in their middle-class homes were exclusively black by U.S. and Brazilian standards.[17] Whenever I visited friends in such apartment buildings, I emphasized my foreign-accented Portuguese and, at times, disclosed my American identity to the doormen to gain entry. I knew that, because of my appearance, the doormen would assume that I did not belong in those buildings. I personally experienced how race intersected with social class to facilitate what Brazilians would likely call class-based and Americans would likely call race-based residential segregation in GV. A black migrant named Letícia, who felt that race shapes blacks' residential options, provides more context for my observations:

So, at times, many times, there is prejudice. For example, if you go to the periphery [suburbs], in the periphery, it's funny, it seems like there are more blacks than whites and what are they [the blacks]? They are discriminated against because really many of them are involved in drugs.

For Letícia, despite there being a small number of blacks in GV, she noticed that they are overrepresented and isolated in the suburbs. She was the only migrant who referred to the residential isolation of blacks in GV or other parts of Brazil. Other migrants, such as Eduardo, highlighted the residential integration of black Brazilians because of its contrast with the hyper-segregation he had observed in the United States.

Historically, people of color (especially blacks of any social class) were denied the opportunity to live in white (middle-class) communities across the United States.[18] Despite the revocation of discriminatory housing laws, residential segregation has persisted, facilitated by informal housing covenants, discriminatory lending policies, and real estate racial steering. Studies suggest that neighborhood racial composition still influences white Americans' residential choices; white Americans simply do not want to live in the same neighborhoods as blacks.[19] In Brazil, however, institutional racism combined with extreme income inequality prevents many black Brazilians from living in middle-class neighborhoods in the absence of overtly racist housing laws.

There is a broad perception in Brazilian society that class inequality trumps racial inequality. Brazilians are more likely to think that blacks live in poorer neighborhoods because of their low SES, rather than that race-based structural conditions keep them in persistent poverty.[20] This perception makes it difficult for Brazilians—and specifically the migrants in this study—to recognize that racial residential segregation exists in Brazilian society. The societal importance of race in the United States served to make migrants more aware of race-based than class-based residential segregation in this country. It contrasted with the class-based segregation in Brazil, where it was not uncommon to see poor blacks, browns, and whites living in the same neighborhood. Through the transnational racial optic migrants noticed that U.S. neighborhoods were highly segregated by race and ethnicity regardless of social class. For them, in GV there was no such thing as black and white neighborhoods, but rather poor and wealthy neighborhoods.

Views of Other Ethno-Racial Groups

Migrants believed Americans' general ignorance made them more prone to dislike other ethnic and racial groups. Fifteen migrants mentioned feeling that Americans had very little knowledge of other ethno-racial groups in the United States or of people from other countries. Brazilians assumed that Americans, by virtue of being citizens of the world's most powerful country, would be more educated and know more about the world than the typical Brazilian. So Americans' lack of such knowledge surprised migrants, including Fabio, a 51-year-old white migrant:

There are some gracious people [Americans] and then you have the Americans . . . they don't want to know what's happening, they have no interest. "Where is Brazil? Oh, the capital of Buenos Aires." Tiffany, when I went to high school, I knew all the industries of the U.S., I knew where the largest producer of corn was, I could get the map of the U.S., the capitals of the U.S., the states, I knew all of that. I think that this is [general] knowledge and the American, to me, has no general knowledge. He knows his little world, that world of his is clearly the best. So, he doesn't need to know anything else, that's the impression I have of the ones I met and interacted with. Of course, you, [with] schooling, college, and university, are different, but the ones I interacted with, I interacted with waiters, painters, those types of people. And it's the same thing here, if I interact with waiters and painters, many of them don't have knowledge.

Owing to his undocumented status and lack of English proficiency, Fabio had to work low-wage jobs in dishwashing and construction, as a restaurant busboy, and as a street food vendor. The majority of Americans he came in contact with were co-workers in these fields who "don't have knowledge." Indeed, there are studies documenting Americans' ignorance of U.S. politics, foreign policy, and historical events, confirming Fabio's perceptions.[21]

Migrants also believed that Americans possessed even less knowledge about Brazil, and that the little that they knew was based on ill-informed stereotypes. Amanda, a white migrant, believed that those stereotypes influenced how Americans viewed her:[22]

AMANDA: Well, when you work, when you work, I don't know . . . Some people, they, they have no idea what kind of, what is Brazil. They think that, well, once a woman came to me and said the word, like monkeys. They think that Brazil is like a place, uh, like a forest. And they, . . . she said, "well, uh, Brazil is a very dangerous place, a lot of violence, a lot of tears." And another time, there was a guy, I was at his house to clean and he had um, a magnet, how do you call that thing that you put on the refrigerator, a magnet? And there was a, a butt, and then he said, there was written Rio de Janeiro, Brazil. And he said, "oh look, Brazil, Rio de Janeiro, yes Brazil, Carnaval, bumbum [butt]." (claps hands once

and laughs) So when they, I think when they talk about Brazil, they think about
sex. That's sad though.

TJ: And do you think any of this affected the way people perceived you because you
were Brazilian and how?

AMANDA: Yes. I think so because they [implied] . . . that was something that was bad
to me. But, sometimes they don't trust you the way they would trust you if you
were like a French person.

TJ: So do you think it was just that you were Brazilian or do you think it was nationality,
or do you think it was also the way you looked or that race was involved too?

AMANDA: Maybe, yes, the race. Yes. Because they think that if you were there [in
the U.S.] to work, you were poor and maybe if you were poor, you can, you want
to steal things.

Amanda makes the explicit connection between race, nationality, and being
an immigrant, which influenced the stereotypes of her and other Brazilians that
Americans she encountered had. She felt her employers were less likely to trust
her because of assumptions they made about nonwhite Brazilian immigrants.

Amanda and other migrants connected Americans' ignorance about Brazil with their dislike of other ethno-racial groups, particularly whites' feelings
toward nonwhites. For 27-year-old Henrique, this was difficult to make sense
of because he felt that Brazilians did not have similar prejudices against other
ethno-racial groups:[23]

One difference is that Brazil is known because it has many immigrants from different countries and everyone lives together in peace. In the U.S., there's this difference,
there's a big immigrant population there, and there's an indifference between different
parts of the U.S. We are very different, Americans and Brazilians, there's a difference.
Yes, here in Brazil, we have a lot of people from other countries, Japan, Portugal, Italy.
We have lots of them in Brazil, Chinese, Jews, in this sense. And in the U.S., there's
a difference in the sense that at times, there's a Jewish person that doesn't like a Hispanic, there's a Hispanic that doesn't like an American, a Puerto Rican that doesn't like
an American, the American doesn't like Puerto Rico.

For Henrique and other migrants, the notion that one American would
dislike another American because of race or skin color was shocking. They
referred repeatedly to the positive social interactions between Brazilians of all

colors, contrasting them with Americans, who seemed to have more strained interracial interactions.

Because of the racialized anti-immigrant sentiment they sensed among Americans toward Hispanic-looking individuals, migrants felt that Americans scrutinized and disliked them more. Felipe, whom I quoted at the beginning of this chapter, assumed that Americans think all foreigners are Hispanic:

There's a joke, I'll tell you a joke that a friend told me about an American going to Mars. If the American goes to Mars and encounters an "ET" [extraterrestrial/alien], he will go to ET and say "que pasa?" because he thinks everyone [every foreigner] in the U.S. is Mexican. He told me this, my friend that lived in the U.S. for 20 years. He said that the American thinks everyone is Hispanic. Everyone is a descendant of the Hispanic. So, he [the American] doesn't differentiate the Brazilian from the Hispanic. It's not important to him. One time I told an American, "I don't speak Spanish, I speak Portuguese." He said, "It's all the same shit."

Felipe's comments suggest that the country's changing ethno-racial demographics have influenced race relations in the United States. Historically, racial discourse has been centered on the relationship between blacks and whites. But the rapid growth of the Latino population, as well as concerns about national security since the terrorist attacks of September 11, 2001, have challenged traditional ethno-racial boundaries, bringing more attention to certain racial relationships, including those between whites and Latinos, Latinos and blacks, whites and Arabs, and Americans and foreigners. Because Brazilians are racialized as Hispanic and Latino, they are often treated as members of those groups, usually for the worse. For Felipe, the fact that white Americans do not recognize the ethnic or linguistic diversity of the Latino population further strains relationships between the groups, usually resulting in discrimination. Felipe's acquaintance's use of the word "shit" also implies disrespect for Spanish and Portuguese and the people who speak these languages.

The transnational racial optic made it easier for migrants to recognize that Americans' general ignorance of other ethno-racial groups facilitated animosity and mistreatment toward nonwhite and illegal-looking immigrants. Respondents painted a picture of Brazil in which Brazilians of all colors get along. Research suggests that there is minimal hostility between Brazilians, but that white Brazilians are the privileged group in interpersonal interactions.[24] However, because migrants perceived a lack of *overt* animosity between racial groups in Brazil, they also perceived the more visible problems between ethno-racial groups in the United States to be bigger. Migrants noted this difference from their pre-migration perceptions of Brazil.[25]

BLACK BRAZILIANS ARE POOR AND FRIENDLY, BUT BLACK AMERICANS ARE BEAUTIFUL AND RACIST

Before arriving, many migrants thought most Americans were white because whites were prevalent on U.S. television programming in Brazil. Migrants also assumed that most black Americans experienced significant hardship because of explicit racism. This was why 16 of 49 migrants told me they were shocked to encounter well-dressed black Americans who lived in nice homes, drove expensive cars, and were well educated. As a black sociologist, I was surprised to hear more than a few respondents discuss black Americans' upward social mobility and physical attractiveness. During my time in Brazil, I noted the vast structural disadvantages of black Brazilians and realized that black Brazilians' marginalized position shaped migrants' perceptions of black Americans. Thirty-one of the 49 migrants said that black Brazilians are thought of as poor, uneducated, and violent.[26] Although migrants praised black Americans' positive attributes, some singled out black Americans as self-segregating and racist toward other ethno-racial groups, especially whites.[27] This observation contrasted with migrants' views of black Brazilians as having harmonious social relationships with nonblack Brazilians. Migration merged these two different perceptions of blacks for migrants.[28] The transnational racial optic helped migrants interpret racial stratification in the United States and Brazil in relation to the social position of blacks in each country.

Before delving into migrants' views, I would like to emphasize that this is a relative comparison focusing solely on black Americans and black Brazilians. It does not fully account for these groups' social positions relative to the general U.S. and Brazilian populations. I also conducted these interviews before the election of President Barack Obama. Therefore migrants' perceptions were more likely shaped by their personal experiences in each country than by the 2008 U.S. presidential election.[29]

Finally, as an African American researcher and outsider, I was stunned to hear migrants' admiration of black Americans' positive attributes, yet at the same time express negative stereotypes about black Brazilians that were unnervingly similar to the ones I have heard ascribed to black Americans. Given my appearance and SES, it was clear that some migrants understood I am considered black in the United States while at the same time asserting that I was not black in Brazil. It is therefore possible that I became the physical embodiment of an accomplished black American for those I interviewed. These examples of how respondents viewed my race and ascribed positive attributes to me as a black American signify the transnational racial optic at work, not only for comparing black Americans and Brazilians, but also in how participants perceived my black/nonblack body and social status during the interview.

Black Americans as Physically Attractive

A number of migrants commented on the physical attractiveness of black Americans relative to black Brazilians, often describing black Americans as beautiful, well dressed, and put together. In my interview with Larissa, a 41-year-old yellow migrant,[30] she spoke about the beauty of the black Americans she interacted with in Newark, New Jersey:

LARISSA: In the U.S., I thought the darker the person, the better off they were. I thought this. It seemed to be better. I lived where there were a lot of blacks. I lived in Newark, everywhere that you went [especially] on Broad Street there were blacks. And they thought I was Hispanic.

TJ: So you said that you think it was better to be black?

LARISSA: It seemed like the blacks in that area, the women only dressed really pretty, so well put together on Broad [Street]. And I, my goodness, I was only cleaning houses and felt so ugly, and wow, those women were so well dressed. The majority [of people] I saw on Broad Street were dressed like that. Well taken care of, and the men too.

TJ: And why did you think this, more or less?

LARISSA: Because when I went to Broad Street, I saw mostly blacks, and the blacks there, they shopped a lot, they were really well dressed, the little girls' hair was so straight, so pretty. Everyone was like this. And they worked in the stores, in the banks, and treated us really well. But they thought I was Hispanic, they didn't know I was Brazilian. I thought being Brazilian was better than being Hispanic.

Like many Brazilians, Larissa links social status with physical markers associated with occupation, style of dress, and cosmetic attributes.[31] Larissa also mentioned seeing blacks working in banks in the United States, which is very uncommon in Brazil.[32] Consequently, she and other migrants presumed black Americans were in a privileged position. However, considering that Larissa lived in Newark, which is one of the country's most dangerous and impoverished cities, it seems she did not have a fully informed view of black Americans' social position. Larissa's reference to the straightness of the little girls' hair as "pretty" is also informative since in Brazil having straight hair (natural or chemically treated) is preferred to very curly (black) hair.[33]

Gustavo, a 37-year-old white migrant, also thought black Americans were physically attractive. Because he had rarely encountered middle-class blacks in Brazil before migrating, he was initially scared when he saw them driving expensive cars in Massachusetts:

I got scared when I saw [U.S.] blacks in nice cars—you know, really expensive cars? I saw that and it scared me because I was thinking this isn't common in Brazil: " Look, the black here can drive a nice car and the black in Brazil can't." I was thinking . . . "those blacks [are] extremely chic (laughs) and beautiful." And this is something that Brazil doesn't really have.

Gustavo used the social position of black Brazilians as a frame of reference for black Americans. His observations about black Brazilians in cars were expressed in other interviews and informal conversations: if a black person is driving a nice car in Brazil, he either stole it or is the chauffeur. Gustavo also described black Americans as *chique*, which means "chic" or "posh" in English. In Brazil, when someone is described as *chique*, it means very fashionable, well dressed, and presentable. Migrants rarely used these words to describe black Brazilians.

For Larissa, Gustavo, and other migrants, the relevance of social status in Brazil was transferred to the U.S. context and used to ascribe positive physical characteristics to black Americans. The characteristics that made black Americans physically attractive were based on markers of high social status in Brazil. If a person has a good job and is well dressed in Brazil, it is usually assumed he or she has a high SES; such individuals often receive better social treatment, such as entrance into exclusive, primarily white, social spaces.[34] For high-SES nonwhite Brazilians, this process is called "social whitening."[35] Although no migrant explicitly stated that black Brazilians were not beautiful, their emphasis on black Americans' beauty implies there is something unattractive about black Brazilians. Having brought their view of the importance of social class, beauty, and appearance from Brazil to the United States, it likely influenced their perception of black Americans' elevated SES and led them to see black Americans as socially white.[36]

Black Americans as Socially Mobile and Respected

Just as Larissa thought that "darker [people] are doing better" in the United States, a few other migrants believed black Americans had more power and wealth than white Americans. This perception was based on those migrants' personal observations of and limited interactions with blacks in the workplace and in residential settings. One of these migrants was Mateus, a 42-year-old moreno who lived in Rhode Island:

We [Brazilians] would say that Americans don't like black people, but after I was there living in the country, I came to see that this wasn't the case because I knew a lot of blacks there. The majority of them have better lives than whites. I lived in an apartment complex, [where] every black person had a nice car and every white person had an ugly car. So at times, I didn't understand this, I said to myself "my God." There in the U.S., the white sometimes fights with the black because the black has more power. I don't know if you noticed this there, the black is well dressed, has nice cars, lives in nice places. I was sometimes perplexed by this. It was something I couldn't resolve.

Mateus's assessment of black Americans' higher SES is based on his perceptions of the blacks in his apartment complex. For him and other migrants, black Americans' social position was at odds with what they had heard before migrating. They could not reconcile some black Americans' upward social mobility with the de facto and de jure racist history of the country. Also evident in Mateus's assessment is his lack of knowledge about the lower social position of blacks relative to the overall U.S. population. Despite the progress that has been made in dismantling overt and legal Jim Crow–style racism, black Americans still have lower levels of education, income, wealth, and health than other ethno-racial groups.[37]

Migrants' lens for interpreting black Americans' social mobility is colored by the hyper-marginalization of black Brazilians, which is more severe than

in the United States. Various studies have found that black Americans are less
structurally disadvantaged than black Brazilians.[38] Telles specifically highlights
how the vastly different socioeconomic positions of these groups is indicative
of Brazil's more unequal vertical relations.[39] Historically, income inequality has
been lower in the United States than in Brazil, and U.S. affirmative action policies have facilitated upward social mobility for more black Americans. Black
Americans are highly visible in media, politics, business, and education. Luiz,
a 43-year-old black migrant who lived in New Jersey, discussed this visibility:

I think that the black American is very important in the U.S., and in Brazil, he is
inferior. [With regard to] social class, at work, in life, in films, they [U.S. blacks] have
more of a chance. Here [in Brazil], the poor population is more black. Here the black
Brazilian is inferior. The black American valorizes himself. And in Brazil, they don't
have the value that exists there. He has more opportunities than the Brazilian, to rise
up and be something. Here, this doesn't exist.

Because of black Americans' higher visibility, Luiz believed that they are
more valued and recognized than black Brazilians, who have fewer educational opportunities and typically work in low-status jobs. Like Luiz, some
Americans believe discrimination is less of a barrier to black Americans' social
mobility because of their visibility in prestigious positions and on television.[40]
But while some blacks have gained access to elite spaces, they represent a minority of the population; black Americans, regardless of social class, continue
to experience racism.[41]

With the global dissemination of U.S. culture, the visibility of black Americans on television cultivates a domestic and global perception that many black
Americans are as wealthy as Oprah, as smart as Obama, or as beautiful as Be-
yoncé. For migrants, seeing black Americans on television and in movie roles
as doctors, CEOs, and attorneys creates the perception that blacks are visible
and respected in U.S. society. On the other hand, black actors and actresses
in Brazil usually portray athletes (especially in soccer), *sambistas* (musicians),
maids, and chauffeurs, but rarely professionals such as doctors or teachers.[42]
Brazilians were used to seeing news stories about black Brazilian criminals before migrating. Therefore, the elevated social position of black Americans was
even more noticeable to them after arriving in the United States.

Black Americans as Politically Active

Some migrants also saw black Americans as more politically active than black Brazilians, and they believed that black Americans' social mobility was the result of their willingness and courage to fight for it politically. I had the following exchange with Gustavo, who earlier described black Americans as *chique*:

GUSTAVO: I think that in the U.S., even though there's [racial] prejudice, I think that the black has more opportunity, even with prejudice. But it's because they struggled and fought for this. I think the black is more present in institutions, in jobs. I think they benefit more than those in Brazil. I think that the black [American], he fights a lot for his dignity. If he senses prejudice in any situation, he tells it and fights. In Brazil, low [marginalized] people lower their heads and stay quiet.

TJ: You talked a little bit about this, when you talked about your perceptions of blacks there in the U.S. and blacks here in Brazil, but do you have other examples?

GUSTAVO: Racially, the difference, I think the difference is that blacks and Americans, they . . .

TJ: There or here?

GUSTAVO: In the U.S., I think that they [blacks] got it, their rights, they got them and positioned themselves in American society. Now, I think that in Brazil, people, the blacks need to fight more, struggle more. It's starting to happen a little bit, the university quotas were recently implemented in Brazil. That already happened in the U.S., I don't remember where, but this happened too. If I'm not mistaken, it was in California, I don't remember. Now, it's been resolved, the issue of quotas. So, I think our blacks need to fight more and struggle more for their rights here. I think that's the difference between Brazil and the U.S., but prejudice exists as much there as it does here.

While Gustavo expressed admiration for black Americans' involvement in achieving social mobility, his comments also implied that black Brazilians are complicit in their own social disadvantage. Given the implementation of university quotas (affirmative action) in Brazil, he and a few other migrants believed that black Brazilians should be more proactive if they want to improve their social position as black Americans have done. Migrants' thoughts about the political involvement of black Brazilians had a "blame the victim" sense about them: black Brazilians are responsible for their lower social position because, unlike black Americans, they have not fought to improve their own lives. Such perceptions, of course, overgeneralize the political activism of blacks in both countries.

Though black Americans' political involvement during and since the Civil Rights Movement has facilitated broad societal change, they remain underrepresented in public office and continue to experience political disenfranchisement.[43] In Brazil, the *Movimento Negro* (Black Power Movement) has gained more prominence in recent decades, but the persistence of the racial democracy ideology has hindered the development of a strong race-based identity for brown and black Brazilians. Thus it has been difficult to replicate a broad social movement like the U.S. Civil Rights Movement.[44] Scholars argue that the system of overt and legal racism in the United States, where blacks were considered a monolithic group regardless of racial ancestry, yielded a solid black racial identity.[45] This was essential for black Americans' political mobilization against racist laws and policies.

Another migrant who discussed black Americans' political activism was Marcêlo, a 55-year-old who racially classified himself as "neutral: not white or black":

TJ: Do you think there's a difference between race in Brazil and the U.S.?

MARCÊLO: Yes.

TJ: What [is the] difference in your opinion?

MARCÊLO: Here, the Brazilian hides a lot, they hide. And in America, no, they expose [fight].

TJ: Racism?

MARCÊLO: Yes, racism . . . blacks, because the American guys, they know their rights. Over here, they are more ignorant, they don't care.

TJ: So, did your experience with other people [in the U.S.] change your opinion about race or color?

MARCÊLO: I also valued, there, I valued the black[s] more, I understood his suffering because there the black[s] fought. There, they had Martin Luther King [Jr.]. Here didn't.

Marcêlo tied black Americans' political involvement to their U.S. citizenship, and he felt that being politically active was a characteristic of being American. However, one cannot consider Marcêlo's views without understanding the culture and role of government stability in addressing blacks' claims for social redress and political activism in each country.

While the United States has been a stable democracy for more than two centuries, Brazil has experienced significant government instability since obtaining its independence from Portugal in 1824.[46] There have been several periods of political unrest, during which protest and public demonstrations against the government were prohibited. The military dictatorship, which lasted from 1964 to 1985, vehemently defended racial democracy ideology and subverted any attempts to organize on the basis of race, removing the "race" question from the Brazilian census for its duration.[47] Since transitioning to democracy in 1985, the Brazilian government has reinstated the collection of race data and has been receptive, especially in recent years, to improving the social position of the black and Indigenous Brazilian populations. Brazil's political history has been much less stable than that of the United States, despite its history of Civil War, Reconstruction, and various political protests over equal rights for all Americans. Its stability, as well as the democratic principles on which the nation was built, eventually made it possible for black Americans to become more included in the political process and assert their rights. Thus migrants used black Brazilians' lack of political activity as a transnational frame of reference for understanding black Americans' political involvement.

Black Americans as Racist

Although many migrants praised the social position and political activism of black Americans, 22 migrants also thought black Americans were racist, especially toward white Americans. One of them was Ricardo, who classified himself as white:

There is racism everywhere. There is racism with the black in Brazil, here it exists, but not to the degree that it does in the U.S. I don't see it, that is my opinion. The black in the U.S. likes his own place, he doesn't mix much either. You see blacks in all social classes, but in general, the blacks, at least in New York where I live[d], he has his own neighborhood, his own club, his own music. This is what I saw, they claim they are not racist, but I see that they stick together to a certain degree. They are people with much culture, tremendous artists, the [black] middle class associates together in one place.

For Ricardo, "sticking together to a certain degree" was racist behavior he associated with middle-class blacks. In fact, many migrants thought that blacks living in separate communities and having separate institutions was racist.

Racista and *preconceito* (prejudiced) were the Portuguese words migrants used to describe this behavior.

In our interviews, however, I learned that during their time in the United States the majority of migrants lived in Brazilian neighborhoods, worked with co-ethnics, attended Brazilian churches, and socialized with fellow Brazilians in their limited leisure time. In other words, migrants practiced the same behavior that they told me made black Americans racist. When some migrants commented on this behavior, I asked if they felt it was racist for Brazilians to live, work, and socialize primarily with Brazilians. They widely responded that it was not. Erika, a 27-year-old morena, said:

TJ: Do you think there's a difference between race in Brazil and the U.S.?

ERIKA: I think every country has its race and prejudice related to race. What caught my attention in the U.S. was the blacks. They really stay away from whites—that caught my attention. This doesn't exist here. Here, there is color prejudice and there's punishment for this. But there isn't, every one [race] living in his own church, community, neighborhood. I thought it was interesting seeing that there.

TJ: Do you think only the blacks live like this in the U.S. or other groups too?

ERIKA: I think it's just the blacks, churches only for blacks.

TJ: When immigrants live in the same community, do you think this is different?

ERIKA: I think so.

TJ: In your opinion, how is immigrants from the same country living in the same neighborhood different from blacks and whites living in different neighborhoods?

ERIKA: I don't understand . . .

TJ: You said that in your experience only blacks live in separate neighborhoods, but you lived in a neighborhood with only Brazilians, socialized only with Brazilians. So my question is, do you think Brazilians living in separate neighborhoods and going to separate churches is different from blacks living in separate neighborhoods?

ERIKA: It's very different.

TJ: How so?

ERIKA: It's a complicated question to respond to, but it was something that caught my attention. I wish I could respond in a better way.

Erika found it difficult to explain why she thought there was a difference between Brazilians and black Americans living in separate neighborhoods and socializing with co-ethnics. As a researcher, I wanted to understand why she felt this behavior was different, so I asked the question in different ways. By the time Erika gave her last response, she seemed nervous, and I did not push further. However, I believe she realized that the behavior she suggested made black Americans self-segregating also applied to her. Because she recognized that this implied she was also racist, she became uncomfortable and deflected the question. This exchange also indicates that Brazilians—in the United States or Brazil—may not directly acknowledge that they also participate in "racist" or self-segregating behavior. Erika's attempt to socially distance Brazilians from the same racist behavior that she ascribes to black Americans further shows the work of the transnational racial optic. By denying the similarities between black Americans' and Brazilians' self-segregating behavior, Erika connects the cordial interracial relations of Brazilian racial discourse with U.S. race relations through the presumed racist behavior of black Americans.

Erika was not the only migrant to suggest that black Americans are self-segregating and racist. Because of residential segregation and/or personal preference, various ethno-racial groups live in homogeneous communities in the United States and therefore are equal-opportunity segregators. Yet because migrants relied on Brazilian racial norms to negotiate race in the United States, they likely noticed this behavior among black Americans because residential segregation levels in Brazil are lower. Since the percentage of African-descended individuals is larger in Brazil than in the United States, migrants perceived that Brazilians of all colors live in racially mixed (albeit class-segregated) communities. Consequently, migrants thought the large presence of black Americans living in certain neighborhoods was racist.

Though migrants of different colors thought black Americans were racist, a few of the black migrants mentioned being unable to socially connect with black Americans. This was the case for Letícia, a 45-year-old with dark-brown skin, black eyes, and straight black hair:

Look, I think, it's like I told you before, from what I saw, it seems that the black there [in the U.S.] is more racist than the white. And like I said at times, I don't know if it is different now because it's been years [since I was in the U.S.]. I cleaned, I worked cleaning a house and they [the owners] were black, they didn't have any type of relationships with whites. They lived, I don't remember the name of the place, but there were only blacks in that area, all the houses were mansions. And one day, I heard a conversation and they [the owners] said they were black and didn't want to mix with anybody. I noticed this there, I don't know what you think, but I noticed that the black seems to want to be better than the white.

Letícia thought her black employers were racist because they lived in an all-black neighborhood and did not mix socially with other racial groups. Like other migrants, she believed blacks Americans were more racist than whites.

Letícia was not the only black migrant to have an uneasy relationship with black Americans. Lucas spoke about his discomfort visiting a black American church:

The blacks [Brazilians] that leave here going to the U.S., I think that they experience a certain difficulty too in interacting with the black [American] community because the identity . . . is not [about] black identity or color, but about nationality. I myself had this experience . . . when I left here [GV], I wanted to learn English quickly, and I had already graduated [from college], but I didn't know how to speak. I went to a place that had a lot of immigrants and few Americans and there were lots of Brazilians, Portuguese, Hispanics, and I couldn't practice English. So, I thought I would find a Baptist church. So, I listened to the choir [on the radio] and thought it was awesome, marvelous. And because I wanted to learn English, I said "I'll socialize with them." So, one day I worked up the nerve and went to that Baptist church to socialize with the people. And I was received in a manner, I wasn't treated badly, but I sensed a coldness. Today, I perceive that I invaded a place that I should not have because there existed a boundary there I could not cross. In my experience living in Brazil, these boundaries are not as defined, but arriving there, I invaded that place and people looked at me, all blacks and I am black, everyone together, but what was at play were other identities, not ethnicity or race. And so, I didn't go back to that place.

When Lucas sought to establish a relationship with the black American community in New Jersey, he realized his nationality and lack of English proficiency were barriers. In contrast to the fluidity of social boundaries in Brazil, in the United States his Brazilian nationality created social distance from members of what he considered to be the same racial group.

Lucas's experience also speaks to the growing importance of ethnicity among U.S. blacks. Increased migration from the Caribbean, Africa, and Latin America in recent decades has produced a more ethnically diverse black population that no longer consists predominantly of African Americans, the descendants of U.S. slaves. Because of the stigmatization of African Americans, these other black groups socially distance themselves from African Americans in an attempt to garner better social treatment from whites.[48] But despite these ethnic group boundaries, blacks of all ethnicities experience racial discrimination and negative social outcomes in the United States.[49]

As black Brazilians, Lucas's and Letícia's experiences highlight the invisibility of Afro-Latin Americans and Afro-Latinos who straddle the ethno-racial divide between blacks and Latinos. The concept of racial *mestizaje* and attempts to racially "whiten" the Latin American population in various countries have at times left Afro–Latin Americans marginalized, and even unacknowledged.[50] Thus concerns about the disadvantaged social outcomes of this group are often overlooked in Latin America. Upon migrating to the United States, Afro-Latinos continue to experience marginalization from Latinos because they may not look "Latin," from black Americans because of their Spanish/Portuguese surnames and accents, and from the larger society because they look black.[51] Lucas's comments demonstrate how being a black Brazilian marginalized him in both countries.

Brazilian migrants' perceptions of black Americans as racist also stemmed from their lack of knowledge about the history of racial inequality in the United States. As a result of overtly racist laws that prohibited blacks of all social classes from living in certain communities or attending the schools of their choice, black Americans had to create their own educational, religious, and cultural institutions.[52] Some migrants were critical of what they perceived as racist and self-segregating behavior among black Americans, which they felt was not as present among black Brazilians. As a consequence of migration, respondents' views of "racist" black Americans contrasted with their pre-migration experiences in Brazil with cordial blacks who were willing to interact with Brazilians of all colors.

EXPERIENCES OF RACIAL AND/OR ANTI-IMMIGRANT DISCRIMINATION

Nearly half of my migrant respondents (24 of 49) discussed their personal experiences with racial discrimination, anti-immigrant discrimination, or a combination of the two during their time abroad. Many mentioned hearing about overt racial discrimination in the United States before migrating, but some were shocked to be the victims of such discrimination. Migrants believed that it stemmed from their racial classification, lack of English language proficiency, or being perceived as Hispanic and/or illegal. This was the case regardless of migrants' racial self-classification; those who classified themselves as white, Hispanic/Latino, or black equally reported experiencing discrimination. A 42-year-old black migrant named Fernando told me about an experience of racial discrimination he had in Massachusetts:

Where I worked with Brazilians, I have a friend that lived in the U.S. for 20 years who told me, "you are black, whites won't like you here." He told me this and this is what happened to me, a white guy wouldn't give me a job because I was black. He told me he didn't have any money [to hire another worker]. But, he didn't say it was because I was black, he didn't say anything. But my friend got the job and told me he [the boss] didn't like blacks. Why didn't he like the work of a black? I am a good worker, I'm honest, I don't fight, I don't say anything. But there was a problem with him [the boss].

Because Fernando has dark-brown skin and short, tightly curled salt-and-pepper hair, it is likely his white U.S. employer perceived him as black. Since both Fernando and his friend were Brazilian immigrants, it is likely that Fernando's race was the basis for this discrimination, and his friend's warning proved to be true. Given the history of black-white race relations in the United States, Fernando's experience is not unusual. Other studies have highlighted similar racial discrimination encountered by "black-looking" immigrants in the United States.[53]

Fernando's experience contrasted with that of a 45-year-old white migrant named Eduardo, who told me he believed darker Brazilians had a more difficult time in the United States than lighter ones. He discussed how being fairer-skinned benefited him:

TJ: Did race have more importance for you in the U.S. than in Brazil?

EDUARDO: Was it important for me?

TJ: Yes.

EDUARDO: My race? Did I consider, for example, me being white in the U.S. more important for me than here? Maybe so for finding work, I think it was much easier in the U.S., I felt that.

TJ: Did you say it was easier?

EDUARDO: It was easier, as a [lighter] Brazilian compared with darker Brazilians, there, they had more difficulty than me finding work, socializing, yes.

TJ: Can you tell me more about this?

EDUARDO: Yes . . . I sometimes felt this. It was clear in Americans' treatment in terms of limiting Brazilians, my community. The treatment was much better, I felt this, for those with lighter skin. It was not only privileged by the Americans, but the Europeans, the Portuguese discriminate against Brazilians with darker skin too, the Italians discriminated [too]. . . . It wasn't very [overt], it was discreet, you could feel it.

Eduardo was white by Brazilian standards but recognized that others did not see him as white like the Americans of Italian and Portuguese ancestry he encountered. Both Eduardo and Fernando's accounts are only subtly based on race because neither was told outright that race was a factor in any particular circumstance.

But some migrants said they were overtly discriminated against for being immigrants and lacking English proficiency. This was the case for Bianca, a 29-year-old morena who lived in New Jersey:

I think like this, they [Americans] constantly watch you in the store, when you go in a store, as soon as you arrive and you don't know how to properly speak English, people would laugh at us. And I felt bad, they were the type of people that followed me around to see I wasn't going to steal anything.

Bianca believed her lack of English proficiency signaled her otherness as an immigrant and influenced Americans' perceptions of and subsequent behavior toward her as a potential criminal. Vinícius, the "Portuguese" migrant I introduced in Chapter 2, also had an overt experience of racist and anti-immigrant discrimination while working for a white client in Florida:

So, I felt a little bit of discrimination . . . when I worked as a salesperson, one time I did business with an older American man. Because I had lived there for many years, I didn't have an accent. Some guys that I worked with called me on the radio [walkie-talkie] and said "I need you to do a job for us" [in Spanish]. So, when I answered him in Spanish, this old guy took the contract . . . he looked, got his check, and asked me "are you Hispanic?" And I said "no, I am Brazilian, but I have lived here for many years." He tore up the check and the contract and said "get out of my house, you Hispanic son of a bitch. He heard me speaking Spanish [with my co-worker], and said "get out of my house, Hispanics aren't welcome in my house."

I didn't know if I should laugh or cry and I got nervous. I had never experienced anything like that.

It appears Vinícius was perceived as white by his American client until he spoke Spanish with some co-workers. Vinícius's use of a foreign language signaled his otherness and nonwhiteness. Speaking English without an accent but also speaking Spanish, identifying as Brazilian, and being labeled as Hispanic elicited a strong racist and anti-immigrant response from that particular American. Although Vinícius was not Hispanic, it did not matter to his client, who grouped Vinícius with other Hispanics. Similar to Felipe's earlier remark about Spanish and Portuguese being "the same shit" for Americans, Vinícius's experience indicates that this American did not differentiate between Brazilians and Hispanics.

For Vinícius and Bianca, language was a social marker that unveiled their status as outsiders in American society. Many migrants recognized the importance of language proficiency in shaping their experiences. Sixty-one percent of migrants spoke little or no English, and it is likely that their limited English hindered their ability to recognize verbally racist behavior when it occurred. However, migrants told me they could detect subtle discrimination by observing nonverbal cues such as body language and voice volume. Some mentioned being followed around stores (like Bianca), and that Americans raised their voices in anger or impatience when the immigrants did not understand English. Like Eduardo, respondents also mentioned having a "feeling" of discomfort or unease in certain interactions with Americans that signaled racial or anti-immigrant discrimination.

In response to the September 11 terrorist attacks in 2001, the U.S. government has instituted extensive background checks and added security to national borders, particularly the U.S. border with Mexico. One unintended consequence has been a rise in some Americans' distrust of perceived outsiders, which has resulted in more racialized anti-immigrant sentiment and attacks against individuals seen as foreign.[54] Increased Latin American immigration and debates on immigration and health reform have further fueled animosity toward Latinos, regardless of their immigration status in the United States.[55] Because the majority of GV migrants were undocumented, many spoke of living in fear, and they discussed being racially profiled by police because they looked as if they might be illegal. Some of their encounters with law enforcement resulted in arrests, after which some migrants were turned over to immigration enforcement and deported. According to migrants, this happened often in Massachusetts towns with large Brazilian communities, where some police departments have been assigned immigration enforcement duties. This is how Gabriel, a 43-year-old *moreno*, was arrested and deported back to GV:

When they [the police] caught me the last time, I was driving in my car, but it wasn't in my name, it was in my friend's name. So, they pulled me over and asked for my documents. And they held for me a long time. I was 500 meters from my house and he [the officer] had been following me and pulled me over. As soon as I got out of the car, he asked for my documents and . . . I told him my documents weren't with me. And I got afraid because of the way he got close to me. He was aggressive. So, I stayed calm and I was afraid that he would do something. So, he told me I could go and then he followed me to my house. He followed me in my house, entered my house and then [came] into my bedroom. Speaking with me, he asked for my documents, my driver's license and passport . . . I gave him my real passport and told him I didn't have a driver's license. He told me I couldn't drive anymore, but he checked my passport inside the car with his computer and called immigration. I'm not sure what happened after that [but I think] he got and filled out a form in his car. He took the form, put it in my passport and told me that in 10–15 days, I needed to appear in court. I turned and told him, "Fine, OK." So, I went inside my house and packed my most valuable things and sent them to Brazil. After that, I stayed at home. After 15 days, they [police] showed up, the same ones from before, and took me to immigration. They came into my house at 6 in the morning, pulled me out of bed in my nightclothes. My jewelry, watch, everything was [left behind] with them, my two passports. I arrived [in Brazil] with the clothes they gave me in jail.

Unfortunately, Gabriel was not the only person to share a story like this. He had migrated to the United States twice by crossing the United States-Mexico border and almost died both times. With medium-brown skin and short, slightly curly black hair, Gabriel was racialized as Hispanic, presumed to be undocumented, and consequently pulled over by the police in his town, which led to his deportation. Gabriel experienced discrimination because most Americans could not distinguish between Latinos and Hispanics and identified Brazilian migrants as looking illegal.

Many respondents also suspected that American employers took advantage of their undocumented status by underpaying them and threatening to report them to the U.S. Office of Immigration and Customs Enforcement (ICE) if they complained of unequal treatment. This happened to Felipe:

When I worked in a restaurant, one time, the manager of the kitchen disrespected us a lot for being illegal in the U.S. I was illegal and he knew that we didn't have papers to work. He exploited us a lot, he didn't respect our hours: "you have to work horrible hours." He verbally disrespected [us] too: "fucking Brazilian guy, stupid Brazilian."

Thus language, immigration status, and "looking" illegal were factors that caused subtle and overt anti-immigrant discrimination for the migrants while in the United States.[56]

When I asked migrants if their experiences of racial and/or anti-immigrant discrimination in the United States would be considered racism in Brazil, the majority believed that they would. However, migrants were quick to claim that Brazil is a more welcoming society and that immigrants have been well received and better incorporated into contemporary society than in the United States. Perhaps this is because GV has primarily been an emigrant-sending rather than immigrant-receiving city, unlike large Brazilian cities such as São Paulo, which are immigrant destinations. Migration from Asia and the Middle East to São Paulo in the mid- and late 1900s was a concern for native Brazilians, who were unsure how these phenotypically nonblack and nonwhite individuals would assimilate. Historian Jeffrey Lesser argues that this non-European immigration has further hybridized a racially mixed Brazil and consequently expanded the notion of what it means to be Brazilian:

As private identities were interpreted for the public sphere, a tug-of-war took place between the leaders of non-European immigrant communities seeking to define social spaces, and politicians, intellectuals, and the press attempting to create the boundaries of Brazilianness. The tension was often expressed as racism . . . prejudice and the ste-reotypes that emerge from it were one way that identity was contested as negotiating positions were expounded and then revised as different publics responded.[57]

Though these groups encountered discrimination, some have intermarried with native Brazilians, become a part of the middle class, and speak a hybrid form of Portuguese mixed with their native languages.[58] Thus immigrants have not been as easily incorporated into Brazil as the GV migrants I interviewed perceived them to be. Again, local discourses on race and ethnicity vary depending on where in Brazil one resides.

Migrants invoked their pre-migration memories of Brazilian race relations, connecting them with their observations and experiences in the United States. The transnational racial optic influenced how migrants viewed U.S. race relations as distinct from Brazilian race relations. As migrants adapted to life in the United States, they noticed that their environments were socially and residentially segregated to a great degree. Also in contrast to Brazil, they observed the relatively higher social position and visibility of black Americans. In addition, migrants encountered substantial racial and anti-immigrant discrimination, unlike any that most had experienced in Brazil before migrating. These findings demonstrate that cordial race relations exist alongside extensive racial inequality in Brazil, which have been documented in other comparative studies of race in the United States and Brazil.[59] What is different about the findings presented here, though, is that they are illustrated at the micro level among migrants who lived in both countries. Migration connected these two racial worlds for my respondents, allowing them to use one racial world as a transnational frame of reference for the other. Through the transnational racial optic, they were able to contextualize their changed social status from mostly white and full citizens in Brazil to primarily nonwhite and undocumented in the United States. In the end, navigating the U.S. racial divide would also affect their readaptation and perceptions of race in GV after returning.

RACIAL CLASSIFICATION AFTER THE RETURN HOME

What changed for me after returning [was that] my experience there and what I learned, that there you are black or white. There doesn't exist an option like here [such as] a mixture with Indio, Asian, no. There in the U.S., I could be wrong, but what I learned is that [you are] white or black. If you have hair that's a little bad [very curly], [for example,] I have a niece who's completely white [in color], whiter than me but with rounder features [less sharp facial features] and her hair is not very good. She would be black in the U.S. and here she never would. So, after I returned, I perceived this huge difference. There, if you are not 100% [straight] hair, eyes, [skin] color, you are black. My niece would be black, I looked at her and didn't understand [this].

Lorena, "human being," age 40, returnee

Although Lorena lived in the United States for only two years, her limited time there had a profound impact on her racial conceptions. Her observations of U.S. racial dynamics became even more pronounced after Lorena returned to GV. Lorena used what she learned about racial classification in the United States to recalibrate her understanding of the Brazilian racial schema: "You are white or black, there doesn't exist an option like here." Lorena's fair-skinned niece represented an overlap between the white and black categories in both countries, and Lorena's migration helped her further understand this "huge difference."

Again, the transnational racial optic was relevant for helping Lorena and other returnees renegotiate their classifications in GV. Reencountering their home context from the perspective of their migration experience made return-ees more cognizant of the racial and social differences between GV and the U.S. cities where they had lived.[1] During their absence from GV society, racial quotas had been put in place in order to increase the number of Afro-Brazilians in federal universities. As a result, returning migrants had to renegotiate their understanding of Brazilian categories and reinterpret the relationship between skin color and racial classification. Returning to Brazil provided an opportunity for them to reflect on their experiences in the United States and on the racial differences in each place. To better illuminate how U.S. migration influenced returnees' perceptions of racial classification in Brazil, I incorporate the per-spectives of 24 of their non-migrant relatives, where appropriate.[2] Comparing the two groups' perceptions of the Brazilian racial schema reveals instances in which returnees brought back U.S. racial ideals and how those ideals influenced returnees' perceptions of their own racial classification.

CHANGES IN RETURNEES' CLASSIFICATIONS

Given that some returnees' self-classifications had changed in the United States, I examined whether returning to Brazil facilitated a similar shift.[3] Lorena, with her fair skin, green eyes, and long, straight, dyed-blonde hair, was one of the few returnees who would have been viewed as white by both Brazilian and U.S. standards. Despite self-classifying as white pre-migration and in the United States, she classified herself as a "human being" (open-ended) and "other: human race" (categorical) at the time of our interview. In other parts of our interview, Lorena revealed that the hyper-importance of racial classification in the United States made her more cognizant of the similarities between people, regardless of race. She now sees herself as part of the human race instead of as a member of a particular racial group or having a particular skin tone. In a sense, her observations in the United States led her to reject the idea of dif-ferences between people based on race or skin color. Nevertheless, aspects of the U.S. racial schema, such as the one-drop rule of black racial classification, remained with Lorena. She connected them with the fluidity of white racial classification in Brazil by negotiating her own and her niece's "black" classifi-

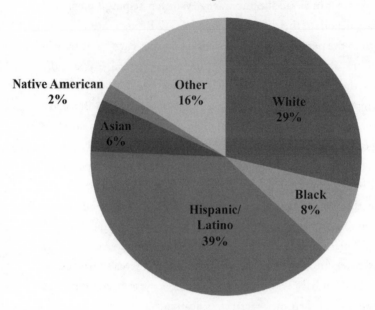

Panel B. Migrants' Race in Brazil Post-Migration

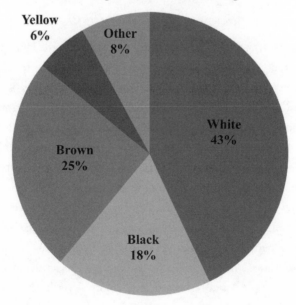

Figure 2. Migrants' Racial Self-Classifications during and after Migration

cation post-migration. Other returnees went through a similar process in re-adjusting to GV racial norms.

U.S. and Post-Migration Classifications

Figure 2 shows returnees' categorical racial classifications in the United States and Brazil post-migration.[4] These figures indicate a noticeable difference between returnees' self-classifications in the two countries.

Table 5 more closely illustrates how returnees' self-classifications shifted between the two migration periods. Notably, eight returnees who self-classified as Hispanic/Latino in the United States reclassified themselves as white in Brazil post-migration. Eleven moved from the "other" category in the United States to the white, black, and brown categories after returning to Brazil. In the United States, most of these returnees self-classified using more than one category, such as "other: black and Latino" or "other: white and Latino" and then self-classified as "black" or "white" respectively post-migration.

Living in the United States, where the white category was more exclusive, led most respondents to classify themselves as nonwhite. But returning to Brazil, where white classification was fluid, most shifted back to the white category because they were white by Brazilian standards. For example, Amanda, a 33-year-old (biracial) white returnee self-classified as white, stating: "When I came back, I said 'I'm home.'" Though Amanda classified herself as Hispanic/Latino in the United States and recognized that Americans did not perceive her as white, she reverted to the white category post-migration since she knew her whiteness could be validated in GV in a way that it was not in the United States.[5]

Though these white returnees' self-classifications did not change, their *understanding* of racial categories in both countries did. Returning to GV further highlighted the differences between the meaning and social importance of racial categories in both countries. Returnees like Felipe, who was once a called a "Brazilian midget" in the United States, said that being white in the United States was different from being white in Brazil. This difference caused confusion for him after his return:

As a result of emigrating, I think that I am not [as] white [as] I thought I was before, no. I think that there in the U.S., we [Brazilians] get confused about our race [racial classification]. We don't know how to place [classify] ourselves, [but] we know that

TABLE 5. MIGRANTS' CATEGORICAL RACIAL SELF-CLASSIFICATIONS
IN THE UNITED STATES AND POST-MIGRATION

Race in the United States	Race in Brazil Post-Migration				
	White	Black	Brown	Other*	Total
White	10	2	1	1	14
	71%	14%	7%	7%	100%
Black	0	4	0	0	4
	0%	100%	0%	0%	100%
Hispanic/Latino	8	1	7	3	19
	42%	5%	37%	16%	100%
Other*	3	2	4	3	12
	25%	17%	33%	25%	100%
Total	21	9	12	7	49
	43%	18%	25%	14%	100%

* Includes Asian American (*amarelo*) and Native American (*Indígena*) classifications.
Note: The dark-gray cells show where returnees classified themselves in similar categories in both countries, which was the case for half of the sample. The light-gray cells show the number of returnees who self-classified in a Brazilian racial category that was different from the one they chose in the United States.

there in the U.S. that we are not white, that we are mixed. But when we return here, you know very well that who you are, who you are here [in GV] also changes, our head [mindset] changes.

While Felipe still classified himself as white when I interviewed him, his time in the United States made him realize he was less white than he had considered himself to be before leaving GV. Before migrating, Felipe self-classified as white, both open-ended and categorical. However, he changed his open-ended classification after migrating to "white but not 100% white." His and other returnees' new awareness of the different standards used for white racial classification in each country, led them to reassess their own racial classification.[6] Returnees inadvertently transported U.S. white racial classification norms back to Brazil, where they viewed themselves through the American white racial lens.

The number of returnees who self-classified as black post-migration was slightly higher after their experiences in the United States. Five returnees moved themselves to the black category after returning. One of them was 30-year-old

Fernanda, who spoke in detail about social segregation in the United States (see Chapter 3). Fernanda self-classified as white before migrating, but now asserts a black racial identity. When I asked for her classification at the time of our interview, she said:

I consider myself black . . . I don't agree that there are various colors. You are black or white. In the U.S., they considered me Latina and white, I didn't consider [see] myself that way. I am Latina. Now, here in Brazil, I am parda, I am yellow. Everyone gives me a classification based on looking at me. [But] I am black, because like I told you, black is black and white is white. It's really confusing, this thing with skin [color]. For me, it's really [confusing], I just have two colors in my head. I don't have this color of parda, yellow, Indigenous, it doesn't exist. You are black or you are white. So, it gets difficult, classification. There are times when I get confused a little bit and that's why for me, there's no difference. It's [you are] black or white.

Fernanda used a U.S. racial lens to negotiate her positionality as a black woman within Brazilian categories to interpret the race of other Brazilians. She saw two racial groups in Brazil—black and white—and her perception became much more pronounced after living abroad. Migration altered her understanding of the Brazilian racial classification system such that she believed it aligned with the U.S. black-white binary.

Although Fernanda was the only returnee to espouse the black-white binary, she was not the only one whose racial self-classification changed after returning. Returnees recognized the different racial norms for white and black classification in four ways by: (1) internalizing the racial norms of their environment; (2) using them to determine their racial classification and related position in the social order; (3) inadvertently transporting those norms when moving from one place to another; and (4) using those norms to reassess their classification in a different place. These findings provide more evidence that racial classification, as a function of race, is a social construction that is malleable across time and between geographical contexts. For returnees, movement across these contexts facilitated a renegotiation not only of racial categories in the two countries, but also of the meanings ascribed to those categories.

Pre- and Post-Migration Classifications

I also compared returnees' pre- and post-migration classifications to assess how any changes could be attributed to living in two countries with different racial schemas (see Table 6). Forty-one of the 49 returnees self-classified in the same Brazilian census category before and after migration. Since returnees were racialized as Latino and experienced racial and anti-immigrant discrimination in the United States, I expected returnees who had self-classified as white before migrating to self-classify as nonwhite after returning. Most, however, did not. The most obvious change in self-classification was among individuals who classified as white before and after migration, but as Hispanic/Latino in the United States. For these individuals, returning to Brazil allowed them to classify themselves as they had before immigrating. Their opinions were similar to those of Amanda.

It is significant, however, that eight returnees changed their racial classifications: four who classified themselves as white before migrating self-classified as nonwhite post-migration, and two returnees who initially self-classified as pardo moved to the black category. One who switched from white to nonwhite was Henrique, who said that in the United States he was mistaken for being Arab. Henrique now classifies as pardo, though he classified himself as white pre-migration and as Hispanic/Latino in the United States. He shared this realization with me:

I know now that the U.S. [has] many white people there. Today, I know that I am not white, but pardo. Even though the Brazilian considers me white, we think that we are white, but I know that I am not white.

Henrique attributed his recognition that he and other Brazilians are not white to his migration experience. But after returning he found that other Brazilians still saw him as white because his physical features were regarded as white in Brazil. Henrique adopted U.S. racial ideals, and they influenced his post-migration classification. He invokes both the U.S. and Brazilian racial schema in his statement: "Even though the Brazilian considers me white, I know I am not white."

Another returnee whose ideas shifted was Renata, the only respondent who used a U.S. ethno-racial category to classify herself post-migration. I discussed Renata at length in Chapter 2 because she switched her classification to nonwhite

TABLE 6. MIGRANTS' RACIAL SELF-CLASSIFICATIONS PRE-MIGRATION
AND POST-MIGRATION

Race Pre-Migration	Race Post-Migration				
	White	Black	Brown	Other*	Total
White	20	1	1	2	24
	83%	4%	4%	8%	100%
Black	0	6	0	0	6
	0%	100%	0%	0%	100%
Brown	0	2	10	0	12
	0%	16%	83%	0%	100%
Other*	1	0	1	5	7
	14%	0%	14%	71%	100%
Total	21	9	12	7	49
	43%	18%	25%	14%	100%

*Includes yellow (*amarela*) and Indigenous (*Indígena*) classifications.
Note: The dark-gray cells indicate where individuals classified themselves in the same categories in Brazil before and after migration. The light-gray cells show where migrants switched from one category to another. Perhaps most notably, nearly all migrants self-classified in the same categories in both time periods.

in the United States. Although she saw herself as white *before* migrating, she adopted a nonwhite classification in the United States and kept it *after returning* to Brazil. In the United States, her open-ended self-classification was yellow and her categorical self-classification was Hispanic/Latino. Post-migration, she classified herself as yellow (categorical) and as Latina when I asked for an open-ended classification. Both her open-ended and categorical classifications shifted during her migration, illustrating that individuals use different words to self-classify when given particular categories or asked for an open-ended classification.[7] Renata recognized that she was not white in the United States, but this recognition continued to influence her racial classification as Latina after returning:

Because before I was white, but after I went there [to the U.S.], I saw there were a lot of that [white] race, much whiter. In reality, I am not white, but yellow because of my family's [mixed] ancestry . . . I would say I'm Latina, I don't see myself as [just] Brazilian, we [Latinos] are all equal, we eat the same food, we are people who have the same customs. Clearly, I'm Brazilian . . . Today, I don't see it like that anymore [differences between Brazilians and Latinos], I see us all the same.

Renata's heightened perception of herself as a Latina during and after migration is unusual since many returnees perceived themselves as culturally distinct and wanted to socially distance themselves from U.S. Latinos.

In addition to asking returnees for their racial classification, I asked if they felt their classification had changed over the course of the migration. Their answers revealed whether the returnees were aware of any changes in their perspective. Forty-three of the 49 returnees told me they did not believe their self-classifications had changed, suggesting that U.S. migration had only subconsciously altered how they negotiated their classifications. Among those 43 were seven of the eight returnees whose classifications did change. Fernanda's and Renata's self-classifications changed radically. These returnees changed their classifications without even being aware of it, indicating how profoundly social context influenced how they perceived themselves and others.

Each of these considerations for how migration influenced returnees' racial classification illustrates the transnational racial optic at work; returnees used the U.S. racial schema to reassess their classifications. Before migrating, returnees saw classification in the context of a wide range of words associated primarily with skin color. However, being in the United States introduced them to five *racial* categories that were more exclusive than Brazilian *color* categories. Returnees remained cognizant of the distinctions between U.S. and Brazilian categories, drawing on their U.S. experiences to renegotiate their place within those categories.

Comparing Returnees' and Non-Migrants' Self-Classifications

A comparison of the racial self-classifications of 24 non-migrants with those of returnees reveals differences that were not apparent from returnees' pre- and post-migration self-classifications.[8] Figure 3 shows both groups' racial classifications using Brazilian census-derived categories.

Returnees and non-migrants self-classified as white in relatively equal numbers.[9] A higher number of returnees self-classified as black, and more non-migrants self-classified in the pardo category.[10] Table 7 shows a cross-tabulation of returnees' and their non-migrant relatives' self-classifications.

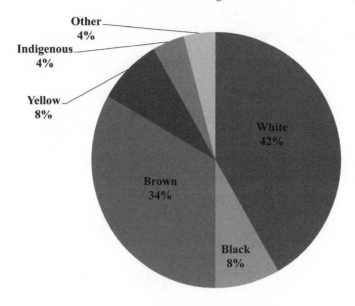

Panel A. Non-Migrants (N=24)

Other
4%

Indigenous
4%

Yellow
8%

White
42%

Brown
34%

Black
8%

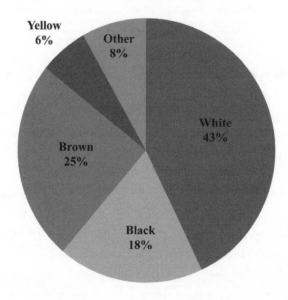

Panel B. Returnees (N=49)

Yellow
6%

Other
8%

White
43%

Brown
25%

Black
18%

Figure 3. Non-Migrants' and Returnees' Racial Self-Classifications

TABLE 7. RETURNEES' AND THEIR NON-MIGRANT RELATIVES' RACIAL
SELF-CLASSIFICATIONS (N = 24)

Returnees' Self-Classification	Non-Migrants' Self-Classification					
	White	Black	Brown	Yellow	Other	Total
White	7	0	2	2	0	11
	64%	0%	18%	18%	0%	100%
Black	0	2	1	0	2	5
	0%	40%	20%	0%	40%	100%
Brown	2	0	2	0	0	4
	50%	0%	50%	0%	0%	100%
Yellow	1	0	0	0	0	1
	100%	0%	0%	0%	0%	100%
Other	0	0	3	0	0	3
	0%	0%	100%	0%	0%	100%
Total	10	2	8	2	2	24
	42%	8%	33%	8%	8%	100%

Note: The dark-gray cells indicate where returnees and non-migrants self-classified in the same categories; light-gray cells show where returnees and non-migrants self-classified in different categories.

Though most migrants reclassified themselves as white post-migration, some shifted to the black category and out of the pardo category. They seemed to align their post-migration classifications more with the U.S. black-white racial binary than with the pardo category, in which most Brazilians classify themselves. Returnees classified themselves as whiter or blacker post-migration relative to racially mixed non-migrants. Given the returnees' negotiation of racial classification in the United States and their observations regarding differences in the white category in each country, this change can likely be attributed to their migration experiences. Returnees brought the U.S. racial schema back to GV and used it to reinterpret racial categories there.

When I asked non-migrants for their racial self-classifications, many thought I was asking if they were racist. These respondents insisted they had no problems with blacks.[11] This response was especially common among non-migrants who classified themselves as white, such as 39-year-old Rodolfo:

TJ: How do you see yourself in terms of race, how do you classify your skin color?

RODOLFO: My color, I don't understand well, my color? (pause) I will tell you the truth, I don't have any problem with race, I have nothing against blacks.

TJ: But, how do you see yourself in terms of skin color? Is there a word you use to classify your skin color?

RODOLFO: Normal. I say normal because I'm not inconsiderate of any color or any race. So, I don't think I'm prejudiced, I think I'm normal.

TJ: You don't have a word that you use to describe your skin color? I'm asking how you classify your skin color.

RODOLFO: Light moreno, white that's burned by the sun because I ride a motorcycle a lot.

With his light skin and short, straight black hair, Rodolfo uses the open-ended racial classification of "light moreno," although he chose white from among the Brazilian census categories. Rodolfo's answer to my question, "white that's burned by the sun," provides another example of the fluidity of the white racial category in Brazil. Similar to most white returnees, non-migrants classified themselves as white even after explicitly disclosing their multi-racial ancestry.

Non-migrants, however, were more likely than returnees to refer to the racial classifications ascribed to them on official documents (e.g., birth certificates) as reasons for self-classifying in particular categories. A 35-year-old non-migrant named Giovana discussed the category written on her birth certificate:

GIOVANA: On my birth certificate, white is written.

TJ: So, how do you classify using Brazilian census categories?

GIOVANA: On the document, it's white.

TJ: Why do you classify like this?

GIOVANA: First, in our culture, the birth certificate says the color. Even though there are people with black [dark] skin, they [officials] say [the person] is parda, light morena, or parda. I know very well that I am a little burned [darker] since I just got back from the beach in Salvador. This corresponds here because [racial] classification refers to skin [color] and hair [texture]. And also, on the birth certificate, [is written] the color from the moment of birth.

With her light skin, dark eyes, and long, straight dark-black hair, Giovana classified as white. She continues to refer to her birth certificate even though I specifically asked for *her* perception of her racial classification. Giovana also suggests that an individual's color is determined by government officials "from the moment of birth," which implies that the classification is unchangeable and that the individual has little agency in determining her own classification. Finally, Giovana mentions how government officials "whiten" individuals with black skin by classifying them as "pardo," which alludes to the aspect of racial democracy ideology that attempts to dilute black phenotypical features in the population through racial mixture.[12]

Giovana's and other non-migrants' references to official documents as the basis for determining their classifications confirm other studies' findings that a government's use of racial categories on official documents, such as birth certificates and censuses, can shape racial discourse and relations.[13] Political scientist Melissa Nobles writes:

> Census data have sustained the linked ideas of Brazilians as 'racially mixed' and of Brazil as a 'racial democracy,' even when there was no political democracy . . . census schedules have been used as the building blocks of social knowledge . . . Censuses provide a lens for examining at close range how race is constructed.[14]

For non-migrants in Brazil, such labels shaped their racial self-classifications.

Curiously, no returnees cited such documents when I asked for their racial classifications. Instead, they used their understanding of U.S. categories as a reference for classifying themselves in the United States and in Brazil post-migration. Although they had been racially socialized in Brazil, returnees' exposure to U.S. categories via migration caused them to think differently about the meaning of racial categories and their positionality in relation to them. Their transnational experiences juxtaposed the United States and Brazilian racial schemas, which is likely why returnees did not refer to the Brazilian documents that categorized them at birth.

SUN EXPOSURE AND SKIN TONE CLASSIFICATION

Many migrants also told me they were "whiter" after returning from the United States. Hearing this was initially surprising, since many returnees had talked at length about not being perceived as white by Americans, which led them to classify themselves as nonwhite in the United States. As our interviews progressed, I learned that returnees felt they were "whiter" post-migration because their skin had lightened from lack of sun exposure. Nineteen returnees mentioned believing that their racial classifications were different *immediately* after returning for this reason. Among these 19 individuals, eight actually did report lighter skin tone classifications immediately after their return.[15] Returnees used the words *branco* (white) and *branquissimo* (very white) to describe their change in skin tone, rather than the word *pálido*, which means "pale." I at first thought it was odd for Brazilians to use a lack of sun exposure to justify classifying themselves differently because it would be similar to a person of color in the United States becoming paler in the winter and changing her racial classification to white. The inverse of this—a white American becoming tan and then classifying as nonwhite—seems impossible. But returnees' perception that their skin color changed because of the climate does not seem as odd if one knows that Brazilians equate their actual skin color with their racial classification. For this reason, I asked the migrants to classify their own skin tone on a scale of one (light) to ten (dark) before, during, and after migration.[16]

Figure 4 shows how returnees, on average, classified their skin tone at each migration stage. The majority classified themselves squarely in the middle, at 5. This is not unusual since Valadarenses see themselves as more racially mixed than other Brazilians. There were some slight differences at each migration stage, with the largest occurring immediately after the migrants' return to Brazil. This shift occurred because, in the United States, migrants realized that they were much darker than very pale white Americans. Also, returnees reported having the lightest skin tones immediately after returning because they felt they were much lighter than fellow Valadarenses after being exposed to less sun abroad. Gustavo was one of these returnees:

When I returned [to Brazil], everyone thought I was much whiter. Because of the snow, there wasn't much sun. I was much whiter for people here. [Now my skin tone] it is much lighter, at number 2, 2 because of the climate. The weather there is much different.

Gustavo rated his skin tone as 4 and had classified himself as white (categorical and open-ended) before migrating. While living abroad he considered himself to be darker and classified his skin tone as a 5, he labeled himself white (open-ended) and Hispanic/Latino (categorical). Immediately after returning, he again self-classified as white (open-ended and categorical) and rated his skin tone as 2 "because of the climate" he had been exposed to in the United States.

Figure 4 also shows that returnees reported darker skin tones when I interviewed them because many felt they had tanned and become much darker since

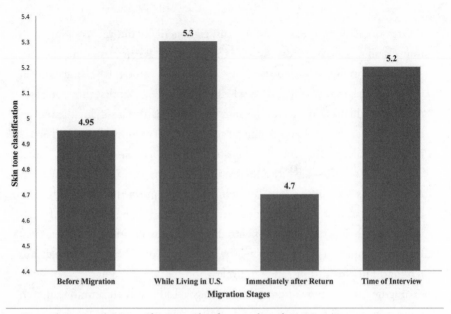

Figure 4. Returnees' Average Skin Tone Classifications throughout Migration

returning to sunny GV. This was true for 13 returnees whose skin darkened over time after their return. Gustavo was also one of those returnees, rating his skin tone as 5 at the time of our interview, which was two years after he had returned.

In comparison with returnees, only three non-migrants shared the perception that sun exposure had affected their racial self-classification. One of those non-migrants was 24-year-old Maurício, who said that being white in Brazil was different because of the tropical climate:

Look [pardo] would be a middle term ok. Not white, because in our country with a tropical climate, even a person who's white [in Brazil], she wouldn't be white like those [people] in the U.S. or Europe. We don't have that type of white because our country is tropical.

Unlike Maurício, most of the other non-migrants who mentioned white racial classification in Brazil tied it to the racially mixed history of the country instead of to the tropical climate.

More returnees than non-migrants expressed the view that lack of sun exposure changes skin color. Therefore I compared both groups' skin tone classifications in order to examine the likely influence of U.S. migration on these findings. On average, non-migrants classified their skin tone as 5, the same as the migrants. This choice would suggest that migration did not substantially influence returnees' self-classifications.

A closer examination of each returnee's skin tone throughout migration, however, demonstrated that 30 returnees reported different classifications between at least two migration stages.[17] Of these 30 returnees, 11 reported a darker skin tone post-migration, which suggests that a change of context influenced their classifications. Ricardo, who vehemently denied being Hispanic, was a returnee who changed his skin tone classification.[18] He rated his pre-migration and U.S. skin tone as 3, but changed it to 1 immediately after returning to GV and at the time of his interview. When I asked why he reported a lighter skin tone than he had before migrating, he replied:

This 3, I [initially] put it thinking about my [skin tone] classification there. My classification here is white. So, I would have to put white as being 1. Here in Brazil, nothing changed . . . My thinking is in relation to what you are asking about in the U.S. and Brazil. Here, there was never much change. I started to think like this [differently about race] there [in the U.S.].

Ricardo describes the U.S. racial schema and credits his experience abroad as making him think differently about the relationship between race and skin color. Though Ricardo had been back in GV for some time, he continued to use the U.S. racial schema as a metric for interpreting his racial and skin tone classifications.

Another returnee who mentioned that the sun made her "whiter" was 43-year-old Stephane, who was externally classified as black by a U.S. justice of the peace:[19]

Look, they [other Brazilians] always teased me, "You got lighter? The time you stayed in the U.S., you are white!" they commented. I said, "no, it's the climate." And I have a sister who told me "wow, you were so black when you left here to go there, you returned white." They [people] used to call me, I had the nickname "preto." My sister said [when I returned] "I don't like you black, I like you white."

Stephane's story implies that lighter skin tone is more highly regarded in Brazil, despite most Brazilians' insistence that racial classification is not important. Stephane's sister's comment that she liked her sister better white than black provides a glimpse into the importance of skin tone and the relative "beauty"

of whiteness, notwithstanding Brazil's persistent claims of being a racial democracy. It is also interesting that Stephane has very light skin, even though
her sister and other family members nicknamed her "preto" before migrating.
"*Preto*," "*pretinho*," and "*neguinho*" are terms families use to describe their
darkest family members.[20]

Returnees' gender and racial self-classifications were influenced by their
perception that sun exposure can change skin color. Twelve of the 19 returnees who mentioned this relationship were women, and eight self-classified as
white.[21] The existing literature on gender and racial classification indicates that
women are more likely to self-classify as lighter than men of the same color,
both in Latin American countries and among ethnic minorities in the United
States.[22] Previous studies also suggest that skin tone is more socially significant
among nonwhites and ethno-racial minorities in the United States and Brazil,
which is contrary to what I found among nonwhite returnees.[23] Social class
also did not influence returnees' views on sun exposure, which was surprising
as higher SES is usually associated with social whitening.

Previous studies of race in Brazil find that Brazilians are likely to associate racial classification with skin tone rather than with ancestry. My findings,
for both Brazilian returnees and non-migrants align with those studies. On
the surface, it seems that the U.S. migration did not strongly alter returnees'
classifications. But closer examination of returnees' self-classifications at each
migration stage showed small differences, both darkening and lightening. In
addition to the anecdotes presented, these changes in self-classification provide evidence that the U.S. migration did alter how returnees thought about
their skin tones in both the United States and Brazil. In recognizing that their
skin tone had changed in the United States owing to less sun exposure, and
in using that physical change to negotiate their skin tone classification in GV,
returnees were using the transnational racial optic to connect the racial norms
of both countries.

Returnees' interpretation of the relationship between sun exposure and
skin color further enhanced their perception that a Brazilian's racial classification can change if his or her skin color changes. U.S. migration, more
specifically the return migration, accentuated this perception for returnees.
Although the notion that race is skin color for Brazilians is not new, the
inclusion of migration as an analytical frame for examining that notion is.

Migration between the two countries facilitated returnees' understanding of how the climate could affect their skin tone and, as a result, their racial classifications in each place. How this happened merits more discussion because migrants' reported racial and skin tone classifications in the United States did not coincide with that perception.

If the idea that sun exposure can change racial classification were to hold, returnees would have had to report lighter skin tones *and* white racial classifications in the United States. However, because returnees recognized that they were darker than white Americans, they reported their skin tones as darkest *and* primarily classified as nonwhite while living there. Returnees believed that losing their tans in the United States made them "whiter" not in the United States, but *after* their initial return to GV. At that stage, returnees reported lighter skin tones and many reverted to classifying themselves as white. And at that point they were probably lighter than the darker non-migrants who had remained in sunny GV.[24]

Migrants also assessed their classifications relative to the people who were around them in both countries. In the United States, migrants used white Americans as the comparison group for evaluating their own skin tone and racial classifications. The return migration prompted a similar renegotiation, but fellow Valadarenses became the comparison group. How returnees subsequently viewed their skin tones in relation to these transnationally connected locations is a function of the transnational racial optic.

ROLE OF EXTERNAL CLASSIFICATION

A thread in this chapter that warrants more discussion is the influence of external racial classification (how other people racially classified returnees) on how returnees viewed themselves. Many of the quotes in this chapter allude to external racial classification as a factor in returnees' negotiation of racial categories in each place. For example, Henrique wanted to be perceived as Latino so that Americans would not think he was a terrorist, and Stephane's sister felt she was whiter post-migration. In each context, a different racial schema influenced how Americans and fellow Valadarenses racially classified the returnees. In turn, those classifications had implications for how returnees perceived themselves and interpreted the racial schemas in both countries.

The returnees were aware that Americans had not perceived them as white, which influenced their decision to classify as nonwhite in the United States. They underwent a similar process upon returning to Brazil, where fellow Valadarenses saw them as white because of their skin color, perhaps leading them to revert to the white racial category. Table 8 shows returnees' *perceived* external racial classifications post-migration and returnees' self-classifications; they are largely consistent, especially for white returnees. However, seven returnees who self-classified as nonwhite believed that other Brazilians saw them as white. These results reflect the fluid white racial classification in Brazil as well as the idea that returnees became whiter after receiving less sun exposure. Returnees' self-classifications were externally validated in Brazil in a way that they were not in the United States.[25]

One's own self-classification will not always match how other individuals and institutions with more power categorize a person. Scholars of racial identity formation argue that individuals learn about their own racial classification through socialization and from interacting with the people and institutions that classify them externally.[26] People may come to see themselves as others see them, which is what happened for returnees whose racial self-classifications in the United States and GV matched how they were externally perceived in both places.

Returnees' experiences renegotiating their racial classifications also influenced how they perceived others in the two contexts. Some returnees wondered what U.S. racial categories would be appropriate for Brazilians in GV. One of these returnees was Luana:

I started to pay attention in the street [in GV] to how that person would be classified [in the U.S.], what race is that person? I still have this in my head, how would that [racial] classification be if it was as important in Brazil as it is there [in the U.S.]? I feel that this classification [from] there is not resolved in my mind. Even if I returned to the U.S., I would still have this doubt. Who am I? Am I white, or Latina, or Hispanic? But it could be that I brought [back] some [racial] ideas and I brought [some] doubts. I still want to study [think about] this more before returning [to the U.S.] to know how to classify myself.

Luana's questions about racial classification in the United States remain as she interacts with other Brazilians. Her "doubt" signals her liminality, the

TABLE 8. MIGRANTS' SELF- AND EXTERNAL RACIAL CLASSIFICATIONS
POST-MIGRATION

Returnees' Self- Classification	Perceived External Classification				
	White	Black	Brown	Other*	Total
White	23	0	0	0	23
	100%	0%	0%	0%	100%
Black	0	5	1	1	7
	0%	71%	14%	14%	100%
Brown	4	0	8	0	12
	33%	0%	67%	0%	100%
Other*	3	0	0	4	7
	43%	0%	0%	57%	100%
Total	30	5	9	5	49
	61%	10%	18%	10%	100%

*Includes yellow (amarela) and Indigenous (Indígena) classifications.
Note: The dark-gray cells indicate where individuals' self and external racial classifications matched; light-gray cells show the inconsistency between the two classifications.

in-betweenness she feels from having lived in both countries. Luana classified herself as white at each migration stage. Even though her self-classification did not change, the migration experience created confusion for her as she struggled to navigate the two racial contexts. Although she is physically back in Brazil, the U.S. racial schema stays with her, illustrating the prominence and mobility of the transnational racial optic as something that individuals carry across national borders. Felipe was another returnee for whom migration changed how he racially viewed Brazilians:

FELIPE: It changed like this, my perception of color changed a little bit in the sense of how I see people [racially]. Because there [in the U.S.], when we are there, I lived there eight, seven years, we see many differences, the racial differences are very much in your day-to-day [life]. You work with an American, an Indian, a Hispanic, a Chinese [person]. So you end up with a divided [confused] head. You become accustomed many times to looking at a person and seeing without knowing them [thinking] "ah, this one is Chinese, ah that one is American, ah that one is black, ah that one is and so on." So I think that the racial perception changes, it becomes sharper, you understand that word?

TJ: More defined?

FELIPE: More defined, from the recognition that there [the U.S.] has more different races. So you get accustomed to that a little bit.

Felipe at least partially acquired the "American obsession" with racial classification and subconsciously brought it back with him to GV. Like Luana, when walking down the street in GV he found himself wondering how the Brazilians he saw in his daily life would be classified in the United States. Living there had made racial differences more noticeable to Felipe and other returnees. While Brazilians usually notice differences in the skin color and hair texture of fellow Brazilians, they do not always explicitly associate those differences with a particular ethno-racial group in Brazil. Thus returnees' experiences in the United States continue to shape how they place Brazilians in distinct racial groups based on their physical features.

Returnees incorporated elements of the Brazilian and U.S. racial schemas to negotiate racial categories in Brazil post-migration. Unlike non-migrants, returnees did not interpret racial or skin color classification as strictly and exclusively Brazilian or American; rather, they saw them as intermingled. While most returnees' pre- and post-migration racial self-classifications were the same, their understanding of Brazilian racial categories and their relationship to skin color changed. Three differences between returnees and non-migrants can be attributed to migration and the transnational racial optic. First, returnees' experience with U.S. categories allowed them to develop a nuanced interpretation of what it means to be white in both countries. Whereas non-migrants often classified themselves as pardo, returnees self-classified in ways that aligned more with the U.S. black-white racial binary. Second, returnees' perception that sun exposure can change skin tone reflected a change in their frame of reference for interpreting their own skin tone. While living in the United States, returnees felt darker than white Americans, but after returning they felt lighter than darker Valadarenses. Finally, some returnees classified themselves and fellow Valadarenses using U.S. ethno-racial categories, demonstrating that they had internalized and remitted those U.S. racial categories.

Racial categories and physical features help individuals determine which racial group they belong to and affect how they are socially positioned. Much of the literature on the social construction of race and racism emphasizes these points.[27] It is significant that U.S. migration influenced not only these returnees' self-classifications, but also how they perceived fellow Brazilians. Migration reconfigured the returnees' understanding of the Brazilian ethno-racial hierarchy, which shaped their perceptions of racial inequality after returning.

CHAPTER 5

RACIALLY MAKING
AMERICA IN BRAZIL

Because like I said, whoever goes [to the U.S.] has this perception,
when you return, [it's] with a more open mind, [you] see that there
is not only this [life in GV], you see that there [in the U.S.] there are
blacks, there are other races [in addition] to Americans, like Latinos,
people from other countries. So, I think our [migrants'] minds
become more opened and upon returning, we share this with our
families and I think we end up opening [the minds] of many people.

Bianca, morena, age 29, returnee

[Return migrants] are treated differently. Everyone that goes
[migrates], independent of color, but the black too, if they return
with money in a privileged situation, they are treated very well. If he
is black, it's as if his color disappears. He still is black, but he is no
longer poor. This person is no longer ashamed, on the contrary, he
[now] has a car. [So] he is good, it's as if [people forget] he never had
anything [before].

Rosângela, black, age 54, non-migrant

Bianca and Rosângela's thoughts demonstrate two ways in which U.S. migration
may influence the lives of all Valadarenses, regardless of whether they migrated
to the United States. Returnees and non-migrants alike agreed that extensive
migration, both to and from the United States, had significantly influenced
the economy and culture of the city. Respondents also felt that migrants return
with a *cabeça diferente*, meaning a "different head" or different mindset. Non-

migrants reported learning about life abroad through their conversations with returnees and are likely influenced by the "open-mindedness" that returnees bring back. This chapter examines migrants' conceptions of broader Brazilian race relations after returning. Specifically, I explore how the transnational racial optic altered returnees' views of racial democracy, racism, and stratification in GV by comparing them with those of non-migrants. I also explore how Valadarenses think the extensive migration back and forth has influenced the conception of race in GV. Race is a social construction that changes over time and across contexts, and people do not always recognize how it affects individuals and relationships. Exploring returnees' and non-migrants' perceptions of race in GV provides insight into how those perceptions move across borders with migrants and subtly influence their views of the home society.

RACIAL DEMOCRACY AMONG VALADARENSES

In 1933, Gilberto Freyre introduced the concept of racial democracy to describe Brazil as a country that: (1) socially accepted interracial marriage; (2) had cordial interracial relations; and (3) lacked racism. Since Freyre's time, nearly all of the literature exploring race in Brazil has used these three attributes to evaluate whether Brazil is the racial democracy Freyre described.[1] I refer to these three attributes as the "tenets of racial democracy." Scholars of Brazilian race relations have used these tenets to interpret racial democracy ideology using three views: (1) the "achieved view"—Brazil is already a multiracial and nonracist paradise; (2) the "oppressive view"—Brazil is racist and has tense interracial relations; and (3) the "aspirational view"—Brazil is a diverse and racist society that aspires to be nonracist.[2] I use these tenets to examine how Valadarenses perceive racial democracy and how U.S. migration influenced those perceptions.

After spending countless hours interacting with Valadarenses, I understood that they did not believe Brazil had achieved an authentic racial democracy. They detested the racism they saw in their country, but they were proud that Brazil had a large population with mixed-race heritage. Most Valadarenses did not use the words "racial democracy" or *democrâcia racial* in our conversations. Instead, their interviews referenced tenets of racial democracy. Most returnees and non-migrants expressed opinions consistent with the aspirational view of racial democracy, while a few returnees and non-migrants expressed opinions consistent with the oppressive view of racial democracy.

Aspirational View of Racial Democracy

Thirty-eight respondents (30 of 49 returnees and 8 of 24 non-migrants) expressed the idea that racial democracy in Brazil is still aspirational. They tended to classify themselves as white and pardo, and described Brazil as a racially mixed society where Brazilians of all skin tones recognize their African ancestry and have high rates of intermarriage. They believed there were no distinct racial groups and that most Brazilians fall in the middle of the black-white color spectrum. These respondents also thought extensive racial mixing was indicative of cordial interracial relations in the larger population. These findings correspond with scholarship on Brazilians' perceptions of racial mixing in their country.[3] One participant who expressed this perception was a 22-year-old moreno non-migrant named Isaac:

Because here in Brazil, there is much mixing . . . because of this mixing, there exist people who are neither light nor very dark. So they're in the middle category, a mixture of race[s], not on one side or the other.

Similarly, other research demonstrates the extensiveness of racial fluidity in Brazil and how it has been associated with the achieved view of racial democracy.[4]

The pervasiveness of the perception that all Brazilians are racially mixed was expressed in many interviews, especially those in which respondents mentioned a famous Brazilian phrase: *todo têm um pé na cozinha,* which translates literally as "everyone has a foot in the kitchen." Felipe, the "white but not 100% white" returnee, used the phrase to explain the prevalence of racial mixture in his family and in Brazil:

We [Brazilians] all have a foot in the kitchen [black ancestry] because my dad was a little lighter than you and my mom is very white. So I consider myself white, but I have a little bit [of black ancestry], I have a foot in the kitchen.

This phrase suggests that all Brazilians regardless of phenotype have African ancestry because of the magnitude of slavery in Brazilian history. This phrase also incorporates the historical image of black slaves as domestics in the kitchen while whites ruled the house, indicating the different social positions ascribed to each group.[5]

In contemporary society, Brazilians use this phrase to discuss their racially mixed heritage, acknowledging their white, black, and Indigenous backgrounds. However, the underlying implication is that having black ancestry—especially for those with a nonblack phenotype—can and should be hidden or relegated to a private space like a kitchen, and should not be subject to public knowledge.[6] The Brazilians studied by sociologist France Winddance Twine enthusiastically discussed their white heritage, proudly displaying photographs of white ancestors while hiding photographs of black ancestors and downplaying their black heritage.[7] Even her respondents with very dark skin tones who had black phenotypes by Brazilian standards participated in such behavior. Twine's findings provide a poignant example of how the phrase "having one foot in the kitchen" can symbolize Brazilians' pride in racial mixture, valuing of white heritage, and denigration of black ancestry all at the same time.

Though most studies of race in Brazil emphasize racial mixing as a fundamental part of Brazilian culture, other research indicates that Brazilians have either downplayed or not acknowledged the explicit purpose of racial democracy ideology: to racially whiten the population.[8] While the belief that all Brazilians are racially mixed was prevalent among the Valadarenses I interviewed, none mentioned being aware that this racial mixing was done to "whiten" Brazilians. Nevertheless, respondents expressing the aspirational view did recognize that racism existed alongside racial mixing in Brazil. One non-migrant who expressed this seeming contradiction was a 24-year-old moreno named Maurício:

It's hard to explain why [racism exists in Brazil] because in reality, whether we want to acknowledge it or not, every Brazilian has a little black blood. There's no way to deny this because it's part of our colonization. But unfortunately, prejudice exists against blacks in Brazil. They are not seen like other people.

Maurício's remarks illustrate that Valadarenses do recognize the simultaneous existence of racial mixing and inequality in their country. His comment that blacks are seen as a separate racial group in the midst of a racially mixed society further supports the notion that Brazil has not achieved Freyre's racial democracy.

Returnees who expressed the aspirational view often referenced the United States because its racial categories and distinct racial groups were the polar opposite of Brazil's. One of these returnees was Vinícius: "The difference is that the Brazilian, he sees that our race [nationality] is a mixture and I think that the American doesn't. The American insists on saying that they are a purer race." For Vinícius, being racially mixed is a marker of having Brazilian nationality, in contrast to the United States, where his perception is that racial purity is more important. Vinícius and other returnees associated the importance of racial purity in the United States with the exclusivity of the white racial group. Another returnee named Lorena connected her understanding of white racial classification in Brazil with that in the United States through her different self-classification in each country:

My color here in Brazil, I am classified [by others] as white. Now we know that in Brazil there is a lot of racial mixture and no one is totally white here. There are many people [who look] completely white but [have] black blood. The white [Brazilian] is very different, huh? The Brazilian has a body shape that is different, has the shape [physique] of the black. So I am classified as white, but I know very well that in my family we have African, black [ancestry].

Unlike whites in the United States, Lorena acknowledged that Brazilians can appear white while acknowledging their black ancestry. For Lorena and other Brazilians, the two are not at odds with each other. Lorena's use of the word "here" suggests she has multiple understandings of the relationship between race, skin color, and ancestry in Brazil. She invokes a transnational understanding of whiteness that influences her view of Brazil as an aspirational racial democracy after migration. Implicit in Lorena's and Vinícius's comments is the idea that white Brazilians are not "really white" in comparison with white Americans; again they are relying on the transnational racial optic to understand the racial mixture tenet of racial democracy in Brazil. Psychologically, these returnees connect nationality and race: to be Brazilian means being racially mixed regardless of phenotype, while to be American means being racially pure or part of what these returnees perceive to be distinct ethno-racial groups. Living in the United States, where returnees observed few interracial marriages, extensive segregation, and clearly defined racial categories, reaffirmed their belief that Brazil is a decidedly interracial society post-migration.

Oppressive View of Racial Democracy

Even though most Valadarenses described Brazil as a racially mixed country, 10 participants (three non-migrants and seven returnees) said that black-white relations were not cordial and that interracial mixing was not common. These individuals self-classified as pardo and black. A strongly held societal belief is that casual and intimate interracial relationships occur often because the Brazilian population is mixed. However, various scholars have contended that intermarriage in contemporary Brazil is exaggerated, and that most Brazilians marry people of the same color.[9] The Valadarenses who expressed ideas consistent with the oppressive view often cited resistance to interracial romantic relationships, especially those between blacks and whites. One of the seven returnees who expressed such a perception was Luiz, a 43-year-old black returnee:

LUIZ: I dated a white woman and her father didn't want it. He didn't like blacks. She ended it because her father didn't like me . . .

TJ: She told you this?

LUIZ: No, her father told her: "you can't date him." [She said] "why dad?" "Because the color black is very bad." So there's prejudice in Brazil, but it's more hidden. But we feel it in our skin, people look at you differently.

As a black man, Luiz attributed his personal experience with interracial dating to racism in Brazil. He also mentions the stigma associated with blackness in Brazil, which may shape some Brazilians' negative views of interracial relationships. Similarly, Márcia, a 26-year-old parda non-migrant, also observed that interracial dating and marriage are not as commonplace as most Brazilians perceive them to be:

The people I know always relate differently to each other. For example, a woman will marry or find a good boyfriend in my family like this, the husband is black and the woman is much lighter. But, generally, where I go, the social rules, you don't see this, you always see the same races together. The woman is white, the man is white. The man is black and so is his wife. I don't see this [mixing as] much. [But among] the people closest to me, there is mixing.

Though Márcia said that racial mixing had occurred in her family, she believed it was not as widespread in the larger society. She also associates finding a "good" partner with having lighter physical features, which is especially the case for lighter women, who are more sought after as romantic partners. While some Brazilians believe the racial mixing in the population represents Brazil's cordial interracial relations, some studies have documented that society penalizes people in interracial relationships.[10] Thus there would seem to be a contradiction between Brazilians' *expressed* attitudes and *actual* practices.

Relatedly, a few returnees mentioned that black-white interracial dating and marriage are not acceptable in their families, and that neighborhoods are not racially integrated. They implied that Brazil is not as socially integrated as previous studies on racial democracy have indicated. One of these was Sérgio, a 46-year-old moreno returnee:

Look, the great majority of people don't give importance to this [but] there are blacks that don't accept a white living in their neighborhoods. Similarly, there are many whites who don't like, for example, a white father that [doesn't want] a black man to date his daughter, but in my opinion, I see that there's discrimination on two parts [both blacks and whites].

Although respondents who expressed the oppressive view did not specifically refer to racial mixing in the Brazilian population, a 47-year-old parda non-migrant named Lígia did:

Here in Brazil, you are white or black. I am not white [but] generally people say, "look you are white." But I'm not white, white normally is another color. Racism exists, but normally people see [race] in black and white. I think it is much simpler, I don't know, than . . . black, white, yellow, brown . . . We [Brazilians] are all mixed. I am the daughter of, my ancestors are Italians mixed with Portuguese, and there's Indian too. My dad was white with very light skin and hair, his hair was very bad [kinky]. The mixture in my family is varied.

Lígia believes most Brazilians see race as "black and white." She was one of a few respondents to express the perception that Brazilians view race as a black-white binary rather than on a racially mixed continuum. Despite expressing this perception, Lígia then self-classified as parda and reemphasized that Brazilians are racially mixed. Many Brazilians use these multifaceted and at times contradictory perceptions to navigate race.

Interestingly, only one respondent actually used the term *democrâcia racial* when speaking with me about Brazilian race relations. This was Lucas, the 43-year-old black returnee who spoke of his experiences attending an African American church.[11] As a sociology professor at the local university in GV, Lucas's perception that Brazil has not achieved racial democracy is quite clear:

I always denied this, that we [Brazilians] are all equal, no, no. [With sarcasm] We are in a racial democracy, in Brazil there isn't prejudice. No, this is not true, this is a lie. In the past and [now] I continue to experience [racism] because there isn't a racial democracy in Brazil. I am a person that has social ascent in Brazil because I am a college professor. But this doesn't take away any risk of experiencing racial discrimination.

In addition to vehemently denying that Brazil is a racial democracy, Lucas also alludes to the falsity of the social whitening hypothesis in Brazil, which suggests that nonwhite Brazilians with a higher socioeconomic status can garner privileged social treatment in predominantly white social spaces.[12]

Comments from these respondents suggest that residential segregation, opposition to interracial relationships, and a fear of black Brazilians all in fact exist. They also suggest that racial democracy, as it is traditionally defined in the literature, is not a reality in Brazil. Note that Lucas characterizes Brazilian racial democracy as hypocrisy. These respondents recognized that while Brazilians share the attitude that everyone is equal and racism is minimal in Brazil, racial inequality exists and it is directed at blacks. For these respondents, the lack of interracial sociability and their direct experiences of racism are incongruent with the notion that Brazil has achieved racial democracy; they take the view that Brazil still struggles with an oppressive racial ideology.

U.S. Migration and Racial Democracy

More Valadarenses expressed opinions consistent with the aspirational view of racial democracy. Returnees (40 of 49) were more likely than non-migrants (8 of 24) to reference tenets of racial democracy in their interviews. Among the returnees, the aspirational view was also expressed more often. Yet some returnees also expressed opinions that overlapped with the oppressive view. Similar to Freyre, migrants' experiences in the United States shaped their perceptions of racial democracy after returning home. Their social positions in the Brazilian racial hierarchy likely influenced their views. While white and some pardo returnees articulated the aspirational view, black and pardo returnees espoused the oppressive view. Just as the transnational racial optic helped migrants negotiate the differences between U.S. and Brazilian race relations during their U.S. migration, the transnational racial optic had a similar influence on their reinterpretation of racial democracy in Brazil post-migration.

For the returnees who expressed the aspirational view, their exposure to U.S. racial categories, living in segregated neighborhoods, and experiencing discrimination likely made Brazilian race relations seem more fluid and cordial post-migration. Because most of these returnees classified themselves as white and pardo, they held a privileged position in the Brazilian racial hierarchy and experienced minimal social exclusion before and after migration. Given the fluidity of the white racial category and their belief that they have racially mixed ancestry, they embody Freyre's vision of a racial democracy yet recognize that racism exists. But for returnees with the oppressive view, observing and interacting with socially mobile black Americans likely highlighted the more marginalized position of black Brazilians. These returnees tended to be black and pardo and did not feel they were fully included in the achieved or aspirational racial democracy rhetoric. Living in the United States made Brazil seem more cordial and aspirational for most white returnees but less egalitarian and more oppressive for black and pardo returnees.

RACISM IN BRAZIL

Nearly all respondents believed that racism exists in Brazil, but many insisted that they personally were not racist and got along with people of all colors.[13] In their interviews with me, both returnees and non-migrants were quick to say they had grown up with blacks and even had black ancestry and relatives. One of these respondents was a 36-year-old white returnee named Isabela:

When I was growing up, I went to a black church, where the majority of the people, including my husband, are black. So I never had that, that barrier, none of that. I never thought about the color [race] of people, for me, everyone is the same.

White respondents like Isabela believed that their close social ties to blacks meant they were not racist. They associated racism with overtly discriminatory and prejudiced behavior. Nicolas, a moreno non-migrant, expressed this view:

Look, where I work, there are whites, lots of girls of the black race there, but with us, I've never seen anyone who has any kind of racism problem. I don't see this—I see everyone the same. We never had this problem there [on job]. I never saw a colleague come close to me, look at a person in a particular way because she is black! I never heard any type of comment like that.[14]

While Nicolas did not comment on the type of work these women did in his office or how their jobs compared with those of his white colleagues, he was insistent that prejudice was not a problem for him or his co-workers. Nicolas's and Isabela's accounts are consistent with the perceptions of racism discussed in other studies.[15] It was difficult for respondents, especially non-migrants, to recognize that racism can be manifested structurally and through unconscious behaviors.[16] Non-migrants instead focused on actual behaviors that could be interpreted as undoubtedly racist, such as calling someone a derogatory name or admitting to disliking someone because of his race. Conversely, returnees' experiences with overt racism and segregation in the United States made them more likely to acknowledge that structural racism, and not just blatantly racist attitudes, affected the opportunities of black Brazilians.

Anti-Black Racism

When I asked returnees and non-migrants to describe racism in Brazil, they told me that anti-black racism was prevalent in GV and throughout the country. Most returnees used the United States as a reference point for describing racism in Brazil. Although most respondents claimed that cordial relations existed between Brazilians of different colors, they also acknowledged that blacks were negatively stereotyped. Such assertions demonstrate the paradoxical relationship between *expressed* positive interracial interactions and *actual* negative structural conditions for black Brazilians, as highlighted in Edward Telles's theoretical explanation of horizontal and vertical Brazilian race relations.[17] Migrants' exposure to middle-class black Americans profoundly influenced their post-migration perceptions of how structural racism affects black Brazilians. Returnees felt that black Brazilians had fewer opportunities for social mobility than black Americans owing to the absence of large-scale political mobilization in Brazil. Their U.S. migration and subsequent return to Brazil allowed them to see the contrast between stratification in the two countries through the transnational racial optic, which shifted their understanding of racism.

Both return migrants and non-migrants cited discrimination against blacks in employment, schooling, and everyday social encounters (e.g., racial profiling, dating), as well as perceptions of all blacks as violent or poor as specific examples of anti-black racism.[18] For Maurício, the 24-year-old moreno non-migrant I quoted earlier, the perceived marginalization of blacks is pervasive:

It's like I said. In high society, they [most Brazilians] think that if you're black, you have to be a domestic [worker] or have a service job [like a maid]. They don't treat them [blacks] like other people, you know? As much in the high social class and in the middle class too. Because it's difficult in our country to see a black as an economist or mayor, you know? Our country, I can't remember having a black president.

Blacks are seen differently from other Brazilians regardless of their social class. They are expected to work in low-status jobs, and even when they seek better employment opportunities, they remain disadvantaged because they lack *boa aparência*, "a good appearance." Rosângela, a black 54-year-old non-migrant, explained:

In terms of work, the black has more difficulty finding a good job compared to a white person. Here, I can be capable, [but] between me and a blonde, the blonde will get the job even if she doesn't have the same capability as me. Because here, appearance in the majority of places comes first. Just like this story I told you, they [employers] don't put "good appearance" in the job ad, [but] at any rate between a black and a white, the white will have advantages in relation to work or anything else.

For Rosângela, having *boa aparência* meant being white and blonde and thus being hired regardless of one's qualifications. Other studies have documented that, from the 1950s to the 1980s, requiring applicants to have *boa aparência* disadvantaged black Brazilians in the labor market.[19] The term was used in employment announcements to exclude or discourage nonwhites from applying. Although the term was declared illegal in the 1980s, studies in 2000 and 2011 by social anthropologist Caetana Damasceno and psychologist Maria Bento found that employers still relied informally on racial (and gender) stereotypes to hire, promote, and fire their employees.[20] Rosângela believes this practice still occurs, even if unofficially, in present-day Brazil.

Other respondents also commented on the importance of physical appearance in Brazil, particularly how Brazilians infer a person's class based on attire or hairstyle, because it can determine how he or she is treated by others.[21] While these features are usually associated with social class, an individual's skin color, hair texture, and other racial markers may also serve as a proxy for social class. Carolina, a 44-year-old morena returnee, explained this relationship with a typical joke made about blacks in Brazil:

Generally they say "black, poor, and thief." So this is a form of prejudice. And when people notice social class, generally they're talking [about] blacks. And at times, people say "ah, this service here wasn't done right, it's black, it's something a black did." So they say that at times. I think it's to humiliate people.

Carolina refers to two popular expressions used to describe blacks. The first expression "black, poor, and thief" (Portuguese: "*preto, pobre, e ladrão*") indicates a broad societal perception that black Brazilians are thieves because of their socially marginalized position. The second expression, "it's something a black did" (Portuguese: "*fazer o preto*" or "*serviço de preto*"), usually means that a task was done inadequately or unsatisfactorily. Carolina and other respondents commented that the reference to poor work implies the inferior quality of tasks done by blacks. Camila, a 48-year-old mixed returnee, mentioned another expression that portrays blacks as suspects and thieves:

For example in Brazil, there's a very weighted term that I'll tell you, if you see a black person stopped [in the streets], he is a suspect. If you see him running, he's a thief. You see? There are some humiliating phrases that people use . . . [Racism] exists cordially. People discriminate, it's all veiled. It's not face to face, but it's veiled. There is racism.

Respondents often shared these expressions with me when I asked how racism is expressed in Brazil, demonstrating their recognition that such phrases are racist or prejudiced and how they relate to the inferior social position of black Brazilians.

The responses of many returnees and non-migrants to my questions about blacks also suggested that blacks are not welcome in elite (read: white) social spaces, such as wealthy neighborhoods or expensive restaurants. Their presence is questioned when they enter such spaces as patrons because black Brazilians are usually assumed to work as domestic employees or chauffeurs. When asked her perception of racism in the United States and Brazil, Amanda, a white returnee, responded by providing an example of how blacks are expected to use the "service" elevator instead of the "social" elevator in expensive apartment buildings:

I think the American people are not so, they are not as racist as Brazilian people. They respect the black people more than the Brazilian ones. There is um . . . a commercial [with Ronaldo "Ronaldinho" de Assis Moreira, the famous Brazilian soccer player]. So, his mother is black and she was waiting for the elevator. And she's black, of course and she's old . . . and was poor, very very poor. Now, she's rich because [of] her son. So, she was waiting for the elevator, I, I imagine that uh, a very rich place going to her apartment maybe. And then there was a, a woman . . . a very fancy, blonde, beautiful, rich woman. Then the woman looked at her and like, up and down and said, "the service elevator is the other one." So the [white] woman was trying to say that . . . she [the black woman] didn't belong. But of course, it was because the woman was black. And then, the woman, the black woman looked at her, said nothing, and then she went to the [social] elevator. Only because the woman was black, she [the white woman] thought the woman was poor.

Given the history of race relations in the United States and Brazil, one might be surprised that Amanda saw Americans as less racist than Brazilians. As a returnee, her frame of reference for interpreting the social position of black Brazilians is the United States. She explicitly ties black Brazilians' social position to structural racism by citing blacks' marginalized status. Amanda feels the United States is less racist because black Americans have more social opportunities.

Gustavo, who spoke at length about black Americans' social mobility in comparison with that of black Brazilians,[22] also perceived black Brazilians to be particularly disadvantaged:

[In] institutions, yes [there's racism]. In Brazil, the black is usually a domestic worker and making minimum wage with the worst jobs. So there's prejudice, he is considered less capable, less intelligent in Brazil. And you can see in all of Brazil that blacks are excluded, they're in the favelas, they're living poorly on the periphery.

The experiences of Amanda, Gustavo, and other returnees in the United States, especially their observations of middle-class black Americans, shaped their post-migration perceptions of anti-black racism, both overt and covert, in Brazil. Returnees directly connected black Brazilians' marginalized social position with pervasive institutional and structural racism.

Cordial Racism

Although return migrants and non-migrants provided detailed examples of anti-black racism in Brazil, many felt this racism was covert. Such racism has been referred to as "cordial racism" in the literature because it is so subtle.[23] Respondents agreed that cordial racism is prevalent in Brazil. Giovana, a 35-year-old light morena non-migrant, believes that although Brazilians acknowledge that racism exists, they will say they are not racist:

Here, the racism is more like a mask, everyone says no [they're not racist], but the majority is. At times they say they are not racist, but they don't really mean it. For instance, my grandfather, he's white, almost transparent, blue eyes, and descended from Italians, and I have a cousin [who] is very brown, she looks like an Indian. And he practically disowned her, saying that she is black and things like that.

Giovana does not explicitly state that her grandfather denies being racist, but she uses his antipathy of the "black" phenotype to illustrate how Brazilians can have racist beliefs without directly stating them. Another returnee, Lorena, discussed how having fairer skin or *boa aparência* covertly privileges lighter Brazilians as an example of cordial racism:

It's very disguised. It's like hidden, why? Because for example, I see this, but I don't participate in this. If you have a job, like a secretary in a school and there's a person with a light appearance [skin tone], tall and a morena person, normally people say [the white] was chosen for her résumé and many times it's because of appearance. I don't do this, but I notice this when there's an important job.

Giovana and Lorena both suggest that while people may say they are not racist, they may in fact hold racist beliefs about individuals that can influence their social and professional interactions, especially with black Brazilians. These comments are particularly informative given the number of Valadarenses who said they were not racist during interviews. Respondents provided examples of how racism exists in Brazil, but they were careful to emphasize that they themselves did not engage in racist behavior. This was especially true for white and pardo respondents, one of whom was Douglas, a 36-year-old white non-migrant:

How can I explain this? I think this way, cordially, I don't have problems in relation to this [being racist] . . . [but] I know that the black here in Brazil has much difficulty in ascending to elevated social classes, as much in school as in work, [there's] much discrimination. It's not that I feel this way [prejudiced], but I see the white as more privileged in our country. It's a latent racism in Brazil. Latent, you understand? Latent means somewhat hidden . . . politically correct: "everything's good and all," but deep down, there is [racism]. Have you noticed this? Not that I act like this, but this is my perception.

Douglas tells me three times he is not racist or does not discriminate against blacks while explaining how he perceives that blacks are treated in Brazil. I found that Valadarenses discussed racism as something that exists concretely but that only abstractly affects black Brazilians. Racism is out there in Brazilian society, but no one I interviewed felt they actively played a part in the manifestation of interpersonal or structural racism aimed toward blacks. Respondents recognized the prevalence of racism in Brazil but felt they were not conscious perpetrators of racist behavior. Such proclamations are not unlike those of white Americans who also deny being racist or prejudiced but are unable to make connections between structural racism and the marginalized position of black Americans. Multiple scholars have argued that overtly prejudiced and anti-black attitudes are not as common among contemporary white Americans as they were in the first half of the twentieth century.[24] However, these scholars also argue that the nature of racism has changed such that white Americans feel they are not complicit in the racial oppression and subsequent inequality that blacks and other ethno-racial minorities experience. A consequence of such behavior is that Brazilians and Americans do not feel inclined to disrupt structural racism or support policies that reduce racial inequality.[25]

Recent studies of racism and racial attitudes in Brazil confirm that Brazilians' perceptions of racism in their country are colored by history and the prevalence of racial democracy ideology.[26] Sociologist Graziella Silva found that middle-class blacks in Rio de Janeiro believe racism is tied to the history of slavery, which results in black Brazilians' continued marginalized social status. She argued that "such a broad definition of racism removes the responsibility from individuals and groups" since racism is rooted in a historical and social process external to individual social actors.[27] France Winddance Twine and Angela Figueiredo have also found that Brazilians believe racism means *expressed* prejudiced behavior in interpersonal interactions.[28] The Valadarenses I interviewed shared views of racism consistent with these findings. However, returnees' experiences of overt discrimination in the United States reinforced a Brazilian view of racism as one that includes cordial prejudiced behavior as separate from the structural mechanisms that disadvantage browns and blacks in Brazil.

Influence of U.S. Migration on the Perceptions
of Brazilian Racism among Returnees

When I asked returnees if they felt their perceptions of racism had changed after living in the United States, roughly 40 percent (19 of 49) said yes. Those individuals thought racism in the United States was greater and more visible than in Brazilian society, but they also believed that Brazilians pay more attention to physical appearance and social class, which can result in discrimination against those perceived as poor. For example, Stephane, a 43-year-old *morena*, observed:

We come back more sensitive and aware that we don't have this prejudice with color, if a person is white, black, or American . . . We learn not to give value to these things [because] everyone is normal . . . We become less prejudiced in terms of race and color.

Because of her experiences in the United States, Stephane associated the hyper-importance of racial classification ("this prejudice with color") in the United States with racism. Curiously, she felt that living abroad made her and other returnees less prejudiced, or caused them to notice skin color less. It appears that her U.S. migration made Stephane both more and less sensitive to racial differences between people: more sensitive in that she recognized the importance of racial classification in the United States, but less sensitive in that those classifications had no bearing on how she treated people of different racial groups in GV. She believed that post-migration she was more able to recognize the humanity of individuals rather than their racial classification. She seems to believe that migration allowed her to adopt a color-blind view of Brazil. Though it could be argued that this view is consistent with the aspirational view of racial democracy (Stephane believes racism exists in Brazil), her experience living in the United States convinced her that racial differences are less important in post-migration Brazil.

A 27-year-old *morena* returnee named Erika also discussed the importance of social class in the United States and Brazil:

Everything is different there in the U.S. I lived there five years and I didn't socialize with them [Americans]. I perceived that they don't like immigrants, and Brazil receives immigrants very well, especially Americans in Brazil. There we are poorly received. Perhaps the U.S. is more prejudiced in terms of color and immigrants . . . I don't think Americans look at social class. [In Brazil] social class is everything, education, clothing, everything.

Erika also emphasized the amount of social segregation and anti-immigrant sentiment she observed in the United States.[29] Seven other returnees also referenced the hyper-segregation they noticed in the United States, which influenced their post-migration perceptions of Brazil as being more racially integrated.

A 38-year-old pardo returnee named Antônio had the opposite perception of Stephane and Erika about the importance of skin color in the United States and Brazil:

My racial classification didn't change; what changed was how people see [racial] classification, how other people classify. I learned a little bit that they [Americans] don't give much importance to skin color. I thought this was good for me so I could grow to learn this. Not that I discriminated against anyone, but for the fact that the Brazilian has this characteristic of sometimes judging others based on skin color. I learned that we [Brazilians] should never do this in our thinking. So, it [immigration] helped me grow.

Contrary to most other returnees' perceptions and studies of race in the United States (and in Brazil for that matter), Antônio expresses the opinion that skin color and racial classification are more important in Brazil. Perhaps this is because Antônio's U.S. experience was largely positive. Despite being undocumented and not speaking much English when he first arrived, he became proficient in English and was eventually able to get a good job as a car salesperson at a dealership in Danbury, Connecticut. Because of the high concentration of Brazilians in that city, his employer recognized the benefit of having a native Brazilian to attract Brazilian customers. As a result, Antônio was able to earn a considerable income and have cordial relationships with his white American co-workers. Being successful despite his medium-brown skin and undocumented status, made Antônio feel that the United States was more accepting of individuals regardless of their skin color or documentation status. For Antônio, his awareness of the importance of physical appearance in post-migration Brazil contrasted with the relative insignificance of appearance and social status in the United States. He brought this view back to Brazil, which influenced his perception of racism there:

Brazil still needs to learn a lot about racism and race [from the U.S.]. Brazil has a lot to learn, [but] it's improved. My view, not that it was discriminatory, but because of the fact that I lived in the U.S. all that time, I know that they [Americans] don't use skin color to classify a person. So, I think that Brazil has much to learn in terms of race.

Antônio used the word "classify" in Portuguese to describe Americans' "use" of skin color. But in this particular context, Antônio felt that Americans do not explicitly *judge* individuals based on skin color, a marker of physical appearance. Other returnees also referred to the greater importance of appearance in Brazil relative to the United States, using it to assess the extent of racism in both countries. Oddly, despite most returnees' encounters with discrimination and being racialized as nonwhite in the United States, they believed that documentation status, rather than skin color or appearance, shaped their position in the American social hierarchy. Returnees also believed in the Horatio Alger stories, which are based on the notion that anyone can realize the American Dream, regardless of background. They felt that being in the United States, even if working in a low-wage job, would provide social mobility in GV after returning. Although returnees felt race was significantly more important in the United States, they also felt social mobility was more equally distributed among Americans of different *races*. This perception contrasted with their views of Brazil, where race did not seem to be as significant as social class: Brazilians of all skin tones struggled to survive financially, and physical appearance privileged some Brazilians over others. The migration experience connected these two perspectives for returnees.

Comparing Racism in Brazil and the United States

In comparing the *questão racial* or the "racial issue" in both countries, returnees emphasized three themes: the extent of racism, the perceived level of segregation, and the importance of social class and physical appearance in each country. Since I have already discussed the latter two, I will now examine returnees' perceptions of the extent of racism in both countries. Twelve returnees believed there was either no racism in Brazil or that it was less of a problem than in the United States given the high levels of social segregation they observed between different U.S. ethno-racial groups. A Latina returnee named Renata expressed this view:

There's a big difference [between race in the U.S. and Brazil]. The Brazilian is more
open, we treat [everyone] well, the black, the white. For example, if you go to a church
here in Brazil, there are blacks, whites, morenos, [and they] are all treated the same.
And in the U.S., I saw that there was a Baptist Church with only blacks, [and one]
with only whites.

However, 11 returnees thought that Brazil and the United States had similar
levels of racism. Natália, a white returnee, stated:

I try to explain [to others] that the vision of race that Americans have is different from
ours. It's not a question of if they are more racist than us, we [Brazilians] can be as racist as them. What distinguishes here, what makes them different [are] the parameters,
the models that we use to be racist and their models.

Natália and other returnees who believed that the United States and Brazil
were equally racist recognized that the parameters for assessing racism are different in both countries. While they acknowledged that racism in each nation
was equally detrimental, they felt it was difficult to say that one is more racist
than the other.

A black returnee named Fernando, who feels both countries are racist toward blacks, believed a key difference between the United States and Brazil is
the enforcement of law and people's awareness of their rights:

FERNANDO: The difference is that there [the U.S.] has laws and they [Americans]
    use the law. And here, there are laws, but I don't know, they're not really followed.
TJ: What types of laws?
FERNANDO: The law is like this. If you call me a *negro*, I can go to court, file a claim,
    and you have to go to the court. There in the U.S., they'll charge you [with a
    crime]. Here, if you go to court . . . a lawyer will enter, talk [to] and pay [the
    judge] and it's all over.[30]

Though he was deported, Fernando told me he became more aware of his
rights, both as an immigrant and as a human being, after returning to Brazil.
While the above exchange oversimplifies how the legal process works in racial
discrimination cases in each country, Fernando's perception about the validity of
the legal system is tied to the culture of the United States and Brazil. Fernando
was not the only returnee to refer to the United States as a place where people
have more rights and where government functions effectively for its people.

While all of their legal references were not related to race, they illustrated the returnees' views of how culture influences the enforcement of law, especially regarding individuals' constitutional rights in each country. These differences influenced returnees' perceptions of the relationship between the law and race in both countries, which in turn shaped their perceptions of racism in each place. For example, a morena named Camila spoke extensively about sharing her perception of the law, individual rights, and race in the United States and Brazil with others in GV:

TJ: Do you ever talk about experiences and perceptions of your life in the U.S.?

CAMILA: Yes, I always discuss this with friends and people who lived there [other returnees], we see a huge difference in relation to the rights that people have there . . .

TJ: What types of rights?

CAMILA: School, education, you know. Because our [Brazilian] constitution says that everyone has the right to health care, education, decent housing. This doesn't happen in our country. It's something that's only on paper. We don't have the right to come and go because many times that we need to go to another city, there's no way to get there.

TJ: Do you also talk with others about your perceptions of race?

CAMILA: I talk about the respect that you have for [general] citizenship, when you respect a person, you automatically respect their race. I know that there in the U.S., they have problems with the racial question [issue], especially in Mississippi, New York. Also in Boston, there's a city [area] that's very violent, Dorchester, Jamaica Plain, where the blacks don't let whites enter. There exists conflict, but in spite of the conflict, I see that the government treats its people equally. There are schools for them [blacks], it's they who self-segregate, and separate, not the government.

In Camila's view, the U.S. government plays an active role in ensuring the "equal" treatment of all Americans regardless of race, whereas she perceives that the Brazilian government does little for its people to promote racial equality or provide access to basic resources. Given the growing income inequality between Americans of different social classes and racial groups, along with the erosion of social welfare programs in recent years, some Americans might disagree with Camila's assessment. But her exposure to life in the United States provided a frame of reference for interpreting how government policies may produce equality between different racial groups in each country. Despite detesting the ineffectiveness of the Brazilian government, Camila also believed that Brazilian society was beginning to pay more attention to the *questão racial*. She linked the diverse ethno-racial histories of the United States and Brazil and discussed how migrants play a role in helping Brazil take social cues from the United States:

Brazil is waking up to this now and the U.S. woke up a much longer time ago than Brazil. Why? The U.S. is a country of immigrants, but Brazil is [also] a country of many races, Indian [Indigenous] mixed with black, white. People have come from abroad and now there is mixture. So they are two similar countries, why? There was much mixing of the races because the U.S. went through the same process as Brazil. The blacks came from Africa, there were Indians just like Brazil. The whites also came from Portugal to Brazil, from Ireland and England to the U.S. So they underwent the same process. It's just that one country woke up before the other. And the U.S. woke up more quickly to this problem [of racism]. And Brazil is waking up now. Why? Because more people are going to school and learning this [racism] is a crime. The Brazilian is studying more, seeing more things. So that's why he is modifying his ideas, discovering he has rights, that he is a citizen. He pays taxes. So he has to take advantage of his rights and all of us, regardless of race, color, sex, we are citizens subject to the law, and there's only one law. We are discovering this, broadening our horizons. So, many of us [migrants] go abroad and come back with new ideas.

Camila explicitly credits the migration experience for her perceptions of social and political changes in Brazil. For her and other returnees, the migration and subsequent return had a significant impact on how they readapted to Brazil, especially increasing their awareness of their rights and the need for civic engagement. Curiously, Camila also believed that having more education makes people more aware of racism. Other studies of racism in Brazil have found a similar perception among Brazilians: that racism is the result of individuals' ignorance and that, over time and with education, racism and racist behavior will fade away.[31] However, those studies also discuss the structural and institutional aspects of racism that perpetuate inequality between black, white, and brown Brazilians.

Surprisingly, eight returnees felt the United States was less racist than Brazil owing to the perceived higher social position of black Americans and the existence of more effective anti-discrimination laws. This is was true for Sofia, a 44-year-old returnee with fair skin, black eyes, and straight, dark-brown hair:[32]

SOFIA: I think that in the U.S. they don't look at the racism of, the skin color, as much as they do in Brazil. In Brazil, skin color has less importance; it is less accepted . . . than in the U.S.

TJ: So you are saying in Brazil that racism, skin color, is less [important]. Is there something else that is more important here in Brazil?

SOFIA: Here in Brazil, it is more, skin color, they look at it more.

TJ: Brazilians look more at skin color?

SOFIA: They look at it more than in the U.S. I think so.

TJ: In what way? Can you provide an example of this difference?

SOFIA: In terms of finding jobs, moving through society as a professional, in school . . .

TJ: Here in Brazil?

SOFIA: When I put my child in school here, I had to fill out a form asking for his skin color.

TJ: And you didn't have to do this in the U.S.?

SOFIA: No. And, my child studies in a class with only whites, he was the only dark one with very curly hair. My goodness! And here, I had to talk with my son about skin color. They classified my son as pardo.

TJ: And in the U.S., would you say there is more racism in terms of skin color?

SOFIA: Less . . . In Brazil, there is more, the U.S. has less. I see that in the U.S., blacks have more opportunities than they do in Brazil.

For a number of returnees, the transnational racial optic affected how they interpreted racism and racial inequality. Although most lived as undocumented and racialized immigrants with few rights in the United States, they believed the United States was a country where the law was respected and equally implemented among U.S. citizens. This perception, along with their observations of middle-class black Americans, altered how they saw the social position of black Brazilians after returning. They concluded that Brazil is a more socially unequal society than the United States because an individual's social class, physical appearance, and inability to fight for his or her rights further marginalizes Brazilians, especially those who are black and socially disadvantaged in other ways (e.g., poor, physically or mentally handicapped). In contrast, some returnees perceived that all people, regardless of race or social class, had greater opportunities for social mobility in the United States and had legal recourse if they experienced discrimination.

INFLUENCE OF U.S. MIGRATION ON RACE IN GV

Given the long history of migration from GV to the United States and its racial influence on returnees, I wondered if U.S. racial ideals were similarly affecting race relations and facilitating returnees' and non-migrants' ability to racially make America in their city. Because non-migrants talked extensively about the impact of U.S. migration on GV, I asked if they felt their migrant relatives were different after returning. Nearly all non-migrants (21 of 24) believed their relatives had changed. Among this group of non-migrants, the majority thought the changes were negative. Non-migrants mentioned that some returnees had difficulty readapting to GV and reconnecting with family they had left behind. They returned money-hungry and complained a lot about GV and Brazil as being poor, corrupt, and disorganized. According to non-migrants, returnees became "Americanized" during their time away, which resulted in their undesirable behavior. Some of the most common phrases non-migrants used to describe returnees were: *voltam fechados* (they return closed off), *se sentem superiores* (they feel superior to non-migrants), and *são insuportáveis* (they are insufferable).

These comments led me to ask whether the non-migrants felt returnees also came back racially Americanized. Most non-migrants (15 of 24) reported that they had not discussed racial issues with returnee relatives either during their time away or after they returned. Among the nine that did, however, non-migrants said their relatives talked about prejudice against Latinos and Latin Americans, and emphasized that Brazilians did not want to be confused with Hispanics. Douglas, a white non-migrant heard about this distinction from other returnees, including his sister, Natália:

Look, this is what I think, the Brazilian in general, he discriminates against Hispanics, Puerto Ricans in the U.S. Many times [the perception you get] from Americans, I have never been there, but the idea that Americans don't really like Hispanics, Mexicans, Puerto Ricans, from Hispanic America. [So] The Brazilian doesn't like to be confused with Hispanics.

This flow of transnational information from their relatives then shaped non-migrants' perceptions of Hispanics and exposed them to U.S. ethno-racial relations. Sociologists Wendy Roth and Elizabeth Aranda found a similar process among non-migrants in the Dominican Republic and Puerto Rico.[33]

Another thing that non-migrants learned about the United States from their returnee relatives was that black and white Americans do not mix socially, especially in romantic relationships. Hugo, a 48-year-old black non-migrant, told me about his brother Luiz's experiences in the United States:

[My brother] interacted and worked with blacks and confirmed what we [Brazilians] already knew from TV, that the black American, he doesn't get involved, for example, in a romantic relationship, a black American, with people of another color. Why? Because he suffered a lot in the past, we see a lot in movies that when a man and woman want to date, if he's of a different race than her, it's like an affront to the family. And here, it's beyond being an affront to the family, the black in relation to the white, the Japanese, or a person of a different race . . . the black, the black American family acts this way, the black acts this way, the majority don't get involved [romantically] with a person of another race.

Though Hugo acknowledged that Brazilians learn about race in the United States from the media, his views were reinforced by his migrant brother's firsthand accounts.[34] Similarly, a 38-year-old morena non-migrant named Denise said she heard about extensive residential segregation between blacks and whites:

I heard that they [Americans] separate themselves, many cities and neighborhoods, I don't know. It's something that doesn't happen in Brazil. Brazilians are all mixed. The Brazilian is Indian, white, black, pardo, yellow, it's all mixed. I had heard that in the U.S., the races separate . . . I had heard [this] directly from people who returned from there and talked about it, that there in the U.S., there is a city that only has blacks. They [returnees] also said that white people couldn't enter [and] that there's confusion.

Some also heard about their relatives' experiences of anti-immigrant discrimination while they were still living abroad. These discussions further shaped non-migrants' perceptions of the United States as a less tolerant country than Brazil. A 19-year old white non-migrant named Olivia believed her migrant sister experienced anti-immigrant discrimination:

When I spoke with my sister? She said she never experienced any racism. The only thing she said was that there, the Brazilian works a lot, like this because [employers knew] she was an immigrant, knew that she was in the country illegally, they work a lot. But not racism.

Interestingly, non-migrants often framed their returnee relatives' experiences of discrimination as a result of their undocumented status. Hardly any non-migrants ascribed their relatives' experiences to racism or being perceived as nonwhite. Most of the migrants who experienced racial discrimination did not share specific details of those encounters with non-migrants because the migrants wanted their relatives in Brazil to think they were having positive experiences.[35] Note that non-migrants' perceptions of race in the United States align with those described by returnees in Chapters 2 and 3: that Brazilians are perceived as Hispanics and that there is social segregation and anti-immigrant discrimination. Returnees in this study shared U.S. racial ideals with non-migrant relatives that overlapped with their perceptions of race in the United States.

Of the 21 non-migrants who felt returnees were different post-migration, only four had responses that were explicitly race-related. This finding was somewhat surprising given that the non-migrants spoke in such detail about the non-racial ways that the U.S. migration influenced returnees. In two of those responses, non-migrants commented that the migrants returned "whiter" because of the climate. As discussed in Chapter 4, this perception was more common among returnees. However, the other two non-migrants mentioned that returnees benefited from living in the United States and from observing Americans who fight for their rights, unlike in Brazil. Lígia, a non-migrant, said:

When they return, they complain about everything because "the U.S. is like this." One thing they brought from there in addition to the Dollar Store and McDonald's is lawsuits. It's interesting, fighting [standing up for oneself] is part of the American culture, to fight for your rights, no matter what its costs. It doesn't matter if you are black or white, if someone steps on your foot, action is taken. Now, here in Brazil, people are starting to do this and I think it's interesting. It's a cool thing they [returnees] picked up, if the black feels offended, he sues. If the white feels offended, he sues. If customers receive bad service, they are suing. So I think it is a positive change [that] these people had there [in the U.S.] and brought here. They learned it [there].

Lígia perceives returnees' adoption of this "American" behavior, filing lawsuits, as a good thing even though returnees "complain about everything." Her perception of returnees' increased civic engagement overlaps with that of returnees. It is through returnees that some non-migrants learn Americans are willing to take legal action when they experience discrimination or a social offense.

In addition, most non-migrants felt that extensive migration between the United States and Brazil had not affected broader GV race relations. One of these non-migrants was Douglas:

Look, [in terms of] the racial question, it [migration] has an influence, yes, but I think it is very small. The immigrant who leaves from here to go there, he has already formed [his] racial thinking, his culture of race is already there. So, if he has a tendency to be racist, he will return from there with this tendency. His perception of being racist will continue the same, this will not change. I don't think it will get worse or better. I think it depends very much on the situation in which he was born, the family, the cultural base that he had. If he grew up hearing his parents talk about not liking blacks . . . he will grow up with that mentality. Now if he grows up with a family structure where people respect each other . . . he will become a person who is able to relate [well] with the world.

Six non-migrants felt that U.S. migration had had a positive racial impact in GV, and three non-migrants specifically mentioned that learning to live with a diverse group of people was a particular benefit. These non-migrants said that, in comparison with GV, the United States is a more global society, with people from around the world. They thought that, as a result, returnees came back with a different frame of mind and were more open to different experiences. One of these non-migrants was Maurício:

[A migrant] has to interact with people from all over the world. In the U.S., there are people from various parts of the world. So, [a return migrant] has a really different perception. Definitely, they return with a very modified head [way of seeing the world], [migration] definitely changes their vision. They return to Brazil with a totally different mindset because there, they see the black race fighting for their rights. Here, blacks are in the minority and prefer to isolate themselves instead of fighting directly. That's the reality. From living with different people, ethnicities, countries, their [return migrants'] perception is different. They don't have this here, the blacks here. They don't have cultural access in relation to this. And in the U.S., whether they [migrants] want to or not, interacting with different races and people, they end up having a totally different perception than the people here [non-migrants].

Maurício believes that black Americans' political activism influences returnees' post-migration racial perceptions, which they share with other Valadarenses. Denise, a 38-year-old morena, credits the back-and-forth movement of returnees with improving GV race relations:

I think it is changing [race relations] for the better, you know, because from the time that many Brazilians, many foreigners, entered the U.S. and vice-versa [Americans came to Brazil], people are understanding more and [so] there is less racism. I think that people are seeking to understand more, I think it is changing, I believe it is. I think it needs to change [because] as human beings, I think we need to understand everyone.

While Denise was not specific about how race relations are improving or between which racial groups, she tied increased racial tolerance in GV with the intercultural awareness that came from migrants living in the United States.

Finally, Rosângela, the non-migrant I quoted at the beginning of the chapter, mentioned that migrants who returned and "succeeded" in the United States regardless of color are treated well in GV. In her opinion, U.S. migration increased the social mobility of returnees, especially the nonwhite ones, such that they receive better social treatment. She also echoed a broad Brazilian societal perception that money contributes to social whitening. However, only a few returnees were able to reach their financial goals while living in the United States and obtain a satisfactory level of financial security. None of those returnees were black.

For the most part, non-migrants did not feel that extensive migration between GV and the United States had a perceptible impact on racial dynamics in the city. Although they acknowledged hearing about race in the United States from returnees during and after migration, non-migrants did not think that the U.S. racial ideals that returnees brought back had *racially* changed GV. This finding is different from what Roth found in Puerto Rico and the Dominican Republic, where non-migrants adopted a pan-ethnic nationality racial schema.[36] Those non-migrants appropriated the U.S. Latino and Hispanic categories as a result of the cross-border diffusion of U.S. ethno-racial categories via migrants and through popular U.S. Latino media sources (e.g., Univisión).

My findings among Valadarense non-migrants suggest a different racialized transnational relationship with the United States for a few reasons. First, owing to language and cultural differences, Univisión and similar forms of

U.S. Latino media are not widely available in Brazil. This means that the cultural norms developed among U.S. Latinos are less accessible to Brazilians, who already perceive themselves to be culturally distinct from Spanish Latin Americans. Second, Brazil is home to large media conglomerates that transmit programming globally, which means that Brazilians are more likely to watch Brazilian and mainstream U.S. television programming that reinforces Brazilian exceptionalism and exposes them to American culture. These media outlets contribute to shaping Brazilians' racial ideals. Though the visibility of Latinos and Hispanics has increased in mainstream U.S. media in recent years, the majority of U.S. programming broadcast in Brazil consist of predominantly white casts with some black Americans and limited representation of other ethno-racial groups.[37] Therefore, Brazilians in general, and Valadarenses specifically, are more likely to encounter U.S. media images from a black-white binary perspective, rather than one with U.S. Hispanics or Latinos.[38] Finally, given Brazilians' reluctance to "notice" race, it is possible that non-migrants did not make more overtly racial observations in our interviews because doing so would be considered racist, which is un-Brazilian.

Like non-migrants, the majority of returnees spoke at length about the economic and cultural impact of U.S. migration in GV but had little to say about a racial impact. My exchange with Fabio, a 51-year-old white returnee, illustrates this point:

TJ: And in what other ways do you think immigration has affected the city? Culturally, economically, in terms of relations between people of different colors?

FABIO: In terms of color, no [impact]. But culturally, of course, whether people want to admit it or not. I'll give you an example of cultural, education [manners]. In the U.S., it's illegal to throw trash in the street. Here, people don't care much about that . . . when they [immigrants] arrive [in the U.S.], they are required to learn quickly that you can be arrested or pay a fine [for littering]. So when they arrive here, they look [for a wastebasket, wondering] "where will I throw my trash?" But, there isn't one. So they learn, culturally they've had this experience. Financially, [migration] affects [GV] a lot, the dollar is [now] low, when the dollar is high, it's better for the city.

TJ: Are there additional ways migration has had an impact in the city?

FABIO: No, I think it's mostly like this, family, culture, and I gave you an economic example.

In short, very few return migrants thought GV race relations were changing due to migration: only eight of 49 thought there was any type of racial impact. These eight returnees had mixed opinions about the racial impact: four believed there had been a positive impact, one thought there was a negative impact, and three did not think the impact was positive or negative.

With regard to positive effects, four returnees believed living in the United States opened their minds through their interactions with people of different backgrounds. These returnees thought this open-mindedness could be passed along in GV as migrants come back and interact with non-migrants. Returnees like Bianca (quoted at the beginning of this chapter) believe their transnational experiences can bring more awareness to fellow Valadarenses and make them more global citizens. Because GV is in a primarily rural state with very few Indigenous- or Asian-descended people, Valadarenses learn about other ethnicities and cultures from return migrants, who play an important role in shaping non-migrants' perceptions of the world beyond GV and Brazil.

Carolina, the one returnee who believed U.S. migration has negatively influenced race relations in GV, commented that children raised in the United States make racist comments. She felt such behavior was not characteristic of Brazilians:

CAROLINA: I think everything is influenced [in GV from migration] . . . because parents who have children there or take their children there and grow up there at times come [back] with conceptions from there and bring them here. So, I think in a certain way, there is an impact . . .

TJ: So, in your opinion, do you have an example of this, or how have you observed this in Valadares?

CAROLINA: Sometimes, I observe their behavior in the mall, they say certain things, their pronunciation . . . They say racist things.

TJ: What types of racist things?

CAROLINA: They talk about other people in a racist way. At times when they're talking, it's the kind of thing that is not ours [Brazilian]. This transition is not from our culture, it's brought [by return migrants].

Though Carolina was not specific about how these children "talk about other people in a racist way," she implied that Valadarenses picked up this behavior in the United States and that it had influenced race relations in GV. Carolina acknowledged the existence of racism in Brazil earlier in our interview, but here she attempts to distance overt displays of racist behavior from Brazilian culture. Like other respondents, she said that she does not participate in this behavior and is not complicit in Brazilian racism.

For Felipe, the returnee who described himself as "white, but not 100% white," the U.S. migration had neither a positive nor a negative impact on race relations in GV. He said that some returnees use U.S. racial categories to classify Brazilians when they come back to GV:

Some people bring [racial ideals from the U.S.] because many people have that obsession of classifying others, "oh, he is this [racially] and calls [another] black, [another] white, [another] Japanese." There are, some people bring [this], but I think the majority do not. The Brazilian in reality is not racist, the Brazilian has no way to be racist because our race is mixed.

In Chapter 4, I discussed how Felipe thought his own perceptions of other Brazilians' racial classifications shifted after the migration experience. Felipe also believed that other returnees might have a similar experience after living in the more race-conscious United States. However, he did not include himself as one of those returnees. Interestingly, he also implied that focusing on racial differences between people is racist, and like Carolina, said that Brazilians cannot be racist.

Felipe's comments illustrate the transnational racial optic at work: while he acknowledged that he notices racial differences between people, which he associates with his experience in the United States, he believed that noticing such differences is racist and therefore un-Brazilian. These two views of race, one more American and the other more Brazilian, conflict with each other in Felipe's mind. Like Felipe, Vinícius, a 31-year-old "Portuguese" returnee, thought that some returnees have a different perception of racial classification:

[Migrants] get accustomed to saying someone went from [being] moreno to black. You get so used to saying that a person is black if they were yellow or pardo. So I think that arriving here, in my point of view, no [ideas are brought back] but maybe they [return migrants] look at a morena person and see them as black [here] like there [in the U.S.].

Vinícius felt this was most apparent among returnees who use the one-drop rule to classify all nonwhite Brazilians as black, which is characteristic of the

U.S. racial system. Both Vinícius and Felipe believe it is possible for returnees to transmit racial views to GV in the form of U.S. racial classification norms.

Gustavo was another returnee who expressed a perception that if race relations in GV are changing, they are doing so almost imperceptibly:

TJ: In terms of race or the importance of race or skin color here, do you think it [GV] is changing as a result of this immigration between Brazil and the U.S.?

GUSTAVO: Look, Tiffany, if it is changing, it is barely noticeable.

TJ: Could you tell me more about how it is barely noticeable?

GUSTAVO: I think that the more the Brazilian has an experience in the U.S. with blacks, working with blacks, he brings this here. But here, he [return migrant] has this way of thinking "oh Brazil is different." There in the U.S., I work with Tiffany because she's black and here no. Tiffany is over there and I stay over here in my social class, she stays in hers, you know? So, I think that there in the U.S. is one way and here is another way . . .

TJ: So, you think that Brazilians have experiences with other groups or nationalities in the U.S., but that it doesn't influence their interactions with other people in GV when they return?

GUSTAVO: I think that if there's an influence, it is very little.

Gustavo highlighted returnees' exposure to black Americans as shaping their post-migration perceptions of race in Brazil. This exchange illustrates how migration changed Gustavo's perception of race and social class in each country. Although Gustavo believed that returnees attempt to distinguish between "here" and "there," he juxtaposed the significance of social class in Brazil with that of race in the United States for influencing blacks' social position and returnees' subsequent interactions with blacks in each country.

Overall, participants' responses to the influence of U.S. migration on GV's culture and economy elicited much more descriptive and in-depth answers than my questions about race relations in GV. Valadarenses' comments about the city's financial dependence on U.S. dollars, the rise in real estate prices, and the opening of "American"-style stores and businesses demonstrated that GV is a place where people, goods, and ideals about culture are transmitted between the city and the United States on a daily basis. However, my attempts to elicit Valadarenses' thoughts regarding how U.S. racial ideals were brought back to GV yielded less conceptually tangible examples of the "racial impact" in GV.

Perhaps this was due to respondents' inability to recognize or unwilling-
ness to disclose where they saw the influence of U.S. racial ideals in GV. After
all, such ideals are considered racist and un-Brazilian. Valadarenses vehemently
oppose what they consider overtly racist or racially discriminatory behavior.
Only a few returnees and non-migrants reported a perception that racial ideals
were being remitted to GV; and none acknowledged personally transmitting or
espousing the racist U.S. attitudes they discussed in the interviews.

Furthermore, even if more respondents had expressed a perception that
U.S. migration was influencing GV racial dynamics, it would be difficult to
disentangle such an influence from pre-existing ideals regarding race and social
stratification in GV and Brazil as a whole. Even though there has been extensive migration and return migration between GV and the United States over
the past 60 years, this project is the first to explore its racial impact. It would
be difficult to evaluate any racial impact without a more thorough investigation of GV's racial dynamics before U.S. migration began.

However, just because Valadarenses may not be able to detect or be willing
to acknowledge a racial impact does not mean that one does not exist. Their
accounts indicate that, for some, the U.S. migration directly or indirectly
influenced their racial perceptions or those of family members or other Valadarenses. It is also possible that respondents were not aware of changes that
resulted from migration. In Chapter 4, I pointed out that most returnees said
their racial self-classifications had not shifted at all throughout the migration
experience. But a review of the racial classifications they reported before, during, and after migration revealed some noticeable shifts for nearly all returnees.
Similarly, returnees' and non-migrants' perceptions of changes in GV's race
relations may not be as noticeable as those in the local economy, where businesses and apartment buildings are constructed with American names, or in
families, where children are left behind in the care of relatives while migrant
parents work abroad. Because ideas associated with race are not visible, it may
be difficult for Valadarenses to recognize how U.S. migration has affected them.
This is especially true since Valadarenses, like many Brazilians, are still inclined
to equate manifestations of racism with overtly racist behavior tied to laws and
language. Therefore, unless returnees have used overtly (U.S.) racist expressions
or behaviors toward other Valadarenses, it is unlikely that respondents would
recognize more subtle changes as indicative of the impact of U.S. migration.

Another issue to consider is whether racial changes may have occurred so slowly over time that they are not perceptible to Valadarenses who have spent their entire lives in GV. Because migration has had other undeniable consequences in the city, it may be difficult for insiders to notice any "racial" differences. Returnees and non-migrants discussed a variety of visible social and cultural practices in GV that have changed over time. Other studies of gender and other social constructions there have found that changes were not immediately recognized by Valadarenses.[39] It is possible that a similar process may occur for racial changes in GV. In addition, people who visit or move to GV from other parts of Brazil, where there are different racial demographics or no extensive migration ties, may pick up on the subtleties of a racial impact in a way that native Valadarenses, both migrants and non-migrants, do not.

Finally, a few returnees recognized that U.S. migration had in fact changed them or their city, even if they could not fully articulate how. They assigned more significance to the racial classification of fellow Valadarenses and noticed differences in racial stratification and inequality between the two countries. These returnees did not perceive GV and/or Brazil in the same way that they had before they migrated.

U.S. migration has had a significant impact on life in GV, but most returnees and non-migrants do not feel this migration has transformed the city racially. Both groups of respondents believe anti-black racism is prevalent and that Brazil is an aspirational racial democracy. For returnees, however, the transnational racial optic transformed their post-migration interpretation of race relations and inequality in GV and Brazil, particularly regarding the greater marginalization of black Brazilians in contrast to that of black Americans. Returnees shared their personal accounts of U.S. race relations with non-migrants. While these conversations provided non-migrants with another lens for viewing race in the United States, their views of Brazilian race relations did not change radically. Although U.S. migration is not racially making America in Brazil in an overt way, returnees' and non-migrants' anecdotes suggest that subtle changes are occurring and may continue in the future. Time will reveal the extent to which U.S. migration transforms racial views in GV and the social consequences this may have for Valadarenses.

CHAPTER 6

SOCIAL CONSEQUENCES
OF THE TRANSNATIONAL
RACIAL OPTIC

From a very young age, I always, I learned very early what my place was, and knowing that place, I sought to arm myself in the best way possible. When people, for example, they called me a monkey in school and I started crying, I was a child . . . the only thing that I always imagined could help me overcome this [racism] was to read and learn as much as possible about my identity so that I could respond to the person that was offending me. So the racial question for me was always clear, it was very defined here [in Brazil]. Arriving in the United States only reinforced it, [so] there were no changes for me, no.

Lucas, black, age 43, returnee

Migration to and from the United States did not extensively alter Lucas's racial conceptions. He had endured significant racism in Brazil before and after migration, as well as in the United States, which reinforced his identity as a black Brazilian. For him, and for other black returnees, the transnational racial optic did not change his racial self-classification or views of racial inequality in Brazil. It did, however, more profoundly influence the racial conceptions of white and pardo returnees, as they inhabited more privileged social positions in Brazil before and after migration.[1]

In this chapter I discuss how differences in race, SES, and gender influenced the extent to which the transnational racial optic shaped returnees' post-migration racial conceptions. Although migration yielded a transnational, or hybrid, Brazilian and U.S. understanding of race for returnees, they could only enact their racial conceptions in one place at a time. Through return migration, the transnational racial optic produced micro-level changes in returnees' racial attitudes and behaviors that in turn changed their interactions with and perceptions of Brazilians in GV and other parts of the country. I refer to these changes as "social consequences" of the transnational racial optic; they are relevant for illustrating how migration can alter macro-level racial discourses and the notions of racial inequality related to such discourses. Ultimately, these social consequences might contribute to a remaking of race in Brazil or, to borrow from sociologists Michael Omi and Howard Winant, facilitate Brazilian racial (re)formations.[2]

THE TRANSNATIONAL RACIAL OPTIC AND RETURNEES' DEMOGRAPHIC CHARACTERISTICS

In interviews, I asked returnees about their migration experiences in order to better understand how the transnational racial optic influenced their perceptions of race relations in the United States and Brazil. Relative to black returnees, the majority of returnees who classified as white and pardo were more aware of differences between Brazilian and U.S. racial categories and more conscious of anti-black structural racism than they had been before migrating.

For white returnees, who inhabited a more privileged social position in the Brazilian "color" hierarchy than pardo or black returnees, race was not very important in Brazil before or after migrating. Race, however, was crucially important for black returnees because of their social disadvantage before migrating. Pardo returnees, who were in the middle of the hierarchy, had mixed experiences with discrimination before migrating. A few felt they were socially disadvantaged because of their color, but the majority did not.

For white and some pardo returnees, living in the United States was a rude awakening, as many of them experienced racial discrimination for the first time. Because white returnees were not "really" white in the United States, they were no longer in a privileged position. They experienced racism, as well as anti-immigrant discrimination for being undocumented. After being treated as nonwhite in the United States, white returnees were forced to reevaluate their racial classification as nonwhite in Brazil. Migration changed how they saw themselves in the U.S. racial hierarchy. While living in the United States, white migrants were categorized with pardo and black migrants, who were more accustomed to being less socially privileged in Brazil before migrating. Most migrants, regardless of race, were racialized as nonwhite and were also undocumented, and they were treated accordingly during their time abroad. Though most white returnees reverted to the white category after returning to Brazil, they had acquired a different understanding of the white category in the United States, which changed how they saw their own whiteness. It was through this process of negotiating different structural positions in each country (due to both race and migration status) that the transnational racial optic altered white and some lighter pardo returnees' racial conceptions.

For pardo returnees, their intermediate position between whites and blacks in Brazil made it more difficult to negotiate their social position in the United States. They became more conscious of their "in-betweenness" when trying to figure out their racial classification. Encounters with the U.S. racial system, especially the black-white divide, made them more appreciative of Brazil's fluid racial categories post-migration. In Brazil they did not have to pick a particular racial category in which to classify themselves because a widely used racially mixed category existed there. Pardos were also more likely than white and black returnees to be invested in the *mestiçagem* aspect of racial democracy ideology. Pardo returnees thought Brazil was more socially integrated than the United States and saw evidence of it reflected in their physical features. When I asked pardos to tell me their racial and skin tone classifications, they expressed pride in having light- to medium-brown skin because it indicated that they were authentically Brazilian.

Though all returnees were aware of the history of black-white U.S. race relations, black returnees were the least surprised to encounter racism in the United States. After all, they had already encountered it overtly and subtly in Brazil. Those experiences heightened their awareness of their blackness before migrating; they expected to be seen and treated as nonwhite by Americans. After returning to Brazil, black migrants realized they would still be racialized as black and would continue to experience racism there. Black returnees' social positions did not change during their migration experiences; they were at the bottom of the racial hierarchy in both countries. The transnational racial optic did not significantly alter their racial conceptions.

CHANGES IN RACE SALIENCE AND CENTRALITY

Social psychologists broadly define salience as the likelihood that a certain identity will be activated in a given situation.[3] The activation of that particular identity is determined by the context of the individual. Correspondingly, race salience is: "the extent to which one's race is a relevant part of one's self-concept at a particular moment or in a particular situation."[4] Therefore, race salience is more indicative of context than it is of an individual's willingness to define herself in terms of race.

Overall, returnees were more aware of differences between Brazilian and U.S. racial categories and more conscious of anti-black structural racism in Brazil than they had been before migrating. However, for white and pardo returnees, issues of race were more salient in the United States because of their more privileged social positions and the prevalence of racial mixture in Brazil. In their post-migration lives, race was not particularly salient until I asked them to speak specifically about it. Some white and pardo respondents said that they hardly thought about race. They also did not feel race was especially important in their interactions with others. White and pardo returnees did not believe that race determined where they lived or that it shaped their social outcomes.

Conversely, for black returnees, race remained salient in their lives because they had been structurally disadvantaged throughout their migration experience. Given black returnees' marginalized social position in both countries, they put less emphasis on the salience of race than white and pardo returnees did. Before, during, and after migration, many black returnees experienced discrimination in their personal and professional lives. These findings suggest that race salience did not produce changes in black returnees' racial perceptions as it did for their white and pardo counterparts.

Therefore, while social circumstances like migration can influence race salience, race centrality is more stable because it "refers to the extent to which a person normatively defines herself with regard to race."[5] Race centrality is associated with how individuals racially perceive themselves across different situations. In other words, how *central* race is to a person can differ from how *salient* race is for that person.[6] Even though a situation may arise in which a person must consider his race, this does not mean that the person always defines herself in relation to that particular classification or that the classification has significant social meaning to that individual. A poignant example of this is Stephane, who initially self-classified as black in the United States after being told she was black by a courthouse official. But she did not classify herself as black before or after that encounter.[7]

For most white and pardo migrants in this study, race was not a central aspect of their lives before or after migration. Although living in the United States made race more salient for them, the migration experience did not make them think about themselves more centrally as racial beings. On the other hand, race was central for black returnees before migrating to the United States and remained a crucial aspect of their identities during the migration and after returning to GV. The few returnees who classified as black had a very strong black racial identity because of their experiences with racism in the United States and Brazil. One race-related realization for black returnees, however, was that despite sharing racial group membership with black Americans, this did not guarantee shared racial solidarity.[8]

How black returnees conceived of their blackness changed as a consequence of their interactions with black Americans. They recognized their cultural, linguistic, and socioeconomic differences from middle-class black Americans. In our interviews, sometimes black returnees used the word "we" when discussing the plight of blacks in Brazil and the United States to signal that they saw me as black in a global diasporic sense. At other times, however, they would state that I was not black by Brazilian standards because of my American nationality, SES, and light-brown skin, which granted me a more privileged social status in Brazil. They were conscious of their blackness and of anti-black racism in Brazil, and migrating to the United States did not change this. Nevertheless, exposure to middle-class black Americans provided a comparative lens for interpreting their own social position in Brazil, which made them more cognizant of their own social disadvantage.

CHANGES IN SALIENCE AND CENTRALITY OF PHENOTYPES AND SOCIOECONOMIC STATUS

Although race was not salient or central in most returnees' lives, skin color and other physical features were. While the phenotypes associated with race were sometimes salient for returnees, those features were not central to most returnees' racial identity. This fact speaks to the importance of physical features in Brazil rather than assigning people to racial groups, as happens in the United States. While Valadarenses, both returnees and non-migrants, did not often talk about specific races, they candidly discussed people's phenotypes in casual conversation. And even though they did not often associate those features as belonging to a particular racial group, it was clear that returnees of all colors made assumptions about other people based on those phenotypes. It was not uncommon for Valadarenses, and Brazilians in general, to use physical features to assess someone's socioeconomic background and treat them accordingly.[9] This tendency is also why most returnees assumed black Americans were more upwardly mobile than black Brazilians.[10]

My Portuguese proficiency and ability to blend into the population allowed me to listen in on conversations about how phenotype shaped social interactions. Because of my skin color, at times I was treated differently depending on the clothing I was wearing, how my hair was styled, or if I let people assume I was Brazilian. When I wore my hair very curly, dressed casually to go shopping, or did not speak to anyone, store attendants ignored me, likely assuming I was a poor black Brazilian.[11] But if I blow-dried my hair straight, dressed more formally, and emphasized my foreign-accented Portuguese to signal my American nationality, store attendants were eager to help me, assuming I was middle class and had money to spend in their establishments.[12] Based on my personal experiences and those of respondents, one can surmise that appearance is especially important in Brazil.[13]

Regardless of social class or race, many returnees were concerned with giving the appearance that they had done well financially in the United States, even if they had not. This was easier for the few returnees who were able to open successful businesses and earn income from rental properties. The majority of returnees, however, struggled to make ends meet in a place where the U.S. dollar was not strong and there were few opportunities for social advancement.

After returning, migrants were more conscious of the importance of social class and appearance in Brazil because they sensed that those attributes were less important in the United States. Our conversations also revealed that social class, rather than nationality, gender, or race, became more salient and central for returnees after migration.[14] Yet despite the importance of social class in Brazil and the fact that all returnees migrated in order to improve their SES, there were hardly any differences in the influence of the transnational racial optic on racial conceptions related to social class. Most migrants had at least completed high school and were from working- and middle-class families. Though a few returnees achieved significant social mobility from successful post-migration ventures, their racial conceptions did not differ much from those of lower-income returnees.

SOCIAL CONSEQUENCES OF THE TRANSNATIONAL RACIAL OPTIC

The transnational racial optic did not just change how returnees thought about racial categories, discrimination, and stratification, but also how they evaluated their social position and that of others in the ethno-racial hierarchies in the United States and Brazil. As returnees navigated race across borders, their altered perceptions had three social consequences for their post-migration lives: (1) a transnational investment in whiteness, (2) more nuanced attitudes regarding black Brazilians and support of racial quotas, and (3) enhanced levels of civic engagement. The impact of each of these consequences on returnees' interactions with other Brazilians has the potential to affect broader race relations in the country.

The Transnational Investment in Whiteness

One social consequence of migration was that returnees became more aware of whiteness in a transnational sense through having to negotiate their racial classification in the United States and Brazil. Returnees were likely exposed to the transnational hegemony of whiteness before migration, given the preference for lighter physical features in Brazil's aspirational racial democracy and returnees' consumption of international media in which whites predominate. However, living abroad and having *direct* exposure to the U.S. racial schema further accentuated returnees' recognition of how whiteness functions across borders. Conscious of the social value that white group membership provides in both places, most of the returnees whose physical features could be considered white in each country classified themselves or attempted to classify themselves as white in each place. But the same was not true for most returnees who were perceived and consequently self-classified as nonwhite in the United States but reverted to the white racial category after returning.[15] Through migration, returnees learned that there were two levels of whiteness: the exclusive level of U.S. whiteness and the more fluid level of Brazilian whiteness. Nevertheless, most returnees' anecdotes, especially those who classified as white before and after migration, indicated a desire to have others recognize them as white because whiteness signified privilege and prestige in both countries.

This recognition was also present in returnees' attempts to socially distance themselves from Latinos, and especially from Hispanics, during their time abroad. Because returnees internalized the negative stereotypes associated with Hispanics, they did not want to be classified with that group. The distinctions returnees made between Latinos and Hispanics illustrated returnees' investment in whiteness in the United States.[16] Returnees more often labeled Brazilians and other "white" South American groups as Latinos while identifying more *mestizo* Mexicans and black Dominicans as Hispanic. In perceiving themselves as "whiter" than Hispanics, returnees were attempting to give themselves a social leg up on the U.S. ethno-racial ladder. Furthermore, in reporting that Americans had treated them better after revealing their Brazilian nationality, some returnees believed they were socially closer to whites than to Hispanics. Because they were not considered white in the United States, given the option, they settled for the Latino rather than the Hispanic label. In doing so, returnees perceived that the Latino label was the whiter of the two labels ascribed to Latin Americans in the United States. Returnees worked within the boundaries of their "nonwhiteness" to get as close as possible to the white category without actually being in it.

After returning to GV, white returnees reported feeling whiter because the U.S. climate, in effect, lightened their skin. Relative to non-migrants who remained in sunny GV, returnees' skin had indeed become lighter. Non-migrants validated and affirmed (white) returnees' change in skin tone, which allowed returnees to fully re-embrace the white racial category, although they clearly recognized that being a white Brazilian was different from being a white American. Returnees also received cues from non-migrants about the higher social value ascribed to whiteness.[17] This external validation of their whiteness was important in helping white returnees revert to that category.

Returnees' enhanced exposure to transnational whiteness via migration further shaped both their romantic partner choices and their beauty standards.

This was true across the board for white, pardo, and black returnees. Because I interviewed returnees in their homes and was often invited to their parties and other social events, I met their spouses, girlfriends and boyfriends, and family members. In most instances, returnees' partners tended to be white or lighter than the returnees. Even among the pardo and black returnees, most said they preferred to date or were attracted to lighter or whiter Brazilians. Although most returnees asserted that they were not racist and liked everyone, they were unlikely to be partnered with or to prefer dating darker Brazilians.[18]

I was also able to get a sense of the relationship between beauty and whiteness in GV through conversations with returnees and others about skin color and hair texture. They casually talked about someone having "bad hair" or "good hair" when describing people's physical features. Often I would hear Valadarenses describe someone with fair skin, light eyes, and long, straight hair as very physically attractive. Because most Valadarenses did not naturally have those features, many—especially women—chemically dyed or straightened their hair and wore contacts to achieve those features. In my trips to a local salon owned by a white returnee, I observed many women doing this. My beautician asked me each time I came for a trim why I did not want to relax or chemically straighten my curly hair.[19] I was told I would look more attractive with my hair straightened and lightened. Even in interviews with some returnees, they made it explicitly clear that while my *café com leite* (coffee with milk) complexion was attractive and Brazilian-looking, my hair was definitely black. Unstated but implied was that my hair was "bad" and considered unattractive. Thus returnees continued to highlight the relationship between beauty and whiteness post-migration.

After their U.S. migration, most returnees clung even more tightly to their Brazilian whiteness. This is likely because they recognized that their own physical features were not aligned with American whiteness. In both places, membership in the white racial category or having physical features closely associated with that category, is a sign of privilege, prestige, and beauty. Whiteness is also defined in opposition to blackness, which means that individuals do not want to be associated with blackness if they want the benefits that come with whiteness. For most returnees, the negativity associated with blackness in Brazil made them cling more strongly to whiteness post-migration. This tendency had implications for returnees' views of black Brazilians and race-based policies like racial quotas.

Returnees' Opinions of Black Brazilians and Racial Quotas

Returnees' time in the United States also made them more conscious of the elevated social mobility that nonwhites, especially blacks, could obtain. In using the transnational racial optic to reevaluate the social position of black Brazilians relative to black Americans post-migration, black, pardo, and white returnees grasped the extent to which black Brazilians faced marginalization. However, at the same time that most returnees voiced admiration for black Americans' social mobility, white and pardo returnees seemed to blame black Brazilians for their disadvantaged position. These returnees mentioned that black Brazilians could not advance socially because they were unwilling to fight for their rights or protest racism as black Americans had done.[20] Though black returnees also thought black Brazilians should organize politically to improve their social standing, they did not blame black Brazilians for their marginalization. In other words, the U.S. migration simultaneously made returnees more sensitive to and resentful of the marginalization of black Brazilians. This "blame the victim" mentality is significant because returnees' perceptions of black Brazilians could affect their behavior toward the few black Brazilians they would encounter in GV. This mentality also shaped returnees' opinions of the racial quotas that have been implemented in Brazilian federal universities to address racial inequality in the country.

In 2001, the Brazilian government under President Fernando Henrique Cardoso implemented racial quotas to increase the number of black Brazilians in civil-service jobs.[21] The first racial quotas in federal universities were implemented in 2003, and each university was responsible for determining eligibility criteria for admission under the quotas.[22] Though blacks and pardos collectively represent slightly more than 50 percent of the Brazilian population, they are significantly underrepresented in Brazil's elite federal universities.[23] Under the quotas, 20 percent of federal university admissions slots are reserved for black, pardo, and Indigenous students.[24] Some universities rely on applicants' self-classification, while others convene special admissions committees that "determine" the racial classification of applicants by viewing photographs or conducting face-to-face interviews.[25] Given the racial mixture in the Brazilian population, critics view the quotas as an American import and argue they will create race-based social divisiveness similar to that in the United States.[26] The quotas have been contentious, and there have been Supreme Court cases arguing against the constitutionality of the policy on the grounds that they are reverse racism.[27]

The twelve returnees who referred to the quotas in our interviews also felt racial quotas were controversial.[28] One of these returnees was Sérgio, a pardo returnee, who noted differences between lower- and middle-class black Americans in his interview:[29]

There is racism in Brazil because of the following. There's a big debate between blacks and whites for space. Right now, there's a huge issue here in Brazil in relation to university quotas. It means that, the black automatically, a law was created to benefit [blacks] but at the same time, it is totally racist because I think blacks and whites should fight for the same space equally. It shouldn't be that because you are darker than me that you get 50% more of an advantage in going to college or any school. Some [supporters] say "well, it's because there are more blacks in the suburbs that don't have resources to go to a private school." There are also many whites who grew up in the suburbs, with the same problems. There are many blacks who are judges, even could be president. . . . So I think it's a racist law.

Returnees clearly recognized that racial inequality existed and was aimed primarily toward black Brazilians.[30] However, some of them fervently believed that introducing policies like racial quotas to address that inequality was racist. Even black returnees were reluctant to support the quotas for the same reason. Therefore, while returnees admired the social mobility of black Americans, they did not support policies like affirmative action.[31]

Shortly after completing my fieldwork and returning to the United States, I received an email in Portuguese from a white friend and colleague in GV, which argued that Brazil did not need racial quotas. The email noted that blacks around the world had achieved major accomplishments in various fields, including: (1) politics—there was a picture of President Barack Obama with the caption "the most powerful politician in the world is black," (2) media—there was a picture of Oprah Winfrey with the caption "the richest and most influential woman in media is black," (3) sports—there was a picture of Tiger Woods with the caption "the best golf player of all time is black," (4) entertainment—there was a picture of Will Smith with the caption "the most popular actor in the world is black," and (5) sciences—there was a picture of astrophysicist Neil deGrasse Tyson with the caption "the most intelligent astrophysicist on earth is black." There were six other examples in the email of blacks who were at the top of their fields.[32] The email ended with the following question: "So why in Brazil do they [blacks] still need racial quotas?" What was both remarkable and ironic about this email was that none of these blacks were Brazilian: 9 of the 11 blacks in the email were Americans who likely benefited from U.S. affirmative action programs before such programs were discontinued. Furthermore, despite the success of these few individuals, most blacks in the United States and around the world remain significantly structurally disadvantaged relative to their white counterparts.

What returnees' perceptions and those of other Brazilians illustrate is that the "success" of a few black Americans is perceived to be representative of most black Americans, and, in this email, of blacks around the world. This success is transnationally transmitted to Brazil through returnees and media images, which have the potential to shape all Brazilians' views of black Brazilians as undeserving of policies like racial quotas. These policies, however, seek to address the structural inequality that most black and many pardo Brazilians experience. Such unsympathetic views of black Brazilians shape returnees' attitudes about racial quotas and could hinder the implementation of anti-discriminatory policies in GV by mostly white politicians who represent Valadarenses at the national level. Returnees' views might subsequently lead to negative interactions with black Brazilians, especially those who are the beneficiaries of racial quotas in university and workplace settings.

Finally, the comments returnees made about the beauty of middle-class black Americans could also yield more anti-black sentiment and negative stereotypes of black Brazilians as poor and unattractive, further reducing their visibility in local GV media. Returnees' direct exposure to "attractive" black Americans shaped their post-migration perceptions of black Brazilians as unattractive. However, given the high visibility of prominent black Americans on the global political, economic, and entertainment stages, it is likely that Brazilians in other parts of the country are exposed to these images of black Americans and ascribe more attractiveness to them because of their higher SES relative to black Brazilians. By "socially whitening" black Americans, Brazilians may in fact not see them as black in comparison with black Brazilians.[33]

Returnees believed black Americans' social mobility could be a model for black Brazilians to follow, but comparisons between the two groups could be a disservice to black Brazilians in a few ways. First, such comparisons often reflect a "blame the victim" mentality and suggest that black Brazilians are to blame for their own social marginalization. Second, such comparisons do not acknowledge black Brazilians' historical efforts to mobilize politically. There has been a long history of resistance and political struggle among black Brazilians, starting with the establishment of *quilombos* during slavery and extending to contemporary Movimento Negro activists.[34] Finally, the comparison between black Americans and black Brazilians does not fully consider how the Brazilian model of "cordial" racism and the historic discourse of racial democracy have systematically disadvantaged black Brazilians. The emphasis on a Brazilian identity in racial democracy discourse, rather than a black racial identity, has probably been the biggest impediment to black political mobilization in Brazil. Furthermore, returnees' views on racial quotas in Brazil indicate that if black Brazilians were to replicate the political strategies used by black Americans, returnees (and likely other Brazilians) would view black Brazilians as racist. There has already been some evidence of this in light of the Movimento Negro's attempts to have pardos reclassified as blacks on the Brazilian census and to include them in racial quotas. White and pardo Brazilians have been resistant to this change because it constitutes the incorporation of a black-white racial binary, which many feel is un-Brazilian and an American import. Most Brazilians do not believe using a U.S.-derived policy will be effective for promoting racial equality in Brazil given the two countries' different histories and norms of racial classification.[35]

Civic Engagement in a Government Not of the People

A third social consequence of the transnational racial optic was returnees' complaints about the inefficiency of the Brazilian government and bureaucracy in comparison with that of the United States. Recognizing the differences between the two countries' governments influenced returnees' civic engagement post-migration. Though this perception initially does not seem race-related, it affected how returnees of different "colors" interacted with the political and bureaucratic systems after returning. Recall that Camila and Fernando, two nonwhite returnees, said that they are now more conscious of the rights they have as citizens after having lived abroad.[36]As a consequence, they and other returnees feel they can be better advocates for themselves and are willing to stand up for their rights if they feel they are being treated unfairly in social encounters. Not only are they concerned about their own well-being, but they also recognize the rights of other people in GV and Brazil. Because returnees were racialized as nonwhite and experienced discrimination in the United States, they felt that living there made them more aware of race-based social inequality. They also observed how Americans, who as citizens did not have deportation fears, were civically engaged and demanded that the government act on their behalf. Because most migrants were undocumented in the United States, they did not actively protest instances of discrimination against themselves or others. However, as citizens of Brazil, after returning they were unafraid and willing to speak out when mistreated by others, especially government bureaucrats in GV. Camila was adamant about this in our interview:

[What I learned from living in the U.S.] was that we have to have respect for everyone regardless of race, color, sex, religion, sexual orientation. We have to respect people for being people, everyone deserves respect. And this is something that changed for me when I returned from there. I no longer accept being treated with disrespect. For example, when I go to city hall or any other public government building, where I pay for the salary of the employee that works there, I don't let them disrespect me. I don't accept that anymore.

After returning, migrants became more vocal in their criticism of the Brazilian government's inefficiencies and failure to serve its people.[37] In sharing their perceptions of the Brazilian and U.S. governments with non-migrants, returnees influenced non-migrants' views of local government and encouraged greater civic engagement. For example, Lígia, a non-migrant I quoted in Chapter 5, told me that returnees and non-migrants are standing up for themselves and filing lawsuits when they experience discrimination. Like other Valadarenses, Lígia attributed this increased civic engagement to the prevalence of transnational migration between GV and the United States.

THE TRANSNATIONAL RACIAL OPTIC
AND BRAZILIAN RACIAL FORMATIONS

In acting on their transnational experiences in GV post-migration, the returnees illustrated how the transnational racial optic yielded micro-level changes in their racial attitudes, which in turn influenced their perceptions of and interactions with other Brazilians post-migration. The cumulative impact of these micro-level changes could lead to macro-level shifts in the social construction of race in GV, and perhaps in other parts of Brazil, where significant U.S. migration and return migration occur. As people move across city and state borders within Brazil, other Brazilians who travel to GV will encounter a city and a group of people whose lives are connected with the United States. Likewise, returnees who relocate to other parts of Brazil will take their altered views of race from the United States with them to those locales, which in turn will shape their interactions with fellow Brazilians. Through this movement, micro-level exchanges of racial ideals between Brazilians may influence racial behaviors, attitudes, and subsequently relations and inequality between Brazilians of different colors at the macro level.

One way migratory movement and transnational ties between the United States and Brazil can change racial discourse in Brazil is through racial formations, which Michael Omi and Howard Winant define as "the sociohistorical process by which racial categories are created, inhabited, transformed, and destroyed."[38] Though this definition seems primarily related to racial categories, Omi and Winant suggest that such categories are given social meaning through racial projects in which "human bodies and social structures are represented and organized."[39] These racial formations yield structural and hierarchical relationships between individuals on the basis of physical features. I have shown how migration to and from the United States yielded changes in returnees' negotiation of racial categories and broader race relations in each country. The nuanced understandings that returnees acquired abroad influenced their perceptions of, interactions with, and attitudes toward the Brazilians they encountered in GV and other parts of Brazil.

Migration in general, and return migration in particular, can facilitate a remaking of race in Brazil. Movement across and within national borders can produce racial formations on a transnational or global scale. That process has begun to unfold in the immigrant-sending context of GV. As Valadarenses continue to travel back and forth between the United States and other countries, they will consciously and subconsciously bring back racial ideals from those places that further influence their own and non-migrants' interpretation of Brazilian race relations. Eventually, returnees' altered micro-level racial perceptions could influence macro-level racial discourses and policies, which could in turn affect racial inequality in GV and Brazil.

CONCLUSION:
TOWARD GLOBAL RACIAL
(RE)FORMATIONS

I think that we are like Stuart Hall, he says that we [people] live in
a situation of a decentered and fragmented identity, that the subject
[person] lives with many identities at the same time and takes on
[embodies] some of them. So this also influences the racial question
and the national[ity] question when talking about migration. So there
exists the image of what a Brazilian is. These images are constructed
apart from narratives, apart from the national image, and when we
[Brazilians] enter into contact with a different country, like the U.S.
for example, we begin to see that there exists another way of looking at
things, a different way. So this dynamic [of migration] also deconstructs
national identities and through that deconstruction of [one] identity,
another is reconstructed. It [migration] provides an opportunity for
these people [migrants] to reconstruct their other identities.

Lucas, black, age 43, returnee

As a sociology professor, Lucas draws on his knowledge of sociological theory
to explain the multifaceted impact that migration can have on individuals, especially how they negotiate their racial and national identities. Though other
returnees could not articulate this impact as concisely and intellectually as Lucas,
their narratives illustrate how immigration to and return migration from the
United States influenced their racial perceptions. Although U.S. migration has
also affected the lives of non-migrants, I devoted more attention to returnees,
whose direct and extended exposure to race in both Brazil and the United States

facilitated the development of a transnational racial optic. The experience and process of moving back and forth between GV and the United States allowed these individuals to see and interpret race with a transnational, or hybrid, U.S.-Brazilian perspective—a unique combination of the two.

The qualitative accounts of Brazilian returnees in GV also poignantly demonstrate that migration, and return migration especially, can be used as analytical tools for comparatively exploring race in and between Brazil and the United States. Shedding light on these individuals' experiences integrates migration scholarship that focuses primarily on the host country with other comparative studies that use race data collected separately in the two countries. In this book I have described the dynamic of the relationship between race and migration in the United States and Brazil in three important ways. First, return migration provides a nuanced vantage point for exploring how migration changes people and countries. Second, Valadarenses' perceptions demonstrate micro-level empirical evidence that race in Brazil and the United States are converging, or beginning to resemble each other. Finally, through the transnational racial optic, migration can transform social constructions of race in multiple contexts. All of these have implications for how migration can influence race in other host and home countries around the globe.

THE NUANCED VANTAGE POINT
OF RETURN MIGRATION

Return migration offers a nuanced perspective for exploring how migration changes not only people and countries, but also the social relations and processes that occur in and between societies. Very little research has examined immigration's impact on home countries. Even less has focused on how return migration affects migrants themselves, the non-migrants with whom they come into contact, or the communities to which they return. Migrants link the economies, cultures, and norms of the host and home countries by sending remittances and maintaining transnational ties.[1] Through the study of returnees and their home countries, researchers learn more about the interconnectedness of host and home countries and about the interactions between returnees and non-migrants, two groups that are affected in different ways by U.S. migration.

The process of returning alters the lens through which migrants see interpersonal relationships, political processes, and broader societal inequalities in their home country. For the returnees whose experiences have been examined in this and other studies, the homecoming elicits a social, cultural, and racial readaptation that is in some ways more psychologically taxing than the initial adjustment to the host society abroad.[2] This "reentry shock" happens when return migrants apply their newly acquired perspectives in the home context, where non-migrant friends and relatives may not understand or be receptive to returnees' new and evolved ideals. For those who migrate from less-developed to more-developed countries, readjustment can be even more difficult. Returnees often confront an internal psychological struggle between national understandings of race in the home and host countries. Return migration can change how migrants perceive themselves and interpret their social positions on the basis of race. Return migration also can affect how migrants interact with and interpret other people's social positions, which can bring about changes in migrants' and non-migrants' racial attitudes, behaviors, and political beliefs.

Examining the experiences of return migrants can also help researchers better assess the selectivity factors that influence both emigration and return migration in various countries. Just as individuals who make the decision to migrate are a select group, so too are the migrants who decide to return home. By exploring differences between return migrants and non-migrants in sending communities, researchers can learn more about the factors that motivate some individuals to migrate and others to remain at home.[3] Comparisons between returnees and non-migrants also illustrate the influence of migration on individuals socially, physically, and mentally.[4] Likewise, comparing migrants who return home with those who remain in the host country yields insights into the extent to which immigrants are being incorporated into host countries. Such comparisons can allow researchers to explore the social inequalities that result from differences in documentation status, education level, English proficiency, occupation, and health outcomes among immigrants of the same nationality in host countries.

Increased global South-North migration has augmented concerns and contentious debates about immigration reform in numerous host countries, including the United States. In such debates, researchers and laypersons usually know very little about the global impact of U.S. migration and how domestic and foreign policies affect people in other countries. Research on return migration and in immigrant-sending cities like GV can provide additional insight into the multifaceted circumstances that shape potential migrants' decision to emigrate. Such research can also illustrate how immigration affects sending communities in home countries. My time living and conducting research in GV helped me further evaluate the far-reaching impact of U.S. social, cultural, and economic influences. Valadarenses are highly dependent on the U.S. economy for their livelihood and survival. The extent of these economic ties became crystal clear to me, as I was in GV at the start of the Great Recession in 2008: construction stopped on high-rise apartment buildings, many returnees' businesses closed, and migrants—victims of subprime lenders and job loss in the United States—returned in unusually high numbers. This sequence of events unfolded in response to the weakening U.S. economy and the eventual collapse of the Lehman Brothers financial firm. In order to draft, legislate, and implement comprehensive and humane immigration reform in receiving countries, an interpretive lens must be directed toward immigrant-sending communities. Otherwise it will be difficult to understand the reasons for and consequences of migration in cities like GV around the globe.

Similarly, exploring return migration in GV and comparable locales minimizes the U.S.-centric lens that dominates U.S. social scientific research and helps scholars connect the local with the global through transnational comparisons and migration research. According to sociologist Nadia Kim:

It is not possible to grasp fully the U.S. immigrants' experiences of "race"/ethnicity—and to avoid reproducing American-centrism in the process—without analyzing the home country and its ties to the U.S. in our theories, methods, and analyses.[5]

Without conducting comparative global migration research, scholars cannot fully comprehend how the United States measures up to other countries on various socioeconomic indicators. This has implications for understanding how U.S. society is progressing, particularly with regard to inequality among different social groups. As American and Western influences grow in rapidly industrializing countries like Brazil, India, and China, these countries will send even more of their citizens to be educated here.[6] Through international research, scholars develop a more critical lens for examining the imperial and cultural influence of the United States and how it affects peoples and societies beyond American shores.

BRAZIL AND THE UNITED STATES ON
RACIALLY CONVERGING PATHS

This examination of how U.S. migration influenced Brazilian return migrants'
racial conceptions provides some micro-level empirical evidence that race in the
United States and Brazil are beginning to resemble each other, as other scholars have suggested in recent years. Sociologist G. Reginald Daniel's comparative examination of Brazil's white-pardo-black racial hierarchy alongside the
multiracial movement in the United States argued that race relations in each
country are converging.[7] Likewise, sociologist Stanley Bailey argued this in a
study of racial identity, attitudes, and politics in Brazil:

It appears to be the case that racial dynamics in the U.S. and in Brazil are like two
ships passing in the night, one showing signs of movement toward mixed-race fram-
ings [U.S.] and the other toward single-race identification [Brazil].[8]

Historically, scholars and laypersons regarded the countries as having very
dissimilar approaches to race-based legislation, racial mixing, and interracial
interactions. But contemporary demographic changes in Brazil and the United
States seem to have brought them racially closer together, as my respondents'
accounts of their experiences in both countries before, during, and after migration indicate.

Over time, researchers have used the black-white racial binary to explain
and interpret U.S. race relations. But increases in interracial marriage and the
resulting multiracial population suggest that racial boundaries are more porous
now than in the past. The growth of the Latino population into the largest
ethno-racial minority is shaping and will continue to shape the relationship
between race, ethnicity, and skin color in contemporary U.S. society. According to Wendy Roth, Latino migrants have transformed views of race in the
United States:

By bringing with them a racialized view of their nationalities . . . Latin American migrants have fostered the view, now accepted by much of mainstream America, that
they do not fit into existing White or Black categories.[9]

As Latin American immigrants in the United States, Brazilians—who have
been infrequently studied—further complicate this relationship. After all, they

are not Hispanic, despite being "Hispanic-looking" to most Americans. Brazilian returnees' experiences provide more confirmation of the racialization of Latinos as a brown ethno-racial group that is distinct from blacks and whites. Brazilian immigrants also illustrate how census-appropriated categories are not "one size fits all" for Latin American-descended individuals in the United States. In the United States there is a government proposal to add "Hispanic" as a separate racial category on the 2020 census.[10] Such a change would likely result in Brazilians not classifying themselves at all, further distancing them socially from Hispanics and having political implications for Brazilian immigrants. Ethno-racial labels are relevant for identity formation and political mobilization; they are also tied to the allocation of government resources. Brazilians' reluctance to self-classify as Hispanic could hinder coalition-building efforts with Hispanics or other Latinos in order to make political claims or to receive resources for Brazilian communities. The case of Brazilians illustrates the complexity of using very specific categories to classify an increasingly diverse and racially mixed populace in the United States. Attempts to classify individuals in the twenty-first-century United States must therefore take into account broader changes in social relations and inequality based on ethno-racial categories.

When specifically examining the applicability of the Latino and Hispanic categories to Brazilians, these migrants' perceptions of and relationships with other Latinos must be considered in light of Brazil's growing global influence. Brazil's economic emergence in recent years contributes to a stronger sense of "Brazilian-ness" for members of its global diaspora. In the United States, this Brazilian exceptionalism facilitates a sense of superiority that leads to social distancing from Hispanics and Latinos. The Valadarenses I interviewed explained how this relationship played out in the United States and Brazil. Economic and social factors also influence how race and culture migrate with people across borders. In confirming the "browning" of America, Brazilian returnees' U.S. experiences illustrate a "Latin Americanization," or more specifically, a "Brazilianization" of U.S. race relations, such that there are three main "racial" groups: whites, (racially mixed) browns, and blacks.[11]

Finally, in recent years, affirmative action policies that use race as a consideration in college admission and employment decisions have been mostly discontinued in the United States on the basis that race has become less salient in determining individuals' social outcomes.[12] Affirmative action was implemented during the Civil Rights Movement to redress the de jure racial discrimination that barred many people of color and women from U.S. colleges and universities, as well as to prevent discrimination in the workplace. However, some Americans hail the two-term presidency of Barack Obama as a sign that the United States is now a color-blind society where race is not as important for shaping social outcomes as it once was: Americans now perceive social class as a greater barrier to mobility than race.[13] These changes in U.S. racial discourse, in addition to demographic trends in interracial marriage and a growing mixed-race population, are similar to some of the tenets associated with Gilberto Freyre's racial democracy ideology.[14] It seems likely, therefore, that a "Brazilianization" of U.S. race relations is under way.

While Brazilian returnees' accounts shed light on the Latin Americanization of the United States, they also illustrate that race, and more specifically racial classification, are becoming more significant in Brazil. In recent years, Brazilians have acknowledged the pervasiveness of racial inequality in their country and have implemented racial quotas to increase the number of black and brown Brazilians in universities. Brazilians are reassessing what it means to be black, white, or pardo for the purposes of determining who is eligible to benefit from quotas.

The adoption of racial quotas and organizing attempts by the Movimento Negro have stirred debate over how this "American import" will affect race relations in Brazil.[15] Brazilians fear racial quotas will create the type of racial animosity that they associate with the United States.[16] Black Brazilian activists have argued that the United States' one-drop rule should be used for racial classification in Brazil, effectively collapsing blacks and browns into one black category on the Brazilian census.[17] Some Brazilians feel that these changes in Brazilian racial discourse signal an impending "Americanization" of Brazilian race relations.[18] Some of my Brazilian respondents found that they left what they perceived to be a more racially conscious United States only to encounter the potential emergence of a U.S.-like black-white binary in Brazil.

My research suggests that both countries are converging through the Brazilianization of U.S. racial discourse and the implementation of U.S.-style affirmative action in Brazil. Some returnees even said they see the United States as a model for addressing anti-black structural racism in Brazil given the sizable black middle class in the United States. Amanda, a white returnee, believes the two countries, more specifically black Americans and Brazilians, will be more socioeconomically similar in a few years:

AMANDA: A lot of Brazilian people think that the black people are like, to work for them.

TJ: To work for them?

AMANDA: Yeah, like, like my maid for example, she's black . . . Things are, nowadays are changing. Black people didn't have a lot of opportunities to get a good job or something.

TJ: How are they [things] changing?

AMANDA: Yes because, nowadays, they [blacks] are getting more space, they are having more opportunities to go to college, to study, to have a good job.

TJ: So, compared to the U.S., do you think it's the same for Brazilian blacks?

AMANDA: No, no, not yet. But maybe in ten years, we're gonna be there.

Though she does not mention racial quotas, Amanda's reference to "blacks getting more space" indicates her recognition that such a policy exists. She believes it will improve the social position of black Brazilians and that they will eventually experience the social mobility of the black Americans Amanda observed in the United States.

Just as they have done in the past, Brazilians and Americans continue to take racial cues from each other in assessing race-based discourse and inequality in their countries. This process is ongoing as both countries' populations grow, their economies evolve, and their citizens migrate and travel between the two places. Brazil has become a popular tourist and study-abroad destination because of its booming economy and ability to attract major athletic events, such as the 2014 FIFA World Cup and the 2016 Olympic Games. The U.S. government and U.S. universities have also promoted extensive and enduring political, cultural, and academic exchanges between the two countries.[19] Therefore, just as many Brazilians, especially those from GV, migrated to the United States in the late twentieth century, Americans are now traveling and temporarily migrating to Brazil in large numbers.[20] The racial ideals they carry with them also have the potential to further "Americanize" Brazilian race relations. Like the Brazilian returnees who had to adapt to U.S. racial norms, these Americans (and other foreigners) acquire Brazilian racial norms and may return to the United States with a more Brazilian racial perspective. Increased migration and further movement between the United States and Brazil will likely accelerate the convergence of race in both countries in the years to come.

INFLUENCE OF THE TRANSNATIONAL
RACIAL OPTIC ON RACE VIA MIGRATION

This comparative study of race in Brazil and the United States through the eyes of Brazilian migrants allowed me to explore how the transnational racial optic influences individuals' racial conceptions and broader social constructions of race. Numerous other studies have shown that immigrating to the United States and other countries forces migrants to reconsider their social position in an environment with different race relations.[21] My focus on return migration illustrates how migrants negotiate their newly acquired perspective on racial issues after they return to their home country.

The returnees I interviewed had the distinct experience of living in two countries with very different (historical) racial discourses; this experience changed how they interpreted and negotiated their structural positions along racial, ethnic, color, and citizenship lines. Returning home altered the vantage point from which they made sense of race in Brazil. At the micro level, returnees had to readjust to the Brazilian racial system by figuring out how to classify themselves and their fellow Valadarenses using Brazilian racial categories. Their understanding of those categories had shifted after being racialized as nonwhite and Hispanic/Latino in the United States. At the macro level, their post-migration understanding of broader Brazilian race relations as more socially cordial, but also more structurally oppressive for blacks, was enhanced through their personal experiences with overt discrimination and observations of middle-class blacks in the United States. Returnees' micro- and macro-level interpretations of race in both countries altered their racial attitudes, behaviors toward black Brazilians, and opinions about social inequality and racial quotas in Brazil. Collectively, these shifts may have longer-term effects on broader social constructions of race in GV and Brazil.

The immigration experience and return migration provided a juxtaposition of race in Brazil and the United States for returnees that influenced their racial readaptation to GV. Their newly acquired transnational racial optic transformed returnees' views of racial classification, race relations, and inequality.

Like Gilberto Freyre, the father of racial democracy ideology, their experiences living in the United States deeply affected how they made sense of race in Brazil after returning. Although Freyre was a white Brazilian (who would likely also have been considered white in the United States), his observation of Jim Crow segregation in the United States was significant in his conceptualization of racial democracy after returning to Brazil. His U.S. migration experience offered a new lens for his perceptions of Brazilian racial mixing and race relations in comparison with those in the United States. Freyre's post-migration development of racial democracy ideology transformed the social construction of race in Brazil, profoundly influencing how racial categories were enumerated, interracial relations were regarded, and racism was evaluated. The narratives of returnees in this study echo Freyre's experience in that their exposure to different racial ideals via migration reshaped individual understandings of race relations.

Although my empirical findings are not highly generalizable beyond this group of Valadarenses, they do illustrate that migration can facilitate changes in racial conceptions at the individual level. In cities like GV that have extensive emigration and return migration, the consolidation of such changes could eventually affect and accelerate broader macro-level racial discourses. According to Roth:

Racial change at the macro level occurs as the cumulative effect of all those people adding, adopting, enacting, and removing racial schemas from their cognitive portfolios. When populations move in the same direction—large portions of a society adopt and use a new schema most often—societal change in racial classifications comes about.[22]

Although I use the perspectives of Brazilian returnees to illustrate the transnational racial optic, I believe this concept can be extended to migrants on the move in other transnational contexts, be they immigrant enclaves in host societies or the neighborhoods of return migrants in their home countries. Migrants are socialized in and develop an understanding of the social world in their countries of origin before migrating. This pre-migration understanding then affects how they understand social relations—one of which can be race—in the countries to which they migrate. Thus the intricacies of racial dynamics in migrants' home societies shape how these individuals negotiate racial dynamics upon their arrival in host societies.

In the United States, one of the largest host countries in the world, the contentious history of race relations presents a challenge for migrants from various countries. How migrants are "positioned" in the U.S. ethno-racial hierarchy can affect their structural incorporation into U.S. society. Migrants who return to their home countries are able to view their home cultures through a hybridized lens that helps them renegotiate ethno-racial relations in their countries of origin. This transnational racial optic can account for changes, although sometimes subtle and subconscious, in these migrants' racial conceptions.

This book is the first to explore these issues. Additional research should explore whether U.S. racial ideals are transmitted back to other immigrant-sending communities, and if so, how such ideals transform social constructions of race in those contexts. In doing so, it will be possible to further examine how migration can lead to a remaking of race or racial formations in transnational social fields. In addition to racial issues, it will also be important to examine the economic, social, and cultural impact of U.S. migration in these communities in order to understand the factors that facilitate U.S. migration and how race influences the migration process.

This research changed how I view race in both the United States and Brazil as a "return migrant" to the United States. In many ways, I had the inverse experience of the Brazilian returnees I interviewed. I arrived in GV with my pre-migration U.S.-formed racial ideals and over time began to develop an understanding of the Brazilian racial system. My personal experiences being racialized as both nonblack and nonwhite have had a subtle impact on the way I think about race now, in particular how I think about skin color. As a lighter-skinned African American from the South, I was not a stranger to (skin) color-ism, particularly because having lighter skin tone and "good" hair were highly desired and valued in the African American community. Still, I and the other African Americans in my hometown and across the United States considered ourselves black regardless of how fair our skin or how straight our hair.

However, living and doing research in Brazil resurrected some issues that I thought I had come to terms with years ago. Upon my "permanent" return to the United States in November 2008, my awareness of variations in skin tone among Americans in general, but especially among black Americans, was significantly heightened. Though I still saw myself as undeniably black in the United States, I would often try to figure out if people I passed on the street would be white, pardo, or black based on their skin tone and hair texture. My time in Brazil talking with locals about race and skin color did not change how I saw myself racially, but it did alter how I viewed Americans and increased my understanding of both the subtle and the glaring differences between race relations in the United States and Brazil. I believe that this shift was indicative of how the transnational racial optic shaped my personal post-migration perceptions of race in the United States. Just as return migration facilitated a shift in Brazilian returnees' racial perceptions, my migration experience affected me. As more people continue to move across international borders, immigration *and* return migration in large numbers have the potential to transform their racial conceptions as well, and to reconstruct race on a global scale.

APPENDIX

Conducting this study was both exciting and demanding. It was exciting because I had long been fascinated by the qualitative differences between the race relations in Brazil and the United States; and it was challenging because I had to conceptualize the project in two languages in two countries. The scholarly commitment and personal investment that qualitative research entails requires meticulous attention to detail, enduring patience, and flexibility to adapt to unpredictable twists and turns. Although I briefly outlined my methods in the introduction and incorporated my ethnographic observations throughout the book, here I elaborate on them and discuss some additional challenges with the hope that they will be useful for others who want to conduct international multilingual research.

CREATING A FOUNDATION IN BRAZIL

Although I lived and conducted research in Governador Valadares in 2007 and 2008, my preparation for carrying out that fieldwork began in 2005, when I started learning Brazilian Portuguese and traveled to Brazil for the first time. As part of an interdisciplinary research team from the University of Michigan,

I attended a research meeting with Brazilian scholars at the Federal University of Minas Gerais in Belo Horizonte, Brazil. We were developing a cross-national survey modeled on the Detroit Area Study (DAS) that would be conducted in Belo Horizonte to assess a broad range of socioeconomic and political indicators.[1] Because of the difficulty measuring race in previous Brazilian surveys, we discussed how to best construct the survey's race question and thought it would be most appropriate to include multiple measures of racial and skin tone classification. This discussion remained with me as I conceptualized the research presented in this book. This meeting was also beneficial because it allowed me to connect with Brazilian scholars who were from GV or had conducted research on the impact of U.S. migration there. These scholars proved to be invaluable, sharing relevant history, background, and literature on the city, connecting me with the local university and other important organizations in GV, and providing feedback on my study design and interview protocols as the project progressed.

I went to GV for the first time in the summer of 2007 to do additional language training, meet relevant contacts, and do some preliminary fieldwork. I became acquainted with Sueli Siqueira, a sociologist from GV, who has conducted extensive research on GV migration in the city, the United States, Italy, and Spain. I also became affiliated with the Centro de Informação, Apoio e Amparo à Família e ao Trabalhador no Exterior (CIAAT), an organization that provided information and support to migrants living abroad and their families in GV. During that summer, I conducted five pre-test interviews (three with return migrants and two with non-migrants), which revealed inaccurately translated words and phrases that respondents misunderstood. This preliminary work, along with feedback from Brazilian researchers in the United States and GV, was immensely helpful in developing the questionnaire I used when I officially began interviewing participants in December 2007.

SAMPLE DEMOGRAPHICS

See Tables 9 through 11 for additional demographic information about return migrants and non-migrants. The demographics of my sample overlap with those in previous studies of Brazilian immigrants in the United States.[2]

TABLE 9. DEMOGRAPHICS OF RETURNEES AND NON-MIGRANTS

Category	Return Migrants (N = 49)	Non-Migrants (N = 24)
Gender: women (%)	53	58
Age: average (years)	40	39
Age: range (years)	20–57	19–54
Income: average ($USD)*	1,507 (std. 1,891)	1,461 (std. 2,222)
Income: median ($USD)	878	1,054
Education Level (%)		
Less than high school	16	8
High school	53	50
College	22	42
Greater than college	8	0
Top 3 Job Types (%)		
Sales/business	41	71
Education: teacher, etc.	18	8
Other	18	21
Currently unemployed (%)	20	13

*Monthly income reported at the time of the interview is converted from Brazilian reals; std = standard deviation.

TABLE 10. RETURNEES' MIGRATION INFORMATION (N = 49)

Returnee	Gender	Age	Years in U.S.	Length of Stay in U.S. (years)	U.S. State(s) of Residence	Non-Migrant Relative
Thiago	M	49	1983–1990	4	NY	Nicolas: brother
Luana	F	45	2006–2007	1	NC, VA	Viviane: sister
Tomás	M	45	1988–2001	5	MA	None
Eduardo	M	45	1983–1991	8	FL, CT	Francisco: brother
Natália	F	38	1989–1994	5	MA	Douglas: brother
Isabela	F	36	1991–2007	16	MA	Samara: sister
Ricardo	M	50	1979–2008	19	FL, SC, NY	None
Jéssica	F	32	2001–2007	6	MA	None
Gustavo	M	37	2002–2005	4	MA	None
Paulo	M	28	2003–2006	4	SC, CA	Marcela: sister
Felipe	M	34	1999–2006	7	MA, CT	None
Fabio	M	51	1983–2004	19	NY, FL	Cecilia: sister
Lorena	F	40	1998–1999	2	MA	Isaac: cousin

Table 10 continued on next page

TABLE 10. RETURNEES' MIGRATION INFORMATION (N = 49) (CONTINUED)

Returnee	Gender	Age	Years in U.S.	Length of Stay in U.S. (years)	U.S. State(s) of Residence	Non-Migrant Relative
Luisa	F	33	1995–2003	8	CT	Giovana: sister
Amanda	F	33	1993–1998	5	CT	None
Mariana	F	24	2000–2003	3	MA	None
Ana	F	45	1984–1999	14	NY, NJ	Denise: sister
Larissa	F	41	1990–2003	11	NJ	Rodolfo: cousin
Vinícius	M	31	1988–2006	13	FL	None
Marcêlo	M	55	1984–2008	18	MA, NY, NJ, PA, FL	Filipe: brother
Henrique	M	27	2004–2007	3	MA, NH	Jorge: brother
Renata	F	46	1984–1999	16	NY	None
Rafaela	F	21	2005–2008	3	GA	Olivia: sister
Sofia	F	44	1990–2002	12	NY, FL	None
Márcio	M	51	1998–2006	8	NJ	None
Ronaldo	M	44	1988–2007	20	NH, MA	Heitor: cousin
Bianca	F	29	1999–2002	13	NJ	None
Sérgio	M	46	2002–2005	3	CT	Kátia: sister
Carolina	F	44	1985–2004	10	NY, NJ	None
Flavio	M	57	1974–1989	12	NY, MD, VA	None
Bárbara	F	48	1991–2002	11	DC, NC	None
Marina	F	39	1999–2006	7	NJ	Lígia: cousin
Luciana	F	41	1988–2007	19	MA	None
Mateus	M	42	1984–1989	5	RI	None
Stephane	F	43	1987–1998	11	VA	None
Juliana	F	41	1994–2001	3	MA	Franciely: sister
Erika	F	27	2000–2006	7	MA	None
Bruno	M	41	1993–2004	11	MA	None
Camila	F	48	1999–2005	5	MA	Lara: sister
Antônio	M	38	2002–2007	6	CT	None
Victoria	F	43	1989–2000	13	CT	None
Fernanda	F	30	2004–2005	1	FL	Marcia: cousin
Rafael	M	38	1987–1990	3	MA	Maurício: cousin
Gabriel	M	43	2001–2007	4	MA	None
Sabrina	F	31	2005–2008	3	FL	Cecicle: sister-in-law
Fernando	M	42	2001–2006	6	MA, CT	None
Luiz	M	43	1990–1994	3	NJ	Hugo: brother
Lucas	M	43	1992–2002	10	NJ, NY, MA	None
Letícia	F	45	1986–1994	8	NY, NJ, MA	Rosângela: sister

Note: Migrants' names are listed by racial classification, beginning with those who self-classified as white, then brown, and then black throughout the migration.

TABLE 11. NON-MIGRANTS' RACIAL AND SKIN TONE CLASSIFICATIONS (N = 24)

Non-Migrant	Gender	Age	Open-Ended Racial Classification	Categorical Racial Classification	Skin Tone Classification	Returnee Relative
Nicolas	M	52	moreno	pardo	4	Thiago: brother
Viviane	F	41	yellow	yellow	6	Luana: sister
Francisco	M	43	white	white	3	Eduardo: brother
Douglas	M	36	white	white	4	Natalia: sister
Samara	F	30	white	white	5	Isabela: sister
Marcela	F	34	white	white	5	Paulo: brother
Cecília	F	52	clara (Light)	white	4	Fabio: brother
Isaac	M	22	moreno	pardo	7.5	Lorena: cousin
Giovana	F	35	light morena	white	3	Luisa: sister
Denise	F	38	morena	pardo	5	Ana: sister
Rodolfo	M	39	normal: white	white	3	Larissa: cousin
Filipe	M	49	white	white	3	Marcelo: brother
Jorge	M	32	white	white	6	Henrique: brother
Olivia	F	19	white	yellow	5	Rafaela: sister
Heitor	M	39	pardo	pardo	3	Ronaldo: cousin
Katia	F	52	more black	pardo	8	Sérgio: brother
Lígia	F	47	parda	pardo	6.5	Marina: cousin
Franciely	F	38	morena	pardo	5	Juliana: sister
Lara	F	52	morena	white	6	Camila: sister
Marcia	F	26	parda	pardo	7.5	Fernanda: cousin
Mauricio	M	24	moreno	Indigenous	5	Rafael: cousin
Cecicle	F	37	black (negra = race)	black (preto = color)	7	Sabrina: sister-in-law
Hugo	M	48	black (race)	black (color)	7	Luiz: brother
Rosângela	F	54	black (race)	other: black (race)	8	Letícia: sister

Note: Non-migrants names are listed in the order that coincides with their returnee migrant relatives in Table 10.

SEMI-STRUCTURED INTERVIEWS AND OBSERVATIONS

My interviews with returnees and non-migrants lasted on average 60 minutes and focused on the following topics: (1) racial and skin tone classifications; (2) perceptions and experiences of racism in the United States and/or Brazil; (3) race relations in the United States and/or Brazil; and (4) the influence of U.S. migration on race and life in GV. I divided my interviews with returnees into five sections. The first section was devoted to collecting immigration-related data; the remaining four sections focused specifically on returnees' recollections of race at four retrospective migration "stages": (1) in Brazil before migrating; (2) in the United States as immigrants; (3) in Brazil immediately after returning; and (4) in Brazil at the time I conducted the interview. This process allowed me to identify changes in returnees' racial conceptions between each stage. Interviews with non-migrants also included immigration-related questions so I could learn what role U.S. migration had played in their lives as residents of GV and relatives of individuals who immigrated to the United States.

After conducting each interview, I took extensive fieldnotes about everything I could remember, from the moment I met the respondent to when I left the interview location. I wrote descriptive details about respondents' physical features, how they were dressed, and their facial expression when I introduced myself as the researcher. Because of my appearance, some respondents were surprised to learn that I was American.[3] My assessment of respondents' phenotypes was useful later as I reviewed their racial conceptions in the transcripts. I also used Brazilian norms and my own physical features as a basis for evaluating how respondents' racial classifications of themselves aligned with how I classified them as the interviewer. Because I was racialized as morena in GV, I classified respondents with skin tones similar to mine as moreno or pardo, those with complexions lighter than mine as white, and those with complexions darker than mine as black. I also recorded how I thought respondents would be classified using U.S. norms in order to further assess how respondents' phenotypes would be racialized in the two contexts.

I usually conducted interviews in locations that were most convenient for the respondents, such as coffee shops and sometimes in their homes. In public places, if anyone else was in earshot of the interview, I noted this and considered how it might have influenced the respondent's answers. If I conducted the interview in a respondent's home, I jotted down my observations of the house and neighborhood to contextualize the socioeconomic background of the respondent. I also noted if anyone else was present in the home during the interview for the same reasons I did so in public places. In most instances, however, the respondent and I were the only ones present during interviews.

Because I lived in GV for the duration of the study, I wrote every day about my observations of life in the city—my daily walks to the gym, weekly trips to the nearby farmers' market, and casual interactions with Valadarenses. Everything I observed and everyone I encountered during my time in the city allowed me to get a better sense of GV-U.S. transnational ties and local discourses related to race. These fieldnotes became especially important after I left GV for contextualizing the rich interview data I collected.

The findings reported in these chapters come from my ethnographic accounts and interviews with 73 Valadarenses: 49 return migrants and 24 non-migrants. When beginning the fieldwork, I had hoped to conduct 100 interviews, 50 with return migrants and 50 with non-migrant relatives, to yield 50 matched return migrant–non-migrant pairs. However, some of the return migrants I interviewed did not have a non-migrant relative, or their non-migrant relative did not live in GV and could therefore not be interviewed. I conducted five additional interviews with return migrants that were not included in the sample, because those individuals were not permanent return migrants. They had become legal U.S. residents or naturalized citizens and were visiting GV temporarily before returning to the United States; their perspectives provided additional insights into the transnational ties between GV and the United States.

MEASURING RESPONDENTS' RACIAL AND SKIN TONE CLASSIFICATIONS

I used four measures to assess respondents' racial classifications: (1) categorical—Brazilian and/or U.S. census-derived categories; (2) open-ended—respondents' self-classification in their own words; (3) perceived external—how respondents believed others classified them; and (4) interviewer-assessed—how I classified the respondents using Brazilian categorical and open-ended categories. These measures are consistent with those used in other studies exploring racial classification in Brazil.[4] For returnees, I used Brazilian categories before and after migration, but I used U.S. categories when asking them to self-classify during

their time in the United States. Given the relationship between racial classification and skin color in Brazil, I also asked respondents for self-ascribed skin
tone classifications using a scale from 1 (light) to 10 (dark). See Table 12 for
returnees' racial classifications over the course of their migration.

I examined and calculated each returnee's mean skin tone over the course
of migration by adding their skin tone self-reports at each retrospective stage
(pre-migration; in the United States; immediately after return; and at the time
of the interview) and then dividing them by 4 (see Table 13). A closer examination of each returnee's skin tone classification at each stage made it easier to
determine which returnees self-classified using the same number on the scale
before, during, and after migration.

Although I used multiple measures for racial classification throughout the
migration process, it was not possible to know with certainty why respondents
self-classified in the ways that they did, or whether those classifications were
accurate at any particular time. Because most respondents were on the move
and lived in the transnational setting of GV, how these people thought about
their racial identities at different times could not be perfectly captured.

TRANSLATING PORTUGUESE AND
THE LANGUAGE OF RACE IN BRAZIL

Learning how the language of race in the United States differs from that in
Brazil brought a unique challenge for migrants during their time in the United
States. The same was true for me as I, a non-native speaker of Portuguese,
talked with Valadarenses about Brazilian conceptions of race. When I first
began interviewing respondents, translation and racial classification issues in
the United States and Brazil led to some insightful as well as some confusing
interviewer-interviewee moments.

The most notable miscommunication was when I asked respondents for
their open-ended racial self-classification using the phrase: "*como você se vê em
relação a raça*" ("how do you see yourself racially?"). I initially included *raça*—the
Brazilian Portuguese translation for race—in this question since other Brazilian
surveys use it when asking for participants' racial classifications. I assumed that
respondents would understand the question phrased in that manner. However,
some respondents believed the word *raça* denoted racism and racial inequality.

TABLE 12. RETURNEES' RACIAL CLASSIFICATIONS THROUGHOUT MIGRATION (N = 49)

Returnee	Open-Ended Race Pre-Migration	Categorical Race Pre-Migration	Open-Ended Race in U.S.	Categorical Race in U.S.	Open-Ended Race at Time of Interview	Categorical Race at Time of Interview	Mean Skin Tone over Migration
Thiago	white	white	white, normal	white	white	white	1.8
Luana	white	white	white	white	white	white	3.5
Tomas	white	white	white	white	white	white	4.3
Eduardo	white	white	white, Brazilian	white	white	white	3.0
Natália	white	white	Foreigner	white	white	white	2.3
Isabela	white/transparent	white	white, but not as white	white	white	white	2.3
Ricardo	white Brazilian, a little dark	white	Brazilian/Latino	white	white	white	2.0
Jéssica	white	white	white, normal	Other: white and Latino	white	white	2.5
Gustavo	white	white	white	Hispanic/Latino	white	white	4.0
Paulo	white	white	not black or white, foreigner	Hispanic/Latino	white	white	5.8
Isabela	white/transparent	white	white, but not as white	white	white	white	2.3
Ricardo	white Brazilian, a little dark	white	Brazilian/Latino	white	white	white	2.0
Jéssica	white	white	white, normal	Other: white and Latino	white	white	2.5
Gustavo	white	white	white	Hispanic/Latino	white	white	4.0
Paulo	white	white	not black or white, foreigner	Hispanic/Latino	white	white	5.8

Table 12 continued on next page

Returnee	Open-Ended Race Pre-Migration	Categorical Race Pre-Migration	Open-Ended Race in U.S.	Categorical Race in U.S.	Open-Ended Race at Time of Interview	Categorical Race at Time of Interview	Mean Skin Tone over Migration
Felipe	white	white	not black, white, or American	Hispanic/Latino	white, but not 100% white	white	4.5
Fabio	white	white	white	Hispanic/Latino	yellowish white	white	4.5
Lorena	white	white	white	white	Human Being	Other: Human Race	3.5
Luisa	white	white	parda, yellow, white	Other: Hispanic/Latino and Asian American	white	white	3.4
Amanda	white	white	Brazilian/Latina	Hispanic/Latino	white	white	4.0
Mariana	morena	white	white	white	white	white	5.0
Ana	light morena	white	light morena	Hispanic/Latino	light morena	white	2.8
Larissa	white	yellow	white or yellow	Asian American	yellow	yellow	2.8
Vinicius	Portuguese	white	Hispanic	Hispanic/Latino	Portuguese	white	5.0
Marcêlo	neutral: not white/black	white	Hispanic	Hispanic/Latino	neutral: not black/white	white	4.0
Henrique	white	white	Latino	Hispanic/Latino	white	pardo	6.3
Renata	white	yellow	yellow	Hispanic/Latino	Latina	yellow	6.9
Rafaela	almost yellow	yellow	not black or white	Asian American	white/yellowish	white	5.0
Sofia	Does not know how to classify	yellow	Does not classify	Asian American	Does not classify	yellow	3.0
Marcio	moreno	white	moreno	white	moreno	white	4.5
Ronaldo	normal, does not classify	Other: white and Indigenous	Does not classify	Other: white and Asian American	normal	Other: white and yellow	5.0
Bianca	morena	white	morena	white	morena	white	7.0
Sérgio	moreno	pardo	moreno	Hispanic/Latino	moreno	pardo	5.0
Carolina	morena	pardo	white	Other: morena	morena	pardo	4.5

Table 12 continued on next page

TABLE 12. RETURNEES' RACIAL CLASSIFICATIONS THROUGHOUT MIGRATION (N = 49) (CONTINUED)

Returnee	Open-Ended Race Pre-Migration	Categorical Race Pre-Migration	Open-Ended Race in U.S.	Categorical Race in U.S.	Open-Ended Race at Time of Interview	Categorical Race at Time of Interview	Mean Skin Tone over Migration
Flavio	moreno	Other: moreno	black	Hispanic/Latino	moreno	Other: moreno	5.5
Bárbara	morena	pardo	Hispanic	white	morena	pardo	5.5
Marina	morena	white	morena	Hispanic/Latino	morena	Other: morena	5.5
Luciana	parda	pardo	parda	none	parda	pardo	3.0
Mateus	moreno	pardo	light moreno	white	moreno	black	3.0
Stephane	morena	pardo	morena	Indigenous	morena	pardo	4.8
Juliana	mulatta	pardo	mulatta	Hispanic/Latino	mulatta	pardo	5.9
Erika	parda	Indigenous	Hispanic	Hispanic/Latino	morena	pardo	6.0
Bruno	moreno	pardo	moreno	Hispanic/Latino	moreno	pardo	6.0
Camila	mixed: not black/white	pardo	mixed person	Hispanic/Latino	mixed person	pardo	6.8
António	dark moreno	pardo	Latino	Hispanic/Latino	pardo	pardo	6.5
Victoria	morena	pardo	morena	Brazilian	morena	pardo	8.0
Fernanda	black	white	much lighter	Other: white and Latina	black	black	6.0
Rafael	moreno	black	moreno	Hispanic/Latino	moreno	black	6.8
Gabriel	moreno	black	moreno	white	moreno	black	8.0
Sabrina	black	pardo	black	black	black	black	7.3
Fernando	black	black	black	black	black	black	7.0
Luiz	black	black	black	black	black	black	8.0
Lucas	black	black	black Hispanic	Other: black and Hispanic/Latino	black	black	8.5
Letícia	black	black	black	black	black	black	10.0

Note: Migrants' names are listed in the order of their racial classifications beginning with those who self-classified as white, then brown, and then black throughout migration.

Returnee	SkinBI	SkinUS	SkinAR	SkinNow	Skin Tone Mean	Change	Std. Deviation
Thiago	2	2	1	2	1.8	Yes	0.5
Luana	3.5	3.5	3.5	3.5	3.5	No	0.0
Tomas	4	6	3	4	4.3	Yes	1.3
Eduardo	3	3	3	3	3.0	No	0.0
Natália	2	3	1	3	2.3	Yes	1.0
Isabela	2	3	2	2	2.3	Yes	0.5
Ricardo	3	3	1	1	2.0	Yes	1.2
Jéssica	2.5	2.5	2.5	2.5	2.5	No	0.0
Gustavo	4	5	2	5	4.0	Yes	1.4
Paulo	6	5	6	6	5.8	Yes	0.5
Felipe	4	6	4	4	4.5	Yes	1.0
Fabio	3	3	6	6	4.5	Yes	1.7
Lorena	4	3	1	6	3.5	Yes	2.1
Luisa	3.5	3	2	5	3.4	Yes	1.3
Amanda	4	4	4	4	4.0	No	0.0
Mariana	5	5	5	5	5.0	No	0.0
Ana	4	2	2.5	2.5	2.8	Yes	0.9
Larissa	3	4	2	2	2.8	Yes	1.0
Vinícius	5	5	5	5	5.0	No	0.0
Marcêlo	4	4	4	4	4.0	No	0.0
Henrique	6	7	6	6	6.3	Yes	0.5
Renata	6	7.5	7	7	6.9	Yes	0.6
Rafaela	5	5	5	5	5.0	No	0.0
Sofia	3	3	3	3	3.0	No	0.0
Marcio	5	5	3	5	4.5	Yes	1.0
Ronaldo	5	5	5	5	5.0	No	0.0
Bianca	7	7	7	7	7.0	No	0.0
Sérgio	5	5	5	5	5.0	No	0.0
Carolina	5	4	4	5	4.5	Yes	0.6
Flavio	5	7	5	5	5.5	Yes	1.0
Barbara	5	5	7	5	5.5	Yes	1.0
Marina	5	6	5	6	5.5	Yes	0.6
Luciana	3	3	3	3	3.0	No	0.0
Mateus	2	3	3	4	3.0	Yes	0.8
Stephane	5	5	4	5	4.8	Yes	0.5
Juliana	5.5	7	5.5	5.5	5.9	Yes	0.8
Erika	6	6	6	6	6.0	No	0.0

Table 13 continued on next page

TABLE 13. MIGRANTS' SELF-CLASSIFICATIONS OF SKIN TONE THROUGHOUT
MIGRATION (N = 49) (CONTINUED)

Returnee	SkinBI	SkinUS	SkinAR	SkinNow	Skin Tone Mean	Change	Std. Deviation
Bruno	6	6	6	6	6.0	No	0.0
Camila	6	7	7	7	6.8	Yes	0.5
Antônio	6	7	6	7	6.5	Yes	0.6
Victoria	8	8	8	8	8.0	No	0.0
Fernanda	7	7	3	7	6.0	Yes	2.0
Rafael	6	7	7	7	6.8	Yes	0.5
Gabriel	8	8	8	8	8.0	No	0.0
Sabrina	7	9	6	7	7.3	Yes	1.3
Fernando	7	7	7	7	7.0	No	0.0
Luiz	8	8	8	8	8.0	No	0.0
Lucas	8.5	8.5	8.5	8.5	8.5	No	0.0
Letícia	10	10	10	10	10.0	No	0.0

Notes: Migrants' names are listed by racial self-classification on a scale from 1 (light) to 10 (dark) , beginning with those who self-classified as white, then brown, and then black throughout migration. Shading identifies the 12 returnees who reported darker classifications at the time of the interview. Italics identify the 28 returnees who reported different skin tone classifications in at least two retrospective migration stages. The remaining 21 returnees reported the same skin tone classification at each migration stage.

SkinBI = skin tone before immigrating; SkinUS = skin tone in U.S.; SkinAR = skin tone after returning; SkinNow = skin tone at time of interview; Change = change in skin tone

Participants thought I was asking them "Are you racist?" when I was actually asking them for their open-ended racial classification. Twenty returnees and 14 non-migrants told me they were not racist after I posed that question.[5] When I rephrased the question to ask "How do you see yourself in terms of [skin] color?" respondents usually held out their arm or hand, looked at the color, and replied with the word they felt best described their color, or *côr*. This experience confirmed what other studies have suggested about Brazilians' perceptions of racial classification: they are tied to actual skin tone, not to distinct racial groups that have intra-group social affinities.[6]

I conducted interviews in Portuguese, but because I am not a native speaker I also hired three Valadarenses to transcribe the audio-recorded interviews. I reviewed each transcript and listened to the corresponding audio-recorded interview to check for accuracy and consistency between the two versions. I made the necessary corrections and imported each transcript into NVivo qualitative software for data analysis. Because I analyzed the interviews in Portuguese, I translated only the excerpts that are printed in this book. There were certain race-related Brazilian colloquialisms and phrases used in interviews that were very difficult to translate for an American audience. Thus it is likely some nuances were lost in translation.

I relied on a grounded theory approach, which means I did not have any preconceived notions about what results would emerge from the data before conducting the fieldwork.[7] Before beginning the qualitative data analysis, I reviewed all of my fieldnotes and took notes on all topics related to race and immigration in the United States, Brazil, and GV that had begun to emerge. I used this list of broad themes to generate the categories for in-depth open and focused coding of the interview transcripts.[8] For example, in Chapters 3 and 4, I did more in-depth analyses to focus on coding categories that referred specifically to return migrants' conceptions of race in the United States and how they compared with their pre-migration conceptions in Brazil. For each of those coding categories, I read all of the interview excerpts to develop a broader idea of how returnees interpreted race in the two contexts. At times, the broader ideas that emerged from these more in-depth analyses resulted in the formulation of "sub-codes" that I used to further explore how movement between GV and the United States influenced returnees' racial conceptions. This was an exhaustive process that continued until no more coding could be done and the coding categories could no longer be deconstructed into smaller sub-codes. I continued to write fieldnotes during this process of data analysis to help me more effectively understand and interpret how returnees negotiated race in both places. This was particularly helpful for identifying whether particular themes were noted among only a few participants or among a larger portion of the sample. I used this analytical approach in each empirical chapter to compare the different stages of the migration process for returnees. I used a similar process to analyze the non-migrant data.

NOTES

INTRODUCTION

1. To protect the respondents' identity and confidentiality, I use pseudonyms that do not overlap with their real names. Throughout the book, I have translated the quotes from the Portuguese interviews and included each respondent's pseudonym and age as reported at the time of the interview.

2. Historically, *morena* referred to a wide range of "brunette" phenotypes, including black, racially mixed, and white individuals with dark hair and eyes. Brazilian anthropologist Gilberto Freyre (1933) used moreno as an overarching term to describe the Brazilian population, since most have dark hair and eyes. Moreno is the most popular informal racial category in Brazil. The Brazilian census equivalent of moreno is the *pardo* category, which also implies racially mixed heritage. Most Brazilians classify themselves as pardo.

3. I use "race" broadly to refer to a single instance or a combination of the following: ethno-racial classification; interpersonal and/or institutional race relations; perceptions and experiences of racial discrimination; and racism. This definition draws on sociologist Eduardo Bonilla-Silva's (1997) "racialized social systems," Ann Morning's (2009) "racial conceptualizations," and Michael Omi's and Howard Winant's (1994) "racial formations" to broadly capture how physical features influence social interactions and stratification, as well as inequality at the interpersonal, structural, institutional, and economic levels, with particular regard to socio-geographic context.

4. See Alba et al. (2005); Kim (2008); Lee and Bean (2007); Roth (2012); Sakamoto et al. (2010); Waters (1999).

5. Racial ideals are characteristics associated with race from a particular country. An example of a U.S. racial ideal is the notion that the United States has a history of overt racism toward people of color. An example of a Brazilian racial ideal is that racial categories are fluid.

6. I use migration, international migration, and transnational migration interchangeably.

7. DeBiaggi (2002); Grasmuck and Pessar (1991); Levitt (2001b, 2007); Pedraza (1991); Takenaka (2000).

8. Alarcón et al. (2009); Assis and Siqueira (2009); Carling (2008); Lee and Bean (2010); Levitt (2000, 2007); Orellana et al. (2001); Pedraza (1991); Rapoport and Docquier (2005); Rivera-Salgado (2003).

9. Aranda (2009); Duany (2002); Flores (2009); Itzigsohn et al. (2005); Kim (2008); Levitt (2001b); Roth (2012); Zamora (2014).

10. A return migrant is an individual who temporarily migrates to another country and then returns to her country of origin permanently or for an extended period of time. I use "returnees" and "return migrants" interchangeably. Some return migrants re-migrate to the same or a different host country after the initial return migration, a process known as "yo-yo migration." However, those individuals again become immigrants. In this book, my focus is on individuals who considered themselves permanent return migrants at the time of the study, regardless of how many times they previously migrated to and returned from the United States.

11. Racial classification refers to the categories used to racially identify a person. In Brazil, it is usually associated with skin tone or *côr*, and in the United States it usually relates to phenotype and ancestry.

12. Levitt and Glick Schiller (2004).

13. Previous studies estimate that 15 to 50 percent of Valadarense migrants return to GV (Assis and DeCampos 2009; Centro de Informação 2007; Goza 1999; Marcus 2009; Martes 2008; Sales 1999; Siqueira 2008, 2009a, 2009b). Given the limited data and number of studies on return migration, it is difficult to determine how Brazilians compare with returnees from other countries who have migrated to the United States and other immigrant-receiving societies. There has been significant return migration to traditional immigrant-sending cities in Mexico (Alarcón 2009; Rendall et al. 2010; CONAPO 2009; Passell and Cohn 2009). For more on qualitative aspects of return migration, see Conway and Potter (2006); Flores (2009); Iredale et al. (2003); Plaza and Henry (2006); Potter et al. (2005); and Tsuda (2009a).

14. Centro de Informação (2007); Goza (1999); Sales (1999); Siqueira (2008, 2009a, 2009b).

15. Humes et al. (2011). The 2010 U.S. census designates "Hispanic" as an ethnic category that is distinct from race since Hispanics can be of any racial group. Thus the term "non-Hispanic whites" refers to whites who do not have Hispanic ethnicity. See Chapter 3 for more on this and the difference between the Latino and Hispanic categories. See also Hirschman et al. (2000); Prewitt (2005); Snipp (2003).

16. Bonilla-Silva (2004); Fu (2008); Lee and Bean (2004, 2010); Lee and Edmonston (2005); Rockquemore and Arend (2002).

17. The "honorary whites" include light-skinned Latinos, many Asian Americans, and Middle Eastern Americans (Bonilla-Silva 2004). Bonilla-Silva suggests this is a tri-racial system, although it could be argued that it is a modified black-white binary system. See the following for how the black-white binary could develop into a black-nonblack binary: Forman et al. (2002); Frank et al. (2010); Lee and Bean (2010); Murguia and Saenz (2002).

18. Araujo (2001); Bailey (2009); Bernardino and Galdino (2004); Fry and Maggie (2004); Xavier and Xavier (2009). See Chapters 5 and 6 for more on quotas in Brazil.

19. Kamel (2006).

20. Bailey (2009); Bonilla-Silva (2004); Daniel (2006).

21. Bailey (2009); Daniel (2006); Degler (1971); Marx (1998); Monk (2013); Nogueira (1955); Pierson (1967); Skidmore (1993); Telles (2004); Van den Berghe (1978).

22. More Africans were brought to Brazil than to any other part of the Americas during the Atlantic slave trade. Consequently, Brazil has the largest number of African-descended people outside of Nigeria. Some scholars have argued that (predominantly unmarried male) Portuguese colonizers' more lax social norms regarding interracial sexual unions, as well as few laws prohibiting interracial marriage, yielded a nation of individuals with a wide range of physical features. This contrasts with the United States, where many of the original European colonists migrated in family units. See Degler (1971) and Skidmore (1993) for more.

23. Bailey (2009); Daniel (2006); Marx (1998); Telles (2004).

24. Fernandes (1965); Freyre (1933); Sansone (2003).

25. Harris (1952); Pierson (1967); Tannenbaum (1947); Wagley (1952).

26. Bailey (2009); Daniel (2006); Degler (1971); Marx (1998); Nobles (2000); Santos and Silva (2005); Sheriff (2001); Telles (2004); Twine (1998).

27. Espiritu (2009); Jacoby (2004); Lee and Bean (2010); Nobles (2000); Pedraza and Rumbaut (1996); Snipp (2003); Vickerman (2007).

28. The legal definition of whiteness shifted in response to the Native American conquest, slavery, the 1880–1920 immigration wave, and westward expansion for the purpose of creating racial boundaries between whites and nonwhites. The definition also included a distinction between legal whiteness and social whiteness for groups who were legally white, such as Irish, Italian, and Jewish immigrants, but who were not socially white, such as the British, and were therefore subject to ethnic discrimination. For more, see Treitler (2013); Feagin (2000); Haney López (1996); and Roediger (2005).

29. Freyre (1951); Lesser (1999); Skidmore (1993); Telles (2004).

30. Iwata (2012); Lesser (1999); Sasaki (1999); Tsuda (2009b).

31. Lesser (2013).

32. Myrdal (1944).

33. Du Bois (1996, p. xiii). This quote is from sociologist Elijah Anderson's introduction to the 1996 version of Du Bois's *The Philadelphia Negro*.

34. Du Bois (1996); Morris (2014).

35. Guimarães (2005); Telles (2004).

36. In developing the ideology after the eugenics movement, Freyre challenged the prevailing scientific argument that racial miscegenation would lead to the biological and cultural degeneracy of the superior (white) racial group. U.S. and Brazilian scholars, however, have harshly criticized Freyre's work, arguing that it encouraged the use of racial mixing to whiten or dilute the African and Indigenous elements in the Brazilian population (Daniel 2006; Guimarães 2001; Sansone 2003; Skidmore 1993; Telles 2004; Twine 1998).

37. Joseph (2013b, 2013c); Marcus (2003); Margolis (1994, 1998); Marrow (2003); Martes (2003; 2007); McDonnell and DeLourenço (2008, 2009).

38. Ethno-racial refers to a combination of ethnicity and race when discussing the ethnic and/or racial origins of individuals. For example, black is considered a racial category, and Latino is ethnic.

39. Margolis (1994, 1998); Mitchell (2003); Sales (1999); Siqueira (2009b).

40. Bailey and Pereira (2010); Marteleto (2012); Padgett and Downie (2009); Rascusen (2010); Reiter and Mitchell (2010); Shannon (2012); Xavier and Xavier (2009).

41. Sociologists Peggy Levitt and B. Nadya Jaworsky (2007) conceptualized what they called the "transnational optic" to illustrate how "economic, political, social, cultural, and religious life are transformed when they are enacted transnationally" (p. 130). Borrowing that term and building on it, I use the "transnational racial optic" to explore how migrants, specifically Brazilian return migrants, enact race transnationally.

42. Joseph (2013a).

43. See the following for more on human social psychological development: Erikson (1959); Herman (2004); Howarth (2002); Hughes et al. (2006); Marcia (1966); Meeus (1996); Mortimer and Simmons (1978); Perry (2002); Proshansky et al. (1983); Relph (1976); Schlegel (1998); Schwalbe and Morgan (1990); Suarez-Orozco and Todorova (2003).

44. Racialization is the process by which an individual or group is ascribed membership, usually by other people, in a particular racial group.

45. External racial classification is how individuals are classified by others. Perceived external racial classification is how individuals perceive they are classified by others. Bailey (2009); Bastos et al. (2009); Itzigsohn et al. (2005); Landale and Oropesa (2002); Loveman et al. (2012); Telles (2004).

46. Foner (1997, p. 358).

47. Brubaker et al. (2004); Cerulo (2002); D'Andrade (1995); DiMaggio (1997).

48. Roth (2012, p. 12).

49. Roth identifies three racial schemas among Dominicans and Puerto Ricans in the United States, the Dominican Republic, and Puerto Rico. The first is the "continuum racial schema," which includes intermediate racial terms between black and white. The second is the "(panethnic) nationality racial schema," which includes nationalities and ethnic groups as well as the panethnic Hispanic/Latino category. She breaks the third schema, the U.S. racial schema, into two sub-schemas. The first is the "traditional U.S. racial schema," in which any mixture of white and black has historically been perceived as black. The second is the "Hispanicized U.S. schema," which includes the white, black, and Hispanic/Latino categories. See Roth (2012) for more.

50. Duany (2002); Flores (2009); Itzigsohn et al. (2005); Kim (2008); Levitt (2001); Roth (2012); Zamora (2014).

51. Kim (2008); Zamora (2014).

52. Conway and Potter (2006); Margolis (2001); Plaza and Henry (2006); Siqueira (2009b); Siqueira et al. (2010); Tsuda (2009a).

53. Aranda (2007); Flores (2009); Levitt (2001).

54. See appendix for more specific demographic information on each respondent.

55. This should not be confused with respondents' self-classifications, which I did not know until I interviewed them.

56. Thirty of 49 returnees obtained tourist visas before migrating, but only 12 were able to obtain green cards or U.S. citizenship.

57. Most of these relatives were siblings or cousins.

58. I discuss the migration experience of returnees in three time periods: (1) before migration (the time in Brazil before migrating to the United States); (2) during migration (their time in the United States as immigrants); and (3) after migration (the period after returning to Brazil).

59. Memory recall is a limitation of most social scientific studies in which respondents are asked to recall events from the recent and distant past (Bernard et al. 1984; Trivellato 1999; Wellman 2007; Wolcott 1994).

60. I am a descendant of slaves and cannot trace my heritage beyond the United States. For more, see Joseph (2014b).

61. See appendix for more on this.

62. President Barack Obama would not be considered black in Brazil, but rather pardo, due to his appearance and racially mixed background. Some would even argue that his status as U.S. president would make him (socially) white in Brazil.

CHAPTER I

1. See Chapters 6 and 7.

2. Carla is a pseudonym.

3. The pizzeria closed in mid-2008, like many other local businesses, signaling the beginning of the Great Recession. See the Conclusion for more.

4. This nickname was used to refer to GV in a New York Times article by James Brooke in 1990.

5. Urban Brazilians and Brazilian immigrants in the United States from large cities like Rio de Janeiro and São Paulo describe people from GV as "caipira," which is a derogatory adjective used to describe people from rural areas (Margolis 1994). The U.S. equivalent for this term would be "redneck" or "backwoods."

6. The micro-region surrounding GV also has significant migration ties to the United States.

7. As a native Southerner, I felt that the hospitable culture of GV was similar to that of the American South. Serteneja is the Brazilian version of U.S. country music.

8. CIAAT (2007). Estimated remittances from the United States to Brazil in 2013 were $2.8 billion, down from $4.9 billion in 2012 (Cohn et al. 2013). The decrease likely derives from the increase in return migration to Brazil due to the 2008 recession and the World Bank's revising its definition of remittances to omit transfers between households (Cohn et al. 2013).

9. Fifteen returnees reported being business owners and/or owning rental properties from which they derive income.

10. Translated from Portuguese.

11. Reis and Machado (2008).

12. Goza (1999); Margolis (1994); Martes (2000); Sales (1999); Siqueira (2009b); Telles (2004).

13. Assis (1995).

14. Siqueira (2009b, p. 67). Translated from Portuguese.

15. Siqueira et al. (2010).

16. Goza (1999); Margolis (1994); Sales (1999).

17. CIAAT (2007); Martes (2008); Reis and Sales (1999); Siqueira (2009b). This term can also be translated colloquially as "making it in America," although it is not a term that Brazilians commonly use.

18. Tourist visas permit recipients to make temporary visits to the United States, but they do not allow migration or employment. Still, many potential Brazilian immigrants acquire tourist visas although they intend to stay and work (Brooke 1990). Given GV's migration history, it is now nearly impossible for anyone from GV to get a tourist visa in Brazil. An alternative is to go to Mexico and cross into the United States at the U.S.-Mexico border, which became a popular option after the restrictions on tourist visas for Brazilians were imposed. In response to high numbers of potential Brazilian migrants flying to Mexico to cross the U.S.-Mexico border in the early 2000s, Mexico also began requiring Brazilians to acquire a tourist visa to visit Mexico (Amaral and Fusco 2005; IOM 2006; Kraul and Gaouette 2005; Rohter 2005).

19. Felipe was one of only four of the 49 returnees who went back to GV because they attained their financial goals. The dollar figures reported here are based on the 2007 currency exchange rate between the Brazilian real and the U.S. dollar.

20. Pastore and Silva (2000); Telles (2004).

21. Valadarenses have also begun migrating to European countries such as Portugal, Spain, and Italy (Siqueira 2009b). Another strategy for Valadarenses who have documentation of

their Portuguese or Italian ancestry is to apply for recognition as an Italian or Portuguese citizen living abroad. If they can secure a European Union passport, that can be used to apply for a U.S. tourist visa. This process privileges "white" Brazilians over mixed and black Brazilians, who likely do not have the proper documentation to do this (Fieldnotes 11/15/2007).

22. DeBiaggi (2002); Fox (2005); Itzigsohn et al. (1999); Levitt (2001a, 2007); Levitt and Schiller (2004); Pedraza (2005).

23. Omi and Winant (1994).

24. For more on race in Brazil and the United States, see Bailey (2009); Daniel (2006); Guimarães (2001); Monteiro and Sansone (2004); Reiter and Mitchell (2010); Telles (2004); and Xavier and Xavier (2009). For more on racial democracy and ideology in Brazil, see Freyre (1933); Guimarães (2006); Reiter and Mitchell (2010).

25. Mineiros are residents of the state of Minas Gerais.

26. IBGE (2010). In Minas Gerais, 45 percent of Mineiros self-classify as white, 44 percent as pardo, and 9 percent as black. Relative to other Mineiros, many more Valadarenses self-classify as pardo. Individuals of Japanese descent generally self-classify as amarelo (yellow) on the census and are concentrated in São Paulo. The 2010 Brazilian census estimates that this group constitutes 1 percent of the population.

27. Telles (2004).

28. See Chapter 5.

29. In the United States, the rule of hypo-descent, also known as the "one-drop rule," excluded individuals with one drop of black (and later nonwhite) blood from the white racial category in order to preserve white racial purity. For more on the history, legacy, and codification of the one-drop rule, see Davis (1991); Haney López (1996); and Feagin (2000). Multiracial individuals now have more flexibility in classifying themselves; however, black-white multiracials are still more likely to classify as black than Asian-white and Latino-white multiracials, who usually classify as white or multiracial (Daniel 1992, 2000; Harris and Sims 2002; Herman 2004, 2011; Khanna 2010; Lee and Bean 2004; Rockquemore and Arrend 2002; Qian 2004).

30. Paim and Pereira (2010); Santos and Silva (2005); Telles (2004).

31. Burgard (2004); Guimarães (2001); Maio et al. (2002); Monteiro and Sansone (2004); Santos and Silva (2005); Souza (2005); Travassos and Williams (2004).

32. Guimarães (2001); Maio et al. (2002); Monteiro and Sansone (2004); Reiter and Mitchell (2010); Santos and Silva (2005); Souza (2005); Travassos and Williams (2004); Twine (1998).

33. Araujo (2000); Figueiredo (2010); Reiter and Mitchell (2010); Silva (2012); Telles (2004).

34. Telles (2004).

35. Telles (2004, p. 232).

36. See Chapter 5.

37. Hall (1991, 2003); Hunt (1997); Kim (2008); Roth (2012); Tomlinson (1999).

CHAPTER 2

1. In Chapters 2 and 4, I use respondents' open-ended racial classifications and descriptions of their physical features to provide additional context on how race and appearance influenced their perspectives. I used each respondent's open-ended racial self-classification because this was a more accurate reflection of how participants viewed their race than either the Brazilian or the U.S. census categories. For some participants, there was inconsistency between their open-ended and categorical classifications as well as between how they self-classified and how I classified them. Whenever such an inconsistency occurs, I include an

endnote to contextualize his or her racial classification. In Chapters 2 and 3, I include information about where migrants lived in the United States to illustrate how their context might have influenced their perceptions.

2. I use the term "migrants" to refer to respondents in Chapters 2 and 3 since these chapters focus on the United States, where they were migrants and not returnees.

3. Roth (2012).

4. Despite differences in the genders, ages, and years of migration, there were many similarities in migrants' perceptions of racial classification in the United States and Brazil.

5. Bailey (2008); Carvalho (2005); Maio et al. (2002); Nobles (2000); Telles (2004).

6. See Telles (2004) for a list of these categories. Roth (2012) refers to this as the "continuum racial schema."

7. Roth (2012); Telles and PERLA (2014); Wade (1996).

8. Jenkins (1996); Loveman (2005); Nagel (1994); Nobles (2000); Roth (2012); Telles (2004).

9. Nobles (2000, p. xi).

10. To ensure "equal" representation between Northern and Southern slaveholding states in the House of Representatives, these census calculations were important for the three-fifths compromise, in which each slave was counted as three-fifths of a person. Only white men who owned property were counted as full citizens, while white women, slaves of African descent, and poor whites were not. Racial categories at times overlapped with social class, gender, and eventually ethnicity (for immigrants) as different groups were incorporated into the nation.

11. McKee (1993).

12. Mora (2014); Rodriguez (2000).

13. De Genova and Ramos-Zayas (2003); Oboler (1995); Rodriguez (2000).

14. De Genova and Ramos-Zayas (2003).

15. Duany (2002); Itzigsohn et al. (2005); Oboler (1995); Rodriguez (2000); Roth (2012).

16. De Genova and Ramos-Zayas (2003); Martes (2007); Joseph (2013b); Oboler (1995).

17. Nobles (2000); Schwarcz (1999).

18. Nobles (2000); Schwarcz (1999).

19. Though the U.S. census asks Hispanic individuals to classify themselves both ethnically (as Hispanic) and racially (e.g., black, white), I combined the categories "Hispanic/Latino" in my interviews for two reasons. First, the existing literature on Brazilian immigrants indicates that they have exposure to both terms in the United States and are usually externally classified as Hispanic (Hollinger 2000; Martes 2007). Second, some returnees used the terms interchangeably during pre-test interviews. Some returnees felt that "yellow" and "Asian/Pacific Islander" best described their skin tone in Brazil and the United States, even though they had no Asian ancestry. Respondents who classified as "other" generally chose "moreno."

20. For this cross-tabulation, I recoded the racial categories to have the same values (e.g., branco = 1, white = 1, etc.). Since the white and black categories are on both the Brazilian and U.S. censuses, I recoded them with the same values. Although the pardo category does not exist in the United States, I recoded it to coincide with the Hispanic/Latino category, since the majority of participants chose this category in the United States, indicating that it most closely matched how they perceived themselves. Martes (2007) and Hollinger (2000) argue that U.S. and Brazilian census-based categories can be aligned in this way, since they are official categories and represent "colloquial" racial categories in both countries. I collapsed the remaining self-classifications into an overall "other" category.

21. Marcus (2003); Marrow (2003); Martes (2007); McDonnell and Lourenço (2009).

22. Bailey and Telles (2006); Maio et al. (2002); Piza and Rosemberg (1999); Silva (1996); Telles (2002); Travassos and Williams (2004).

23. Barth (1969); Cornell and Hartmann (1997); Jenkins (1994); Nagel (1994).

24. Cornell and Hartmann (1997); Nagel (1994); Roth (2012).

25. I thought she would be white in the United States.

26. Since Vinícius's skin tone was closer to mine, he likely would not have been considered white in the United States.

27. For more on the 2005 London bombings and the death of Jean Charles de Menezes, see IPCC (2007).

28. Bailey (2009); Cornell and Hartmann (1997); Hall and DuGay (1996); Nagel (1994); Roth (2012).

29. Cornell (1988); Davis (1991); Espiritu (1992); Feagin (2000); Nagel (1994).

30. She categorically classified herself as Hispanic/Latino while living in the United States.

31. Other studies of Latin American immigrants also note different conceptions of whiteness in the United States and Latin America, which these migrants must negotiate (Haney López 1996; Roth 2012; Vidal-Ortiz 2004). The literature on the one-drop rule has suggested that once a "white-looking" person reveals mixed ancestry, he or she is no longer perceived as white by others in the United States who are aware of this ancestry (Davis 1991; Feagin 2000).

32. Bonilla-Silva (2004); Fu (2008); Lee and Bean (2004, 2010); Lee and Edmonston (2005); Rockquemore and Arend (2002).

33. Huber et al. (2008); Jaret (2002); Jonas (2006); Pulido (2007).

34. Margolis (1998); Marrow (2003); McDonnell and Lourenco (2009).

35. See Joseph (2013b) for a more detailed discussion.

36. Most Brazilians who fill out the U.S. census check off "Some Other Race" and write in "Brazilian" (Barker 2012; Margolis 1994; Martes 2007; Siqueira and Jansen 2008).

37. Argentina and Chile are considered to be two of the "whitest" Latin American countries, where the majority of the population has very fair skin and straight hair (Graham 1990; Minority Rights Group 1995).

38. See Joseph (2013b) for more.

39. Margolis (1994, 2007).

40. Economist (2009).

41. Padgett and Downie (2009).

42. Margolis (2007, p. 218). "Race" is used as a nationality here, as in the Brazilian people.

43. Margolis (2007).

44. Margolis (2007, p. 217).

45. Joseph (2013b); Marrow (2003); Martes (2007); McDonnell and Lourenco (2009).

46. I asked, "Which classification do you consider most important?" There were five possible responses: (1) being Brazilian; (2) social class; (3) race/color; (4) nothing; and (5) other. None said race/color was most important.

47. For more on how Latino immigration is changing ethno-racial demographics and relations in the South, see Jones (2011); Lippard and Gallagher (2011); López-Sanders (2011); Marrow (2011); McClain et al. (2011); and McDermott (2011).

48. Thirty-two reported that their racial classification was not important. After asking each participant how he/she racially self-classified using Brazilian and U.S. census-derived categories, I asked: "How important is this classification for you?" There were four responses: (1) very important, (2) important, (3) not important, and (4) not important at all.

CHAPTER 3

1. Amaral (2006, 2013); Bailey (2009); Schwartzman (2007); Telles (2004).

2. Twelve migrants reported observing tense race relations without identifying specific ethno-racial groups.

3. I thought Luana would be considered white in Brazil, but not in the United States.

4. Bobo (2001, 2011); Bonilla-Silva (2003); Schuman et al. (1997).

5. Bobo (2011); Bonilla-Silva (2003); Feagin (2000); Parks and Hughey (2011); Wise (2013).

6. Fryer (2007); Fu (2008); Qian and Lichter (2007); Wang and Kao (2007).

7. Petrucelli (2001); Schwartzman (2007); Silva and Reis (2012); Telles (2004).

8. Petrucelli (2001); Schwartzman (2007); Silva and Reis (2012); Telles (2004).

9. Osuji (2013); Petrucelli (2001); Ribeiro et al. (2009); Silva (2012); Telles (2004).

10. Schwartzman (2007); Telles (2004).

11. Batson et al. (2006); Fryer (2007); Fu (2008); Lee and Edmonston (2005); Qian and Lichter (2007); Wang and Kao (2007).

12. Charles (2005); Emerson et al. (2001); Harris (1999); Iceland and Scopilliti (2008); Krysan (2002); Massey and Denton (1993).

13. The pre-migration socioeconomic status and ethno-racial background of immigrants influences their incorporation in the United States (Alba and Nee 2003; Nee and Sanders 2001; Portes and Rumbaut 1996; Portes and Zhou 1993). Because of racial stratification in Brazil, higher-SES migrants who have professional occupations or study in U.S. institutions of higher education are likely to classify and be perceived as white in Brazil, and maybe in the United States as well. Their SES would probably ease their social incorporation and minimize their residential segregation from white Americans. Consequently, their experiences would likely be very different from the return migrants I interviewed in GV.

14. I devote more attention to migrants' perceptions of black Americans later in this chapter.

15. Amaral (2013); Morais et al. (2003); Telles (2004).

16. Amaral (2013); Morais et al. (2003); Telles (2004).

17. Some of these empregadas lived in a separate room in their employers' homes, while others lived in poor (and mostly black) neighborhoods on the city's outskirts.

18. See the following for more on U.S. residential segregation: Charles (2003); Emerson et al. (2001); Feagin (2000); Harris (1999); Massey and Denton (1993).

19. Charles (2005); Emerson et al. (2001); Harris (1999); Krysan (2002); Massey and Denton (1993).

20. Bailey (2009); Guimarães (2001); Santos and Silva (2005); Telles (2004).

21. Ackerman and Fishkin (2004); Berinsky (2004); Rutherford (2004); Ungar (2008).

22. Amanda is biracial: her mother is white, and her father is black. However, she classifies as white because of her light-brown skin and slightly curly light-brown hair.

23. Henrique is the migrant from Chapter 2 who wanted to be perceived as Latino because he was afraid of being mistaken for Middle Eastern.

24. Petrucelli (2001); Silva and Reis (2012); Telles (2004).

25. Telles (2004).

26. This view coincides with Telles's (2004) theory of negative vertical relations in Brazil as compared with those in the United States. See Chapter 5 for more on return migrants' and non-migrants' perceptions of blacks in Brazil. These stereotypes of black Brazilians are similar to widely held stereotypes of black Americans (Bobo 2001, 2011; Bobo et al. 2012; Schuman et al. 1997).

27. See Joseph (2014a) for more.

28. I found these perceptions common among migrants regardless of gender, race, and where they lived in the United States.

29. I conducted my last interviews for the project in September 2008. Obama's name was not mentioned during any interviews. Had I conducted this research a year later, after the election, I imagine more respondents would have commented on the election of Obama as an additional indicator that black Americans had more opportunities than black Brazilians.

30. Though Larissa self-classified as yellow, she would be likely be considered white in Brazil and the United States, with her light skin, hazel eyes, and shoulder-length, straight blonde hair.

31. Schwartzman (2007); Telles (2004).

32. I did not see any black or pardo bank tellers or bankers when conducting financial business in GV or other parts of Brazil. However, many of the security guards at banks were black men.

33. Caldwell (2003); Telles (2004). The issue of hair texture is also relevant in the United States and other parts of the Americas, where the good (white/straight) versus bad hair (black/curly) debate is ongoing (Caldwell 2003; Candelario 2000; Mercer 1987; Patton 2006).

34. While attributes such as appearance, attire, and occupation are also associated with higher SES in the United States, these factors are especially important in Brazil given the emphasis on social class (Paim and Pereira 2010; Segatto and Frutuoso 2006; Telles 2004).

35. Schwartzman (2007); Telles (2004). Brazilians who do not look white must usually declare their social status (e.g., education or occupation) in order to benefit from social whitening. While middle-class Americans of color may also benefit from their high social status, it does not reduce their likelihood of experiencing discrimination or lead to their being perceived as racially white.

36. Twine (1998) also found that black Brazilians in a small town in the state of Rio de Janeiro thought black Americans were more beautiful than their Brazilian counterparts.

37. Bobo (2011); Carter (2005); Massey (2007); Shapiro (2004); Williams et al. (2007).

38. Bailey (2009); Figueiredo (2010); Silva (2012); Telles (2004).

39. Telles (2004).

40. Bobo (2011); Bonilla-Silva (2003); Gallagher (2003).

41. Bobo (2011); Feagin (2000); Lamont and Fleming (2005); Massey (2007); Pager and Shepherd (2008).

42. Araujo (2000); Twine (1998).

43. Dawson (1995); Schildkraut (2005); Segura and Bowler (2011); Verba et al. (1993).

44. Daniel (2006); Marx (1998); Paschel and Sawyer (2008); Sansone (2003); Telles (2004).

45. Bailey (2009); Daniel (2006); Davis (1991); Marx (1998); Telles (2004).

46. Skidmore (1993); Telles (2004).

47. Nobles (2000); Skidmore (1993); Telles (2004).

48. Jackson (2010); Model (1995); Vickerman (2007); Waters (1999).

49. Krysan (2002); Massey (2007); Rogers (2004); Vickerman (2007); Waters (1999); Williams et al. (2007).

50. Golash-Boza (2011); Jones (2011); Oboler and Dzidzienyo (2005); Paschel and Sawyer (2008); Telles and Bailey (2013); Wade (1996); Zamora (2014).

51. Flores (2009); Itzigsohn and Dore-Cabral (2000); Roth (2012).

52. Feagin (2000).

53. Rogers (2001); Roth (2012); Sakamoto et al. (2010).

54. Huber et al. (2008); Jaret (2002); Jonas (2006); Pulido (2007).

55. Huber et al. (2008); Jaret (2002); Jonas (2006); Pulido (2007).

56. See Joseph (2011b, 2013d) for more on the health implications of this discrimination.

57. Lesser (1999, p. 6).

58. Lesser (1999, 2003, 2013).

59. Bailey (2009); Silva (2012); Silva and Reis (2012); Telles (2004); Twine (1998).

CHAPTER 4

1. Most returnees returned to GV after 2000 because of documentation status concerns, because they were deported or feared deportation, in order to be reunited with family, and/ or after reaching their financial goal. See Joseph (2011a) for more on their reasons for returning. Other studies on return migration to GV and Brazil indicate similar reasons for returning home (Assis and DeCampos 2009; Marcus 2009; Margolis 2001; Reis and Sales 1999; Siqueira 2009a, 2009b). Just as the Valadarenses and Brazilians who emigrate are a selective group, so too are those who make the return migration.

2. See appendix for more on the non-migrant sample.

3. See Chapter 2 for returnees' pre-migration and U.S. racial classifications.

4. To account for the possible differences that occurred as migrants readapted to living in GV, I ran cross-tabulations to compare returnees' categorical racial self-classifications at two time periods: (1) immediately after their return and (2) at the time of the interview. There was much consistency across the racial categories between the two sets of classifications. The post-migration results come from the time of the interview. See appendix for each returnee's categorical and open-ended racial classifications before, during, and after migration.

5. Given that most migrants did not reach their financial goals in the United States, it is unlikely that returnees whitened their classifications because they had achieved a higher social class.

6. See Chapter 2 for more.

7. See Chapter 2 for more on how census categories influence racial classification and racial identity formation.

8. See appendix for non-migrants' racial classifications and other demographic information.

9. The specific categories chosen by the four returnees who classified as "Other" were: (1) white and yellow; (2) moreno; and (3) human race. The specific category for the one non-migrant who classified as "other" was negra.

10. I found similar results among the 24 returnee and non-migrant pairs.

11. See appendix for more.

12. Bernardino (2002); Daniel (2006); Dávila (2003); Freyre (1933); Hordge-Freeman (2013); Telles (2004); Xavier and Xavier (2009).

13. Nobles (2000); Telles (2004).

14. Nobles (2000, pp. 5–6).

15. See appendix for returnees' skin tone classifications at each migration stage.

16. These are retrospective classifications. Just as I asked returnees to recall their racial classifications at each migration stage, I also asked for their self-ascribed skin tone classifications.

17. See appendix.

18. See Chapter 2.

19. See Chapter 2.

20. These are also considered terms of endearment for close family members and friends (Caldwell 2007; Melo 2012; Racusen 2010). Terms such as negão and pretinha/o (negrito/a in Spanish) are used similarly in other Latin American countries, but they are sometimes considered offensive. The English equivalent of these terms would be "big black man" or "little black woman" (Lancaster 1991; Rivero 2002). These terms can have a derogatory meaning

in some contexts, such as when they are used to refer to black Latin Americans as childish, ignorant, or lazy (Andrews 2008; Cirqueira 2010; Melo 2012; Rivero 2002; Sharman 2001).

21. The racial classifications of the other 11 returnees were: black (N=4), brown (N=5), and "other" (N=2). "Other" refers to returnees who self-classified as yellow (amarela), Indigenous (Indígena), or "other" using Brazilian census categories. Since only a few returnees classified themselves in these categories, I report their numbers together in this chapter.

22. DeCasanova (2004); Hunter (2002); Landale and Oropesa (2002); Rezende and Lima (2004); Rockquemore (2002); Telles (2002, 2004).

23. DeCasanova (2004); Hunter (2002); Landale and Oropesa (2002); Rezende and Lima (2004); Rockquemore (2002); Telles (2002).

24. In two trips to GV after conducting the research in 2009 and 2011, Valadarenses who remembered me commented on how "white" I had become since conducting my fieldwork there in 2007. They recognized that my skin tone had lightened after I returned to the less sunny United States.

25. See Chapter 2 for returnees' self- and perceived external racial classification in the United States.

26. Cornell (1996); Cornell and Hartmann (1997); Jenkins (1996); O'Donoghue (2004); Perry (2002); Phinney and Onwughalu (1996); Quintana (2007); Stevenson (1995).

27. Bonilla-Silva (1997); Feagin (2000); Omi and Winant (1994).

CHAPTER 5

1. Bailey (2004); Daniel (2006); Degler (1971); Dulitzky (2005); Guimarães (2005); Reis (1996); Sheriff (2001); Telles (2004); Telles and Bailey (2013); Twine (1998).

2. See Joseph (2013c) for a more detailed discussion. Freyre's perception of Brazilian race relations in comparison with those in the United States in the 1930s represents the achieved view. However, more contemporary works argue that Brazil is not the racial democracy that Freyre conceived. Most studies find that Brazil's racial climate is still oppressive or aspirational. More recent studies that are consistent with the oppressive view argue that Freyre's explicit emphasis on racial mixing has overshadowed extensive anti-black racial prejudice and facilitated an oppressive denial of racial inequality in Brazil; see Munanga (2004); Telles (2004); and Twine (1998). On the other hand, studies that align with the aspirational view, posit that Brazil is not yet an authentic racial democracy, but that it aspires to be; see Bailey (2009); Reis (1996); and Sheriff (2001). These scholars suggest that Brazilians' belief in racial democracy should not be construed as a denial of racial discrimination, but as a national ideal of social inclusion for which Brazilians strive. They compare Brazilians' belief in racial democracy to that of Americans who believe in the tenets of the U.S. Constitution (liberty, freedom, equal rights for all) yet recognize that those democratic ideals have not been fully achieved.

3. Carvalho et al. (2004); Guimarães (2006); Silva and Reis (2012); Telles (2004).

4. Bailey (2009); Guimarães (2006); Telles (2004); Twine (1998).

5. Amorim (2010); Htun (2005).

6. Amorim (2010); Htun (2005).

7. Twine (1998).

8. Daniel (2006); Dulitzky (2005); Skidmore (1990, 1993); Telles (2004). In the 1920s and 1930s, Brazilian congressional bills and constitutional amendments sought to prohibit and limit the immigration of Asians and "any colonists 'of the black race'" in order to further whiten the Brazilian population (Skidmore 1990, p. 23).

9. Osuji (2013); Petrucelli (2001); Schwartzman (2007); Telles (2004).

10. Guimarães (2003); Reiter and Mitchell (2010); Sheriff (2001); Telles (2004); Twine (1998).

11. See Chapter 3.

12. Schwartzman (2007); Telles (2004).

13. This was the case for 44 of 49 returnees and all 24 non-migrants.

14. This is a direct translation from Portuguese, and Nicolas's use of the word "meninas" or "girls of the black race" should not be interpreted as similar to the racist use of "boy" as a denigration of black manhood or personhood in the United States during the pre–Civil Rights Movement era. It is common in Brazilian Portuguese to use meninas to refer generally to women, even though the literal translation in English is "girls."

15. Silva (2012); Telles (2004); Twine (1998).

16. An example of an unconscious behavior associated with racism is clutching one's purse or being afraid when passing a black person in the street.

17. See Telles (2004) for more.

18. See Figueiredo (2010) and Silva (2012) for more on the black middle class in Brazil.

19. Bento (2000); Damasceno (2000, 2011); Paim and Pereira (2010); Telles (2004).

20. Bento (2000); Damasceno (2000, 2011).

21. Adelman and Ruggi (2008); Segatto and Frutuoso (2006).

22. See Chapter 3.

23. Bailey (2009); Telles (2004); Twine (1998).

24. Bobo (2001, 2012); Bonilla-Silva (2003); Kinder and Sears (1981); Schuman (1997).

25. Bailey (2009); Bobo (2011); Bonilla-Silva (2003).

26. Bailey (2009); Silva (2012); Silva and Reis (2012); Telles and Bailey (2013).

27. Silva (2012, p. 513).

28. Figueiredo (2010); Twine (1998).

29. Erika is the returnee who accused black Americans of being self-segregating and racist while not perceiving the same behavior as racist among Brazilians (Chapter 3).

30. I have left "negro" in Portuguese from the interview transcript, even though it is also an English word. This term in Portuguese is a politically loaded racial category that refers to blacks in Brazil and is different from "preto," which is a color category on the Brazilian census. However, in certain contexts like this one, the word can be interpreted as an insult like the offensive "n-word" in the United States.

31. Bailey (2009); Silva (2012); Telles (2004).

32. Sofia does not classify herself racially, but feels that others classify her as white in Brazil.

33. Aranda (2007); Roth (2012).

34. Luiz is the black returnee whose white ex-girlfriend's father did not want them to date in Brazil because Luiz is black.

35. See returnee Carolina's account in Chapter 1.

36. Roth (2012).

37. Amaral (2002); Araujo (2000); Dávila (2001); Lozano (2007); Tufte (2000).

38. Amaral (2002); Araujo (2000); Dávila (2001); Lozano (2007); Tufte (2000).

39. Martes and Fleischer (2003); Siqueira (2009b); Levitt (2007).

CHAPTER 6

1. See Chapters 4 and 5 for more. In this chapter, pardo refers to returnees who did not self-classify as white or black, but instead as racially mixed using terms such as moreno and mulatto.

2. Omi and Winant (1994).

3. Gurin and Markus (1988); Sellers et al. (1998); Stryker and Serpe (1994); Turner et al. (1994).

4. Sellers et al. (1998, p. 24).

5. Sellers et al. (1998, p. 25).

6. Banaji and Prentice (1994); Cross (1991); Phinney (1992); Sellers et al. (1998).

7. See Chapter 2.

8. See Chapter 3.

9. See specific quotes on this from returnees Erika and Antonio in Chapters 4 and 5.

10. See Chapters 3 and 5 for more.

11. Even when dressed casually in the United States, I have been able to receive good customer service when shopping or eating in a restaurant.

12. Temporarily changing my hair texture made me look more pardo rather than black because of my skin tone.

13. See Chapter 5.

14. Research suggests, however, that social class is tied to race, even though Brazilians see social class as more important than race for determining social outcomes. See Chapter 1 for more.

15. See Chapters 2 and 4.

16. See Chapter 3.

17. See Chapter 4 for the remark that Stephane's sister made about liking Stephane better as white than black.

18. For more on Brazilians' dating and marital partner preferences, see Osuji (2013); Petrucelli (2001); Telles (2004); and Twine (1998).

19. This beautician, who had very dark skin and long, straight, black hair extensions, would have been considered black in the United States and in Brazil.

20. See Chapters 3 and 5.

21. Boston and Nair-Reichert (2003). Quotas have also been implemented for women and handicapped individuals in other sectors of the Brazilian government (Htun 2004).

22. Bailey and Pereira (2010).

23. Bailey and Pereira (2010); Boston and Nair-Reichert (2003); Telles (2004); Xavier and Xavier (2009).

24. Bailey and Pereira (2010); Xavier and Xavier (2009).

25. Bailey and Pereira (2010).

26. Bailey and Pereira (2010); Kamel (2006).

27. Bailey and Pereira (2010); Kamel (2006).

28. Four non-migrants directly referenced racial quotas in Brazil and were not supportive of the policy.

29. See Chapter 3.

30. See Chapter 5.

31. The U.S. federal government instituted the first affirmative action policies in 1964 to desegregate public schools, attack racial employment discrimination, and undertake "affirmative" recruitment of racial minorities and women in jobs (Boston and Nair-Reichert 2003; Bowen and Bok 2000). In 1969, President Richard Nixon issued Executive Order 11458 to increase the number of federal contracts awarded to minority businesses (Boston and Nair-Reichert 2003; Bowen and Bok 2000). By the early 1980s, such policies extended to local governmental agencies. Both programs were successful, and institutions of higher learning implemented similar policies to increase the number of minority and women students (Boston and Nair-Reichert 2003; Bowen and Bok 2000). U.S. colleges and universities

had the autonomy to determine how to implement affirmative action, either by reserving a set number of spaces for minority applicants or considering race in admissions decisions to increase campus diversity. Since the 1980s, the constitutionality of affirmative action in higher education has been contested repeatedly, and many cases have reached the Supreme Court (Boston and Nair-Reichert 2003; Bowen and Bok 2000). The most recent case was Schuette v. the Coalition to Defend Affirmative Action in April 2014, in which the court upheld a Michigan constitutional amendment that prohibits the use of affirmative action for admission to the state's public universities. In response to the controversy surrounding affirmative action in the United States, most of the policies have been discontinued to make race less of a factor in hiring and admission policies.

32. These were Venus and Serena Williams (tennis players), Ben Carson (surgeon), Lewis Hamilton (British race car driver), Usain Bolt (Jamaican sprinter), and Michael Steele (former chairman of the Republican National Committee).

33. Non-migrants did not personally say that black Americans were more attractive than black Brazilians, although a few did mention hearing about black Americans' social mobility from returnees.

34. Quilombos are historically black rural communities that were founded by runaway slaves and were relevant sources of slavery resistance. The descendants of these slaves still inhabit these isolated lands and have conserved African culture, religion, and languages. For more see Almeida (1998) and Telles (2004).

35. Bailey (2009); Bernadino (2002); Bernardino and Galdino (2004); Boston and Nair-Reichert (2003); Fry and Maggie (2004); Htun (2004, 2005).

36. See Chapter 5.

37. Returnees lived in the United States before the 2008 recession when there was less gridlock between Democrats and Republicans.

38. Omi and Winant (1994, p. 55).

39. Omi and Winant (1994, p. 55).

CONCLUSION

1. Aranda (2007); Flores (2009); Grasmuck and Pessar (1991); Levitt (2001a, 2007); Pedraza (1991).

2. Assis and DeCampos (2009); Conway and Potter (2006); Flores (2009); Iredale et al. (2003); Margolis (2001); Phillips and Potter (2005); Plaza and Henry (2006); Potter et al. (2005); Siqueira (2009b); Tsuda (2009a).

3. See Joseph (2011a) for more on the reasons for migrating.

4. See Joseph (2011a, b) for more on these changes.

5. Kim (2008, p. 248).

6. Buga and Meyer (2012); Downie (2011); García et al. (2013); Goodman (2012); Mc-Murtrie (2012); Shannon (2012).

7. Daniel (2006).

8. Bailey (2009, p. 8).

9. Roth (2012, p. 189).

10. Krogstad and Cohn (2014); López (2013); Ríos et al. (2014). The Census Bureau is considering combining race and ethnicity in the 2020 Census. The question would read as follows: "What is Person 1's race or origin?" under which there would be seven categories— White; Black, African American, or Negro; Hispanic, Latino, or Spanish origin; American Indian or Alaska Native; Asian; Native Hawaiian or Other Pacific Islander; and some other race or origin. Respondents would be able to write in specific ethnicities under each "race."

11. As in Latin America, the percentage of Asian-descended and Indigenous persons in the United States is currently much smaller than the share of whites, browns, and blacks. However, the projected growth of the Asian population will likely yield additional shifts in future U.S. race relations.

12. Bobo (2011); Bobo et al. (2012); Boston and Nair-Reichert (2003).

13. Bobo et al. (2012); Bonilla-Silva (2003); Hunt (2007); Hutchings (2009); Schuman et al. (1997).

14. See Chapter 5 and Joseph (2013c).

15. Kamel (2006); Telles (2004).

16. Kamel (2006); Telles (2004).

17. Bailey and Telles (2006); Guimarães (2006); Loveman et al. (2012); Telles (2004).

18. Bailey (2009); Daniel (2000, 2006); Kamel (2006); Skidmore (2003); Xavier and Xavier (2009).

19. Goodman (2012).

20. Adoema Idoeta (2011); Downie (2011, 2012); Romero (2011); Whitefield (2012).

21. Duany (2002); Itzigsohn (2009); Kim (2008); Roth (2012); Zamora (2014).

22. Roth (2012, p.182).

APPENDIX

1. For more on the DAS, see Clemens et al. (2002).

2. Margolis (1994, 1998); Martes (2000); Siqueira (2009b).

3. See Joseph (2014b) for more.

4. Bailey (2009); Bastos et al. (2009); Loveman et al. (2012); Maio et al. (2002); Schwartzman (2007); Telles (2004).

5. During the interviews I did not provide specific categories when I initially asked for respondents' self-ascribed open-ended racial classifications, and it was in fact the first question on racial classification.

6. The following studies used the word raça when asking participants for their racial classifications: Bailey (2009); Nobles (2000); Nogueira (1985); Oliveira et al. (1985); Silva (1996); Telles (2004).

7. Glaser and Strauss (1967).

8. Emerson et al. (1995).

REFERENCES

Ackerman, Bruce, and James S. Fishkin. 2004. *Deliberation Day*. New Haven, Conn.: Yale University Press.

Adelman, Miriam, and Lennita Ruggi. 2008. "The Beautiful and the Abject: Gender, Identity and Constructions of the Body in Contemporary Brazilian Culture." *Current Sociology* 56(4): 555–86.

Adoema Idoeta, Paula. 2011. "Americans Eye Opportunities in Brazil's Booming Economy." *BBC Brasil*, March 11. http://www.bbc.co.uk/news/world-latin-america-12745667.

Alarcón, Rafael, Rodolfo Cruz, Alejandro Díaz-Bautista, Gabriel González-Konig, Antonio Izquierdo, Guillermo Yrizar, and René Zenteno. 2009. "La Crisis Financiera en Estados Unidos y su Impacto en la Migración Mexicana." *Migraciones Internacionales* 5(1): 193–210.

Alba, Richard, and Victor Nee. 2003. *Remaking the American Mainstream: Assimilation and Contemporary Immigration*. Cambridge, Mass.: Harvard University Press.

Alba, Richard, Rúben Rumbaut, and Karen Marotz. 2005. "A Distorted Nation: Perceptions of Racial/Ethnic Group Sizes and Attitudes Toward Immigrants and Other Minorities." *Social Forces* 84(2): 901–19.

Alegría, Margarita, William Sribney, Megan Woo, Maria Torres, and Peter Guarnaccia. 2007. "Looking beyond Nativity: The Relation of Age of Immigration, Length of Residence, and Birth Cohorts to the Risk of Onset of Psychiatric Disorders for Latinos." *Research in Human Development* 4(1&2): 19–47.

Almeida, Alfredo Wagner Berno de. 1998. "Quilombos: Tema e Problema." In *January dos Pretos: Terra de Mocambeiros*. São Luis, Brazil: Sociedade Maranhense de Direitos Humanos.

Amaral, Ernesto Friedrich. 2006. "Race Segregation in Brazil: A GIS Approach." Paper
    presented at the annual meeting of the Population Association of America, Los Ange-
    les, Calif., March 29–April 1.
————. 2013. "Racial and Socioeconomic Segregation: An Analysis of Three Brazilian
    Metropolitan Areas." *Revista Redes* 18(1): 248–62.
Amaral, Ernesto Friedrich, and Wilson Fusco. 2005. "Shaping Brazil: The Role of Inter-
    national Migration." Washington, D.C.: Migration Policy Institute (June).
Amaral, Roberto. 2002. "Mass Media in Brazil: Modernization to Prevent Change." In
    Latin Politics, Global Media, edited by E. Fox and S. Waisbord, pp. 38–45. Austin:
    University of Texas Press.
Amorim, Laura Maia. 2010. "Dilemas na Tradução de Muse & Drudge ("Musa e Mula"),
    De Harryette Mullen: Negritude, Dissonância e Miscigenação." *Terceira Margem*
    23(Julho/Dezembro): 139–51.
Andrews, George Reid. 2008. "Disapora Crossings: Afro-Latin America in the Afro-At-
    lantic." *Latin American Research Review* 43(3): 209–24.
Aranda, Elizabeth. 2007. *Emotional Bridges to Puerto Rico: Migration, Return Migration,
    and the Struggles of Incorporation.* Lanham, Md.: Rowman and Littlefield.
————. 2009. "Puerto Rican Migration and Settlement in South Florida: Ethnic Iden-
    tities and Transnational Spaces." In *Caribbean Migration to Western Europe and the
    United States: Essays on Incorporation, Identity, and Citizenship*, edited by A. M. Cer-
    vantes-Rodríguez, R. Grosfoguel, and E. Mielants, pp.111–30. Philadelphia: Temple
    University Press.
Araujo, Clara. 2001. "Potencialidades e Limités da Políticas de Cotas no Brasil." *Estudos
    Feministas* 9(1): 231–52.
Araujo, Joel Zito. 2000. *A Negação do Brasil: O Negro na Telenovela Brasileira.* São Paulo:
    Editora SENAC.
Assis, Gláucia de Oliveira. 1995. "Estar Aqui, Estar Lá . . . Uma Cartografia da Vida Entre
    Dois Lugares." PhD diss., Departmento de Sociologia, Universidade Federal de Santa
    Catarina, Florianópolis, Santa Catarina, Brazil.
Assis, Gláucia de Oliveira, and Emerson César DeCampos. 2009. "De Volta Para Casa:
    A Reconstrução de Identidades de Emigrantes Retornados." *Tempo e Argumento* 1(2):
    80–99.
Assis, Gláucia de Oliveira, and Sueli Siqueira. 2009. "Mulheres Emigrantes e a Configu-
    ração de Redes Sociais: Construindo Conexões Entre o Brasil e os Estados Unidos."
    Revista Interdisciplinar da Mobilidade Humana 17(32): 25–46.
Bailey, Stanley R. 2004. "Group Dominance and the Myth of Racial Democracy: Antira-
    cism Attitudes in Brazil." *American Sociological Review* 69(5): 728–47.
————. 2008. "Unmixing for Race Making in Brazil." *American Journal of Sociology*
    114(3): 577–614.
————. 2009. *Legacies of Race: Identities, Attitudes, and Politics in Brazil.* Palo Alto, Calif.:
    Stanford University.
Bailey, Stanley R., and Edward E. Telles. 2006. "Multiracial versus Collective Black Cat-
    egories: Examining Census Classification Debates in Brazil." *Ethnicities* 6(1): 74–101.
Bailey, Stanley R., and Michelle Pereira. 2010. "Racial Quotas and the Culture War in
    Brazilian Academia." *Sociology Compass* 4(8): 592–604.
Banaji, M. R., and D. A. Prentice. 1994. "The Self in Social Contexts." *Annual Review of
    Psychology* 45: 297–332.
Barker, Alexandra. 2012. "United States Census Bureau: Your Community by the Num-

bers." Paper presented at Brazil Week—Healthcare and Portuguese-Speaking Immigrants in the United States: The Case of Massachusetts. Harvard University, Cambridge, Mass., April 20.

Barth, Frederick. 1969. *Ethnic Groups and Boundaries: The Social Organization of Culture Difference.* Boston: Little, Brown.

Bastos, João, Samuel Dumith, Ricardo Santos, Alúsio Barros, Giovani Duca, and Ana Nunes. 2009. "Does the Way I See You Affect the Way I See Myself? Associations between Interviewers' and Interviewees' "Color/Race" in Southern Brazil." *Caderno Saúde Pública* 25(10): 2111–24.

Batson, Christie D., Zhenchao Qian, and Daniel T. Lichter. 2006. "Interracial and Intraracial Patterns of Mate Selection among America's Diverse Black Populations." *Journal of Marriage and Family* 68(August): 658–72.

Bento, M. 2000. "A Raça e Gênero no Mercado de Trabalho." In *Trabalho e Gênero: Mudanças, Permanências e Desafios*, edited by M. I. B. da Rocha, pp. 295–307. São Paulo: Editora 34.

Berinsky, Adam. 2004. *Silent Voices: Public Opinion and Political Participation in America.* Princeton. N.J.: Princeton University Press.

Bernardino, Joaze. 2002. "Acão Afirmativa e a Rediscussão do Mito da Democracia Racial no Brasil." *Estudos Afro-Asiáticos* 24(2): 247–73.

Bernardino, Joaze, and Daniela Galdino. 2004. *Levando a Raça a Sério: Ação Afirmativa e Universidade.* Rio de Janeiro: DP&A Editora.

Bernard, H. Russell, Peter Killworth, David Kronenfeld, and Lee Sailer. 1984. "The Problem of Informant Accuracy: The Validity of Retrospective Data." *Annual Review of Anthropology* 13: 495–517.

Bianchi, Fernanda, Maria Cecilia Zea, and John J. Echeverry. 2002. "Racial Identity and Self-Esteem Among Black Brazilian Men: Race Matters in Brazil Too!" *Cultural Diversity and Ethnic Minority Psychology* 8(2): 157–69.

Bobo, Lawrence D. 2001. "Racial Attitudes and Relations at the Close of the Twentieth Century." In *America Becoming: Racial Trends and Their Consequences*, vol. 1, edited by N. J. Smesler, W. J. Wilson, and F. Mitchell, pp. 264–301. Washington, D.C.: National Academies Press.

———. 2011. "Somewhere between Jim Crow and Post-Racialism: Reflections on the Racial Divide in America Today." *Daedalus* 140(2): 11–36.

Bobo, Lawrence D., Camille Z. Charles, Maria Krysan, and Alicia D. Simmons. 2012. "The Real Record on Racial Attitudes." In *Social Trends in American Life: Findings from the General Social Survey since 1972*, edited by P. V. Marsden, pp. 38–82. Princeton, N.J.: Princeton University Press.

Bonilla-Silva, Eduardo. 1997. "Rethinking Racism." *American Sociological Review* 62(3): 465–80.

———. 2003. *Racism without Racists: Color-Blind Racism and the Persistence of Racial Inequality in the United States.* Lanham, Md.: Rowman and Littlefield.

———. 2004. "From Bi-Racial to Tri-Racial: Towards a New System of Racial Classification in the USA." *Ethnic and Racial Studies* 27(6): 931–50.

Boston, Thomas, and Usha Nair-Reichert. 2003. "Affirmative Action: Perspectives from the United States, India and Brazil." *Western Journal of Black Studies* 27(1): 3–14.

Brooke, James. 1990. "Town That Uncle Sam Built, You Might Say." *New York Times*, November 30.

Bowen, William G., and Derek Bok. 2000. *The Shape of the River: Long-Term Conse-*

quences of Considering Race in College and University Admissions. Princeton, N.J.: Princeton University Press.

Brubaker, Rogers, Mara Loveman, and Peter Stamatov. 2004. "Ethnicity as Cognition." *Theory and Society* 33: 31–64.

Buga, Natalia, and Jean-Baptiste Meyer. 2012. "Indian Human Resources Mobility: Brain Drain versus Brain Gain." San Domenico de Fiesole, Italy: European University Institute, Robert Schuman Centre for Advanced Studies. http://cadmus.eui.eu/bitstream/handle/1814/23482/CARIM-India-RR-2012-04.pdf?sequence=1.

Burgard, Sarah. 2004. "Race and Pregnancy-Related Care in Brazil and South Africa." *Social Science & Medicine* 59(6): 1127–46.

Caldwell, Kia Lilly. 2003. " 'Look at Her Hair': The Body Politics of Black Womanhood in Brazil." *Transforming Anthropology* 11(2): 18–29.

———. 2007. *Negras in Brazil: Re-Envisioning Black Women, Citizenship, and the Politics of Identity.* New Brunswick, N.J.: Rutgers University Press.

Candelario, Ginetta. 2000. "Hair Race-ing: Dominican Beauty Culture and Identity Production." *Meridians* 1(1): 128–56.

Carling, Jorgen. 2008. "The Human Dynamics of Migrant Transnationalism." *Ethnic and Racial Studies* 31(8): 1452–77.

Carter, Prudence. 2005. *Keepin' It Real: School Success beyond Black and White.* Oxford, U.K.: Oxford University Press.

Carvalho, José Alberto Magno de, Charles H. Wood, and Flavia Andrade. 2004. "Estimating the Stability of Census-Based Racial/Ethnic Classifications: The Case of Brazil." *Population Studies* 58(3): 331–43.

Carvalho, Marília. 2005. "Quem é Negro, Quem é Branco: Desempenho Escolar e Classificação Racial de Alunos." *Revista Brasileira de Educação* 28: 77–95.

Centro de Informação, Apoio e Amparo à Família e ao Trabalhador no Exterior (CIAAT). 2007. "Um Estudo sobre a Imigração em Governador Valadares." Governador Valadares, Brazil.

Cerulo, Karen A. 2002. "Establishing Sociology of Culture and Cognition." In *Culture in Mind: Toward a Sociology of Culture and Cognition,* edited by K. Cerulo, pp. 1–12. New York: Routledge.

Charles, Camille Zubrinsky. 2003. "The Dynamics of Racial Residential Segregation." *Annual Review of Sociology* 29: 167–207.

———. 2005. "Can We Live Together? Racial Preferences and Neighborhood Outcomes." In *The Geography of Opportunity: Race and Housing Choice in Metropolitan America,* edited by X. Briggs, pp. 45–79. Washington, D.C.: Brookings Institution Press.

Cirqueira, Diogo Marçal. 2010. "A Mística do Racismo: Narrativas de Estudantes Negras/os Universitários sobre Racismo na Educação Formal." *Itinerarius Reflectionis* 2(9): 1–22.

Clemens, Judi, Mick P. Cooper, and Kathy Powers, eds. 2002. *The Detroit Area Study 1952–2001: Celebrating 50 Years.* Ann Arbor: University of Michigan Press.

Cohn, D'Vera, Ana Gonzalez-Barrera, and Danielle Cuddington. 2013. "Remittances to Latin America Recover—but Not to Mexico." *Pew Research Hispanic Trends Project.* Washington, D.C.: Pew Research Center (November 15).

Consejo Nacional Población (CONAPO). 2009. "Encuesta sobre Migración en la Frontera Norte de México (EMIF)." Secretaría de Gobernación, Estados Unidos Mexicanos. http://www.conapo.gob.mx/en/CONAPO/Encuesta_sobre_Migracion_en_la_Frontera_Norte_de_Mexico_2009.

Conway, Dennis, and Robert B. Potter. 2006. "Caribbean Transnational Return Migrants as Agents of Change." *Geography Compass* 1: 1–21.

Cornell, Stephen. 1988. *The Return of the Native: American Indian Political Resurgence.* New York: Oxford University Press.

———. 1996. "The Variable Ties That Bind: Content and Circumstance in Ethnic Processes." *Ethnic and Racial Studies* 19(2): 265–89.

Cornell, Stephen, and D. Hartmann. 1997. *Ethnicity and Race:Making Identities in a Changing World.* Thousand Oaks, Calif.: Pine Fore.

Cross, William. 1991. *Shades of Black: Diversity in African American Identity.* Philadelphia: Temple University Press.

Damasceno, Maria Caetana. 2000. "'Em Casa de Enforcado Não Se Fala em Corda': Notas Sobre a Construção Social da 'Boa Aparência' no Brasil." In *Tirando a Máscara. Ensaio Sobre o Racismo no Brasil,* edited by A. Guimarães and L. Huntley, pp. 165–99. São Paulo: Paz e Terra.

———. 2011. *Segredos da Boa Aparência: Da "Cor" à Boa Aparência No Mundo do Trabalho Carioca (1930–1950).* Rio de Janeiro: EDUR, UFFRJ.

D'Andrade, Roy. 1995. *The Development of Cognition Anthropology.* New York: Cambridge University Press.

Daniel, G. Reginald. 1992. "Beyond Black and White: The New Multiracial Consciousness." In *Racially Mixed People in America,* edited by M. P. P. Root. Thousand Oaks, Calif.: Sage Publications.

———. 2000. "Multiracial Identity in Brazil and the United States." In *We Are a People: Narrative and Multiplicity in Constructing Ethnic Identity,* edited by J. Burroughs and P. R. Spickard, pp. 153–77. Philadelphia: Temple University Press.

———. 2006. *Race and Multiraciality in Brazil and the United States: Converging Paths?* University Park: Pennsylvania State University Press.

Dávila, Arlene M. 2001. *Latinos, Inc: The Marketing and Making of a People.* Berkeley: University of California Press.

Dávila, Jerry. 2003. *Diploma of Whiteness: Race and Social Policy in Brazil, 1917–1945.* Durham, N.C.: Duke University Press.

Davis, James. 1991. *Who Is Black? One Nation's Definition.* University Park: Pennsylvania State University Press.

Dawson, Michael. 1995. *Behind the Mule: Race and Class in African-American Politics.* Princeton, N.J.: Princeton University Press.

DeGenova, Nicholas, and Ana Y. Ramos-Zayas. 2003. "Latino Racial Formations in the United States: An Introduction." *Journal of Latin American Anthropology* 8(2): 2–17.

DeBiaggi, Sylvia Duarte Dantas. 2002. *Changing Gender Roles: Brazilian Immigrant Families in the United States.* El Paso: LFB Publishing.

DeCasanova, Erynn Masi. 2004. "'No Ugly Women': Concepts of Race and Beauty among Adolescent Women in Ecuador." *Gender and Society* 18(3): 287–308.

Degler, Carl N. 1971. *Neither Black nor White: Slavery and Race Relations in Brazil and the United States.* Madison: University of Wisconsin Press.

DiMaggio, Paul. 1997. "Culture and Cognition." *Annual Review of Sociology* 23: 263–87.

Downie, Andrew. 2011. "How Brazil Is Sending 75,000 Students to the World's Best Colleges." *Time World* (São Paulo), September 21.

———. 2012. "Why Is Your Boss Moving to Brazil?" *Time World* (São Paulo), February 2.

Duany, Jorge. 2002. *The Puerto Rican Nation on the Move: Identities on the Island and in the United States.* Chapel Hill: University of North Carolina Press.

Du Bois, W. E. B. 1903. *Souls of Black Folk.* Chicago: A. C. McClurg.
———. 1996 [1899]. *The Philadelphia Negro: A Social Study.* Philadelphia: University of Pennsylvania.
Dulitzky, Ariel. 2005. "A Region in Denial: Racial Discrimination and Racism in Latin America." In *Neither Enemies nor Friends: Latinos, Blacks, Afro-Latinos,* edited by A. Dzidzienyo and S. Oboler, pp. 39–59. New York: Palgrave.
Dzidzienyo, Anani. 2005. "The Changing World of Brazilian Race Relations?" In *Neither Enemies nor Friends: Latinos, Blacks, Afro-Latinos,* edited by A. Dzidzienyo and S. Oboler, pp. 137–55. New York: Palgrave.
The Economist. 2009. "Brazil Takes Off: Now the Risk for Latin America's Success Story Is Hubris." November 12.
Emerson, Michael O., Karen J. Chai, and George Yancey. 2001. "Does Race Matter in Residential Segregation? Exploring the Preferences of White Americans." *American Sociological Review* 66(6): 922–35.
Emerson, Robert, Rachel Fretz, and Linda Shaw. 1995. *Writing Ethnographic Fieldnotes.* Chicago: University of Chicago Press.
Erikson, Erik H. 1959. *Identity and the Life Cycle.* New York: International Universities Press.
Espiritu, Yen Le. 1992. *Asian American Panethnicity: Bridging Institutions and Identities.* Philadelphia: Temple University Press.
———. 2009. ""They're Coming to America": Immigration, Settlement, and Citizenship." *Qualitative Sociology* 32: 221–27.
Feagin, Joe. 2000. *Racist America: Roots, Current Realities, and Future Reparations.* New York: Routledge.
Fernandes, Florestan. 1965. *A Integração do Negro na Sociedade de Classes.* São Paulo: Dominus Editora.
Figueiredo, Angela. 2010. "Out of Place: The Experience of the Black Middle Class." In *Brazil's New Racial Politics,* edited by B. Reiter and G. Mitchell, pp. 51–63. Boulder, Colo.: Lynne Rienner.
Flores, Juan. 2009. *The Diaspora Strikes Back: Caribeño Tales of Learning and Turning.* New York: Routledge.
Foner, Nancy. 1997. "What's New about Transnationalism? New York Immigrants Today and at the Turn of the Century." *Diaspora* 6(3): 355–75.
Forman, Tyrone A., Carla Goar, and Amanda Lewis. 2002. "Neither Black nor White? An Empirical Test of the Latin Americanization Thesis." *Race and Society* 5: 65–84.
Fox, Jonathan. 2005. "Unpacking 'Transnational Citizenship'." *Annual Review of Political Science* 8: 171–201.
Frank, Reanne, Ilana Redstone Akresh, and Bo Lua. 2010. "Latino Immigrants and the United States Racial Order: How and Where Do They Fit In?" *American Sociological Review* 75(3): 378–401.
Freyre, Gilberto. 1933. *Casa Grande e Senzala.* Rio de Janeiro: Editora Record.
———. 1951. *Brazil: An Interpretation.* New York: Knopf.
Fry, Peter, and Yvonne Maggie. 2004. "Cotas Raçiais: Construindo um País Divido?" *Econômica* 6(1): 153–61.
Fryer, Roland G. Jr. 2007. "Guess Who's Been Coming to Dinner? Trends in Interracial Marriage over the 20th Century." *Journal of Economic Perspectives* 21(2): 71–90.
Fu, Xuanning. 2008. "Interracial Marriage and Family Socio-economic Well-being: Equal Status Exchange or Caste Status Exchange?" *Social Science Journal* 45(1): 132–55.

Gallagher, Charles A. 2003. "Miscounting Race: Explaining Whites' Misperceptions of Racial Group Size." *Sociological Perspectives* 46(3): 381–96.

García, Ofelia, Mercè Pujol-Ferran, and Pooja Reddy. 2013. "Educating International and Immigrant Students in United States Higher Education: Opportunities and Challenges." In *English-Medium Instruction at Universities: Global Challenges*, edited by A. Doiz, D. Lasagabaster, and J. M. Sierra, pp. 174–95. Bristol, U.K.: Short Run Press.

Glaser, Barney G., and Anselm Strauss. 1967. *The Discovery of Grounded Theory: Strategies for Qualitative Research.* Edison: Aldine Transaction.

Golash-Boza, Tanya. 2011. *Yo Soy Negro: Blackness in Peru.* Gainesville: University Press of Florida.

Goodman, Allan E. 2012. "Remarks to the Brazil-United States Conference: Partnership for the 21st Century- United States-Brazil Educational Partnership: Science without Borders." Presented at Institute of International Education Brazil-United States Conference, New York, April 9.

Goza, Franklin. 1999. "Immigrant Social Networks: The Brazilian Case." http://iussp2005.princeton.edu/download.aspx?submissionId=50570.

Graham, Richard, ed. 1990. *The Idea of Race in Latin America, 1870–1940.* Austin: University of Texas.

Grasmuck, Sherri, and Patricia Pessar. 1991. *Between Two Islands: Dominican International Migration.* Berkeley: University of California Press.

Guimarães, Antonio Sérgio. 2001. "Race, Class, and Color: Behind Brazil's Racial Democracy." *NACLA Report on the Americas* 34(6): 28–29.

———. 2003. "Como Trabalhar com "Raça" em Sociologia." *Educação e Pesquisa* 29(1): 93–107.

———. 2005. "Racial Democracy." In *Imagining Brazil*, edited by J. Souza and V. Sinder, pp. 119–40. Lanham, Md.: Lexington Books.

———. 2006. "Depois da Democracia Racial." *Tempo Social* 18(2): 269–87.

Gurin, Patricia, and Hazel Markus. 1988. "Group Identity: The Psychological Mechanisms of Durable Salience." *Review Internationale de Psychologie Sociale* 1(2): 257–74.

Hall, Stuart. 1991. "The Local and the Global: Globalization and Ethnicity." In *Culture, Globalization, and the World-System: Contemporary Conditions for the Representation of Identity*, edited by A. King, pp. 19–39. Binghamton: State University of New York Press.

———. 2003. "The Whites of Their Eyes: Racist Ideologies and the Media." In *Gender, Race, and Class in the Media: A Text Reader*, edited by G. Dines and J. M. Humez, pp. 18–22. Thousand Oaks, Calif.: Sage.

Hall, Stuart, and Paul DuGay. 1996. *Questions of Cultural Identity.* Thousand Oaks, Calif.: Sage.

Haney López, Ian F. 1996. *White by Law: The Legal Construction of Race.* New York: New York University Press.

Harris, David R. 1999. "Property Values Drop When Blacks Move In, Because . . .": Racial and Socioeconomic Determinants of Neighborhood Desirability." *American Sociological Review* 64(3): 461–79.

Harris, David R., and Jeremiah Joseph Sims. 2002. "Who Is Multiracial? Assessing the Complexity of Lived Race." *American Sociological Review* 67(4): 614–27.

Harris, Marvin. 1952. "Race Relations in Minas Velhas, a Community in the Mountain Region of Central Brazil." In *Race and Class in Rural Brazil*, edited by C. Wagley, pp. 47–81. Paris: UNESCO.

Herman, Melissa. 2004. "Forced to Choose: Some Determinants of Racial Identification in Multiracial Adolescents." *Child Development* 75(3): 730–48.

———. 2011. "Methodology and Measurement in the Study of Multiracial Americans: Identity, Classification, and Perceptions." *Sociology Compass* 5(7): 607–17.

Hirschman, Charles, Richard Alba, and Reynolds Farley. 2000. "The Meaning and Measurement of Race in the United States Census: Glimpses into the Future." *Demography* 37(3): 381–93.

Hollinger, David. 2000. *Postethnic America.* New York: Basic.

Hordge-Freeman, Elizabeth. 2013. "What's Love Got to Do with It?: Racial Features, Stigma, and Socialization in Afro-Brazilan Families." *Ethnic and Racial Studies* 36(10): 1507–23.

Howarth, Caroline. 2002. "Identity in Whose Eyes? The Role of Representations in Identity Construction." *Journal for the Theory of Social Behaviour* 32(2): 145–62.

Htun, Mala. 2004. "From 'Racial Democracy' to Affirmative Action: Changing State Policy on Race in Brazil." *Latin American Research Review* 39(1): 60–89.

———. 2005. "Racial Quotas for a 'Racial Democracy'." *NACLA Report on the Americas* 38(4): 20–27.

Huber, Lindsay Perez, Corina Benavides Lopez, Maria C. Malagon, Veronica Velez, and Daniel G. Solorzano. 2008. "Getting beyond the 'Symptom,' Acknowledging the 'Disease': Theorizing Racist Nativism." *Contemporary Justice Review* 11(1): 39–51.

Hughes, Diane, James Rodriguez, Emilie P. Smith, Deborah J. Johnson, Howard C. Stevenson, and Paul Spicer. 2006. "Parents' Ethnic–Racial Socialization Practices: A Review of Research and Directions for Future Study." *Developmental Psychology* 42(5): 747–70.

Humes, Karen, Nicolas Jones, and Roberto Ramirez. 2011. "Overview of Race and Hispanic Origin: 2010." 2010 United States Census Briefs # C2010–BR-02. Washington, D.C.: U. S. Census Bureau (March).

Hunt, Darnell M. 1997. *Screening the Los Angeles "Riots": Race, Seeing and Resistance.* Cambridge, U.K.: Cambridge University Press.

Hunt, Matthew O. 2007. "African-American, Hispanic, and White Beliefs about Black/White Inequality, 1977–2004." *American Sociological Review* 72(3): 390–415.

Hunter, Margaret L. 2002. ""If You're Light You're Alright": Light Skin Color as Social Capital for Women of Color." *Gender and Society* 16: 175–93.

Hutchings, Vincent L. 2009. "Change or More of the Same? Evaluating Racial Attitudes in the Obama Era." *Public Opinion Quarterly* 73(5): 917–42.

Iceland, John, and Melissa Scopilliti. 2008. "Immigrant Residential Segregation in United States Metropolitan Areas, 1990–2000." *Demography* 45(1): 79–94.

Independent Police Complaints Commission (IPCC). 2007. "Stockwell One: Investigation into the Shooting of Jean Charles de Menezes at Stockwell Underground Station on 22 July 2005." London: IPCC (November).

Instituto Brasileiro de Geografia e Estatística (IBGE) [Brazilian Institute of Geography and Statistics]. 2010. Brazilian Census. Rio de Janeiro, Brazil.

International Organization for Migration (IOM). 2006. "Brazil Profile." Geneva, Switzerland: IOM (last updated 2013).

Iredale, Robyn, Fei Guo, and Santi Rozario, eds. 2003. *Return Migration in the Asia Pacific.* Northampton, Mass.: Edward Elgar.

Itzigsohn, José. 2009. *Encountering American Faultlines: Race, Class, and the Dominican Experience in Providence.* New York: Russell Sage Foundation.

Itzigsohn, José, and Carlos Dore-Cabral. 2000. "Competing Identities? Race, Ethnicity, and Panethnicity among Dominicans in the United States." *Sociological Forum* 15(2): 225–47.

Itzigsohn, José, Silvia Gorguli, and Obed Vazquez. 2005. "Immigrant Incorporation and Racial Identity: Racial Self-Identification among Dominican Immigrants." *Ethnic and Racial Studies* 28(1): 50–78.

Itzigsohn, José, Carlos Dore-Cabral, Esther Hernandez Medina, and Obed Vazquez. 1999. "Mapping Dominican Transnationalism: Narrow and Broad Transnational Practices." *Ethnic and Racial Studies* 22(2): 316–39.

Iwata, Miho. 2012. "Embodied Stories of Foreign Migrants: Negotiating the Racial Landscape in Contemporary Japan." Paper presented at annual meeting of the Eastern Sociological Association, New York, February 25.

Jackson, Regine O. 2010. "Black Immigrants and the Rhetoric of Social Distancing." *Sociology Compass* 4(3): 193–206.

Jacoby, Tamar. 2004. *Reinventing the Melting Pot: The New Immigrants and What It Means to Be American.* New York: Basic Books.

Jaret, Charles. 2002. "Troubled by Newcomers: Anti-Immigrant Attitudes and Actions during Two Eras of Mass Migration." In *Mass Migrations to the United States: Classical and Contemporary Periods,* edited by P. G. Min, pp. 19–61. Blue Ridge Summit, Penn.: Altamira Press.

Jenkins, Richard. 1994. "Rethinking Ethnicity: Identity, Categorization and Power." *Ethnic and Racial Studies* 17(2): 197–223.

———. 1996. *Social Identity.* London: Routledge.

Jonas, Susanne. 2006. "Reflections on the Great Immigration Battle of 2006 and the Future of the Americas." *Social Justice* 33(1): 6–20.

Jones, Jennifer. 2011. "Making Race in the New South: Mexican Migration and Race Relations in Winston-Salem, North Carolina." PhD diss., Department of Sociology, University of California at Berkeley.

Joseph, Tiffany. 2011a. "Race and 'Making America' in Brazil: How Brazilian Return Migrants Negotiate Race in the United States and Brazil." PhD diss., Department of Sociology, University of Michigan at Ann Arbor.

———. 2011b. "My Life Was Filled with Constant Anxiety': Anti-Immigrant Discrimination, Undocumented Status, and their Mental Health Implications for Brazilian Immigrants." *Race and Social Problems* 3(1): 170–81.

———. 2013a. "Race, Migration, and the Transnational Racial Optic." Paper presented at annual meeting of the American Sociological Association, Denver, Colo., August 20.

———. 2013b. "Latino, Hispanic, or Brazilian: Considerations for Brazilian Immigrants' Racial Classification in the United States" In *The Discourse and Politics of Immigration in the Global North,* edited by J. Capetillo, G. Jacobs, and P. Kretsedemas, pp. 275–92. New York: Routledge.

———. 2013c. "How Does Racial Democracy Exist in Brazil? Perceptions from Brazilians in Governador Valadares, Minas Gerais." *Ethnic and Racial Studies* 36(10): 1524–43.

———. 2013d. "Falling through the 'Universal' Coverage Cracks: Latin American Immigrants' Healthcare Access in Boston." Paper presented at annual meeting of the Robert Wood Johnson Foundation Health Policy Scholars, Princeton, N.J., June 6.

———. 2014A. "United States Blacks Are Beautiful but Brazilian Blacks Are not Racist': Brazilian Return Migrants' Perceptions of United States and Brazilian Blacks." In *Re-Positioning Race: Prophetic Research in a Post-Racial Obama Age,* edited by S. Barnes, Z. Robinson, and E. Wright II, pp. 151–71. Albany: SUNY Press.

————.[2014b] "A (Black) American Trapped in a ('Non-Black') Brazilian Body: Reflections on Navigating Multiple Identities in International Fieldwork." Unpublished.

Kamel, Ali. 2006. *Não Somos Racistas: Uma Reação Aos Que Querem Nos Transformar Numa Nação Bicolor.* Rio de Janeiro: Editora Nova Fronteira S.A.

Kaufman, Florian K. 2008. "Emigrant or Sojourner? The Determinants of Mexican Labor Migration Strategies to the United States." PhD diss., Department of Economics, University of Massachusetts at Amherst.

Khanna, Nikki. 2010. ""If You're Half Black, You're Just Black": Reflected Appraisals and the Persistence of the One-Drop Rule." *Sociological Quarterly* 51(1): 96–121.

Kim, Nadia. 2008. *Imperial Citizens: Koreans and Race from Seoul to LA.* Palo Alto, Calif.: Stanford University Press.

Kinder, Donald R., and David O. Sears. 1981. "Prejudice and Politics: Symbolic Racism versus Racial Threats to the Good Life." *Journal of Personality and Social Psychology* 40(1): 414–31.

Kraul, Chris, and Nicole Gaouette. 2005. "Brazilian Illegal Immigration into United States Is Targeted by Mexico." *Los Angeles Times*, September 15.

Krogstad, Jens Manuel and D'Vera Cohn. 2014. "U.S. Census Looking at Big Changes in How It Asks about Race and Ethnicity." FactTank News in the Numbers Website. http://www.pewresearch.org/fact-tank/2014/03/14/u-s-census-looking-at-big-changes-in-how-it-asks-about-race-and-ethnicity/.

Krysan, Maria. 2002. "Community Undesirability in Black and White: Examining Racial Residential Preferences through Community Perceptions." *Social Problems* 49(4): 521–43.

Lamont, Michèle, and Crystal Fleming. 2005. "Everyday Antiracism: Competence and Religion in the Cultural Repertoire of the African-American Elite." *Du Bois Review: Social Science Research on Race* 2(1): 29–43.

Lancaster, Roger. 1991. "Skin Color, Race, and Racism in Nicaragua." *Ethnology* 30(4): 339–53.

Landale, Nancy, and R. S. Oropesa. 2002. "White, Black, or Puerto Rican? Racial Self-Identification among Mainland and Island Puerto Ricans." *Social Forces* 81(1): 231–54.

Lee, Jennifer, and Frank D. Bean. 2004. "America's Changing Color Lines: Immigration, Race/Ethnicity, and Multiracial Identification." *Annual Review of Sociology* 30: 221–42.

————. 2007. "Reinventing the Color Line: Immigration and America's New Racial/Ethnic Divide." *Social Forces* 86(2): 561–86.

————. 2010. *The Diversity Paradox: Immigration and the Color Line in Twenty-First Century America.* New York: Russell Sage Foundation.

Lee, Sharon M., and Barry Edmonston. 2005. "New Marriages, New Families: United States Racial and Hispanic Intermarriage." *Population Bulletin* 60(2): 3–36.

Lesser, Jeffrey. 1999. *Negotiating National Identity: Immigrants, Minorities, and the Struggle for Ethnicity in Brazil.* Durham, N.C.: Duke University Press.

————. 2003. *Searching for Home Abroad: Japanese Brazilians and Transnationalism.* Durham, N.C.: Duke University Press.

————. 2013. *Immigration, Ethnicity, and National Identity in Brazil.* New York: Cambridge University Press.

Levitt, Peggy. 2000. "Migrants Participate across Borders: Toward an Understanding of Forms and Consequences." In *Immigration Research for a New Century: Multidisciplinary Perspectives,* edited by N. Foner, R. G. Rumbaut, and S. J. Gold, pp.459–479. New York: Russell Sage Foundation.

———. 2001a. "Transnational Migration: Taking Stock and Future Directions." *Global Networks: A Journal of Transnational Affairs* 1(3): 195–216.

———. 2001b. *The Transnational Villagers*. Berkeley: University of California Press.

———. 2007. *God Needs No Passport: How Migrants Are Transforming the American Religious Landscape*. New York: New Press.

Levitt, Peggy, and B. Nadya Jaworsky. 2007. "Transnational Migration Studies: Past Developments and Future Trends." Annual Review of Sociology 33:129–56.

Levitt, Peggy, and Nina Glick Schiller. 2004. "Conceptualizing Simultaneity: A Transnational Social Field Perspective on Society." *The International Migration Review* 38(3): 1002–39.

Levitt, Peggy, and Mary Waters. 2002. *The Changing Face of Home: The Transnational Lives of the Second Generation*. New York: Russell Sage Foundation.

Lippard, Cameron D., and Charles A. Gallagher. 2011. *Being Brown in Dixie: Race, Ethnicity, and Latino Immigration in the New South*. Boulder, Colo: First Forum Press.

López, Nancy. 2013. "Killing Two Birds with One Stone? Why We Need Two Separate Questions on Race and Ethnicity in the 2020 Census and Beyond." *Latino Studies* 11: 428-438.

López-Sanders, Laura. 2011. "Is Brown the New Black? Immigrant Incorporation and the Dynamics of Ethnic Replacement in New Destinations." PhD diss., Department of Sociology, Stanford University, Palo Alto, California.

Loveman, Mara. 2005. "The Modern State and the Primitive Accumulation of Symbolic Power." *American Journal of Sociology* 110(6): 1651–83.

Loveman, Mara, Jeronimo O. Muniz, and Stanley R. Bailey. 2012. "Brazil in Black and White? Race Categories, the Census, and the Study of Inequality." *Ethnic and Racial Studies* 35(8): 1466–83.

Lozano, José-Carlos. 2007. "Latin America: Media Conglomerates." In *The Media Globe: Trends in International Mass Media*, edited by L. Artz and Y. R. Kamalipour, pp. 99–117. Lanham, Md.: Rowman and Littlefield.

Lucas, Robert E. B. 2005. "International Migration to the High-Income Countries: Some Consequences for Economic Development in the Sending Countries." In *Are We on Track to Achieve the Millennium Development Goals?*, edited by F. Bourguignon, B. Pleskovič, and A. Sapir, pp. 127–62. New York: World Bank and Oxford University Press.

Maio, Marcos Chor, Simone Monteiro, Dóra Chor, Eduardo Faerstein, and Claudia S. Lopes. 2002. "Cor/Raça no Estudo Pró-Saúde: Resultados Comparativos de Dois Métodos de Autoclassificação no Rio de Janeiro, Brasil." *Caderno Saúde Pública* 21(1): 171–80.

Marcia, James E. 1966. "Development and Validation of Ego-Identity Status." *Journal of Personal Social Psychology* 3(5): 551–58.

Marcus, Alan P. 2003. "Once Again: Brazilians Are Not Hispanic." *Brazzil*, October 3.

———. 2009. "Brazilian Immigration to the United States and the Geographical Imagination." *Geographical Review* 99(4): 481–98.

Margolis, Maxine. 1994. *Little Brazil: An Ethnography of Brazilian Immigrants in New York City*. Princeton, N.J.: Princeton University Press.

———. 1998. *An Invisible Minority: Brazilians in New York City*. Boston: Allyn and Bacon.

———. 2001. "With New Eyes: Returned International Immigrants in Rio de Janeiro." In *Raízes e Rumos: Perspectivas Interdisciplinares em Estudos Americanos*, edited by S. Torres, pp. 199–211. Rio de Janeiro: 7Letras.

———. 2003. "Na Virada do Milênio: A Emigração Brasileira para os Estados Unidos." In *Fronteiras Cruzadas: Etnicidade, Gênero, e Redes Sociais*, edited by A. C. B. Martes and S. Fleischer, pp. 51–72. São Paulo: Paz e Terra.

———. 2007. "Becoming Brazucas: Brazilian Identity in the United States." In *The Other Latinos: Central and South Americans in the United States*, edited by J. L. Falconi and J. A. Mazzotti, Chapter 10. Cambridge, Mass.: Harvard University Press.

Marrow, Helen. 2003. "To Be or Not to Be (Hispanic or Latino): Brazilian Racial and Ethnic Identity in the United States." *Ethnicities* 3(4): 427–64.

———. 2011. *New Destination Dreaming: Immigration, Race, and Legal Status in the Rural American South*. Palo Alto, Calif.: Stanford University Press.

Marteleto, Letícia J. 2012. "Educational Inequality by Race in Brazil: 1982–2007: Structural Changes and Shifts in Racial Classification." *Demography* 49(1): 337–58.

Martes, Ana Cristina Braga. 2000. *Brasileiros nos Estados Unidos: Um Estudo Sobre Imigrantes em Massachusetts*. São Paulo: Paz e Terra.

———. 2007. "Neither Hispanic, nor Black: 'We're Brazilian.'" In *The Other Latinos: Central and South Americans in the United States*, edited by J. L. Falconi and J. A. Mazzotti, pp. 231–56. Cambridge, Mass.: Harvard University Press.

———. 2008. "The Commitment of Return: Remittances of Brazilian Emigrés." In *Becoming Brazuca: Brazilian Immigration to the United States*, edited by C. Jouet-Pastre and L. J. Braga, pp. 125–50. Cambridge, Mass.: Harvard University Press.

Martes, Ana Cristina Braga, and Soraya Fleischer, eds. 2003. *Fronteiras Cruzadas: Etnicidade, Gênero e Redes Sociais*. São Paulo: Paz e Terra.

Marx, Anthony. 1998. *Making Race and Nation: A Comparison of the United States, South Africa, and Brazil*. New York: Cambridge University Press.

Massey, Douglas, and Nancy Denton. 1993. *American Apartheid*. Cambridge, Mass.: Harvard University Press.

———. 2007. *Categorically Unequal: The American Stratification System*. New York: Russell Sage Foundation.

McClain, Paula D., Gerald F. Lackey, Efrén O. Pérez, Niambi M. Carter, Jessica Johnson Carew, Eugene Walton, Candace Watts Smith, Monique L. Lyle, and Shayla C. Nunally. 2011. "Intergroup Relations in Three Southern Cities." In *Just Neighbors?: Research on African American and Latino Relations in the United States*, edited by E. Telles, M. Sawyer, and G. Rivera-Salgado, pp. 201–40. New York: Russell Sage Foundation.

McDermott, Monica. 2011. "Black Attitudes and Hispanic Immigrants in South Carolina." In *Just Neighbors? Research on African American and Latino Relations in the United States*, edited by E. Telles, M. Sawyer, and G. Rivera-Salgado, pp. 242–65. New York: Russell Sage Foundation.

McDonnell, Judith, and Cileine De Lourenco. 2008. "Brazilian Immigrant Women: Race, Ethnicity, Gender, and Transnationalism." In *Becoming Brazuca: Brazilian Immigration to the United States*, edited by C. Jouet-Pastre and L. J. Braga, pp. 151–73. Cambridge, Mass.: Harvard University Press.

———. 2009. "You're Brazilian, Right? What Kind of Brazilian Are You? The Racialization of Brazilian Immigrant Women." *Ethnic and Racial Studies* 32(2): 239–56.

McKee, James B. 1993. *Sociology and the Race Problem: The Failure of Perspective*. Urbana: University of Illinois Press.

McMurtrie, Beth. 2012. "China Continues to Drive Foreign-Student Growth in the United States." *Chronicle of Higher Education* (November 12).

Meeus, Wim. 1996. "Studies on Identity Development in Adolescence: An Overview of Research and Some New Data." *Journal of Youth and Adolescence* 25(5): 569–98.

Melo, Margareth Maria de. 2012. "Identidades Negras Entrelaçadas no Curso de Pedagogia." *Revista da ABPN* 4(8): 156–69.

Mercer, Kobena. 1987. "Black Hair/Style Politics." *New Formations* 3(winter): 33–54.

Minority Rights Group, eds. 1995. *No Longer Invisible: Afro-Latin Americans Today.* London: Minority Rights Publications.

Mitchell, Christopher 2003. "Perspectiva Comparada sobre Transnacionalismo entre Imigrantes Brasileiros nos Estados Unidos." In *Fronteiras Cruzadas: Etnicidade, Gênero, e Redes Sociais,* edited by A. C. B. Martes and S. Fleischer, pp. 33–50. São Paulo: Paz e Terra.

Model, Suzanne. 1995. "West Indian Prosperity: Fact or Fiction?" *Social Problems* 42(4): 535–53.

Monk, Ellis. 2013. "Color, Bodily Capital, and Ethnoracial Division in the United States and Brazil." PhD diss., Department of Sociology, University of California at Berkeley.

Monteiro, Simone, and Livio Sansone. 2004. *Etnicidade na América Latina: Um Debate sobre Raça, Saúde e Direitos Reprodutivos.* Rio de Janeiro: Ed. Fiocruz.

Mora, G. Cristina. 2014. *Making Hispanics: How Activists, Bureaucrats, and Media Constructed a New American.* Chicago: University of Chicago Press.

Morais, Maria da Piedade, Bruno de Oliveira Cruz, and Carlos Wagner de Albuquerque Oliveira. 2003. "Residential Segregation and Social Exclusion in Brazilian Housing Markets." *Texto para Discussão* 951(April): 1–39.

Morning, Ann. 2009. "Toward a Sociology of Racial Conceptualization for the 21st Century." *Social Forces* 87(3): 1167–92.

Morris, Aldon. 2014. *The Scholar Denied: W. E .B. Du Bois and the Birth of American Sociology.* Berkeley: University of California Press.

Mortimer, Jeylan T., and Roberta G. Simmons. 1978. "Adult Socialization." *Annual Review of Sociology* 4: 421–54.

Munanga, Kabengele. 2004. *Rediscutindo a Mestiçagem no Brasil: Identidade Nacional Versus Identidade Negra.* Belo Horizonte, Brazil: Autêntica.

Murguia, Edward, and Rogelio Saenz. 2002. "An Analysis of the Latin Americanization of Race in the United States: A Reconnaissance of Color Stratification among Mexicans." *Race and Society* 5(1): 85–101.

Myrdal, Gunnar. 1944. *American Dilemma: The Negro Problem and Modern Democracy.* New York: Harper and Row.

Nagel, Joane. 1994. "Constructing Ethnicity: Creating and Recreating Ethnic Identity and Culture." *Social Problems* 41(1): 152–76.

Nee, Victor, and Jimmy M. Sanders. 2001. "Understanding the Diversity of Immigrant Incorporation: A Forms-of-Capital Model." *Ethnic and Racial Studies* 24(3): 386–411.

Nobles, Melissa. 2000. *Shades of Citizenship: Race and the Census in Modern Politics.* Palo Alto, Calif.: Stanford University Press.

Nogueira, Oracy. 1955. *Tanto Preto, Quanto Branco: Estudo de Relações Raciais.* São Paulo: EDUSP.

Oboler, Suzanne. 1995. *Ethnic Labels, Latino Lives: Identity and the Politics of (Re)Presentation in the United States.* Minneapolis: University of Minnesota Press.

Oboler, Suzanne, and Anani Dzidzienyo. 2005. "Flows and Counterflows: Latinas/os, Blackness, and Racialization in Hemispheric Perspective." In *Neither Enemies nor*

Friends: Latinos, Blacks, Afro-Latinos, edited by A. Dzidzienyo and S. Oboler, pp. 3–35. New York: Palgrave.

O'Donoghue, Margaret. 2004. "Racial and Ethnic Identity Development in White Mothers of Biracial, Black-White Children." *Affilia* 19(1): 68–84.

Oliveira, Lucia Elena, Rosa Maria Porcaro, and Tereza Cristina Araújo Costa. 1985. *O Lugar do Negro na Força de Trabalho*. Rio de Janeiro: IBGE.

Omi, Michael, and Howard Winant. 1994. *Racial Formation in the United States: From the 1960s to the 1990s*. New York: Routledge.

Orellana, Marjorie Faulstich, Barrie Thorne, Anna Chee, and Wan Shun Eva Lam. 2001. "Transnational Childhoods: The Participation of Children in Processes of Family Migration." *Social Problems* 48(4): 572–91.

Osuji, Chinyere. 2013. "Confronting Whitening in an Era of Black Consciousness: Racial Ideology and Black-White Interracial Marriages in Rio de Janeiro." *Ethnic and Racial Studies* 36(10): 1490–1506.

Padgett, Tim, and Andrew Downie. 2009. "The One Country That Might Avoid Recession Is . . . " *Time Magazine*, March 5.

Pager, Devah, and Hana Shepherd. 2008. "The Sociology of Discrimination: Racial Discrimination in Employment, Housing, Credit, and Consumer Markets." *Annual Review of Sociology* 34: 181–209.

Paim, Altair dos Santos, and Marcos Emanoel Pereira. 2010. "Estereótipos, Boa Aparência, e a Secretária Executiva." *Passo Fundo* 6: 29–40.

Parks, Gregory, and Matthew Hughey. 2011. *The Obamas and a (Post) Racial America?* New York: Oxford University Press.

Paschel, Tianna S., and Mark Sawyer. 2008. "Contesting Politics as Usual: Black Social Movements, Globalization, and Race Policy in Latin America." *SOULS Interdisciplinary Journal of Black Politics, Society and Culture* 10(3): 197–214.

Passell, Jeffrey S., and D. Cohn. 2009. "Mexican Immigrants: How Many Come? How Many Leave?" Pew Hispanic Center, Washington, D.C. http://pewhispanic.org/reports/report. php?ReportID=112.

Pastore, José, and Nelson do Valle Silva. 2000. *Mobilidade Social no Brasil*. São Paulo: Makron Books.

Patton, Tracy Owens. 2006. "Hey Girl, Am I More Than My Hair? African American Women and Their Struggles with Beauty, Body Image, and Hair." *NWSA Journal* 18(2): 24–51.

Pedraza, Silvia. 1991. "Women and Migration: The Social Consequences of Gender." *Annual Review of Sociology* 17: 303–25.

———. 2005. "Assimilation or Transnationalism? Conceptual Models of the Immigrant Experience." In *Cultural Psychology of Immigrants*, edited by R. Mahalingham, pp. 419–27. Mahwah, N.J.: Lawrence Erlbaum.

Pedraza, Silvia, and Rubén G. Rumbaut. 1996. *Origins and Destinies: Immigration, Race, and Ethnicity in America*. Belmont, Calif.: Wadsworth.

Perry, Pamela. 2002. *Shades of White: White Kids and Racial Identities in High School*. Durham, N.C.: Duke University Press.

Petrucelli, José Luis. 2001. "Seletividade por Cor e Escolhas Conjugais no Brasil dos 90." *Estudos Afro-Asiaticos* 23(1): 29–51.

Phillips, Joan, and Robert Potter. 2005. "Incorporating Race and Gender into Caribbean Return Migration: The Example of Second-Generation "Bajan-Brits." In *The Experience of Return Migration: Caribbean Perspectives*, edited by R. B. Potter, D. Conway, and J. Phillips, pp. 69–88. Aldershot, U.K., and Burlington, Vt.: Ashgate.

Phinney, Jean S. 1992. "The Multigroup Ethnic Identity Measure: A New Scale for Use with Diverse Groups." *Journal of Adolescent Research* 7(2): 156–72.

Phinney, Jean S., and Mukosolu Onwughalu. 1996. "Racial Identity and Perception of American Ideals among African American and African Students in the United States." *International Journal of Intercultural Relations* 20(2): 127–40.

Pierson, Donald. 1967. *Negroes in Brazil: A Study of Race Contact at Bahia.* Carbondale, Ill.: Southern Illinois University Press.

Piza, Edith, and Fulvia Rosemberg. 1999. "Color in the Brazilian Census." In *From Indifference to Inequality: Race in Contemporary Brazil,* edited by R. Reichmann, pp. 37–51. University Park: Pennsylvania State University Press.

Plaza, Dwayne, and Frances Henry. 2006. *Returning to the Source: The Final Stage of the Caribbean Migration Circuit.* Mona, Jamaica: University of West Indies Press.

Portes, Alejandro, and Rubén Rumbaut. 1996. *Immigrant America: A Portrait.* Berkeley: University of California Press.

Portes, Alejandro, and Min Zhou. 1993. "The New Second Generation: Segmented Assimilation and Its Variants." *Annals of the American Academy of Political and Social Science* 530(1): 74–96.

Potter, Robert, Dennis Conway, and Joan Phillips. 2005. *The Experience of Return Migration: Caribbean Perspectives.* Burlington, Vt.: Ashgate.

Prewitt, Kenneth. 2005. "Racial Classification in America: Where Do We Go from Here?" *Daedalus* 134(1): 5–17.

Proshansky, Harold M., Abbe K. Fabian, and Robert Kaminoff. 1983. "Place-Identity: Physical World Socialization of the Self." *Journal of Environmental Psychology* 3: 57–83.

Pulido, Laura. 2007. "A Day without Immigrants: The Racial and Class Politics of Immigrant Exclusion." *Antipode* 39: 1–7.

Qian, Zhenchao. 2004. "Options: Racial/Ethnic Identification of Children of Intermarried Couples." *Social Science Quarterly* 85(3): 746–66.

Qian, Zhenchao, and Daniel T. Lichter. 2007. "Social Boundaries and Marital Assimilation: Interpreting Trends in Racial and Ethnic Intermarriage." *American Sociological Review* 72(1): 68–94.

Quintana, Stephen M. 2007. "Racial and Ethnic Identity: Developmental Perspectives and Research." *Journal of Counseling Psychology* 54(3): 259–70.

Rapoport, Hillel, and Frédéric Docquier. 2005. "The Economics of Migrants' Remittances." IZA Discussion Paper no. 1531. Social Science Research Network, March. Available at SSRN: http://ssrn.com/abstract=690144.

Racusen, Seth. 2010. "Opportunities and Challenges for the Afro-Brazilian Movement." In *Brazil's New Racial Politics,* edited by B. Reiter and G. Mitchell, pp.127–47. Boulder, Colo.: Lynne Rienner.

Reis, Ellem Saraiva, and José de Renó Machado. 2008. "Imigração, Risco e Família. Novas Configurações Familiares e Direitos Humanos em Governador Valadares." *Revista Interdisciplinar da Mobilidade Humana* 16(31): 229–37.

Reis, Fabio. 1996. "Mito e Valor da Democracia Racial." In *Multiculturalismo e Racismo: O Papel da Ação Afirmativa nos Estados Democráticas Contemporâneos,* edited by J. Souza, pp. 221–32. Brasília: Ministério da Justiça.

Reis, Rossana, and Teresa Sales. 1999. *Cenas do Brasil Migrante.* São Paulo: Boitempo.

Reiter, Bernd, and Gladys L. Mitchell, eds. 2010. *Brazil's New Racial Politics.* Boulder, Colo.: Lynne Rienner.

Relph, Edward. 1976. *Place and Placelessness*. London: Pion Limited.

Rendall, Michael S., Peter Brownell, and Sarah Kups. 2010. "Declining Return Migration from the United States to Mexico in the Late-2000s Recession." Labor and Population Series Report WR-720–1, February. Santa Monica: RAND.

Rezende, Claudia Barcellos, and Marcia Lima. 2004. "Linking Gender, Class, and Race in Brazil." *Social Identities* 10(6): 757–73.

Ribeiro, Carlos, Antonio Costa, and Nelson Do Valle Silva. 2009. "Cor, Educação e Casamento: Tendências da Seletividade Marital no Brasil, 1960 a 2000." *DADOS: Revista de Ciências Sociais* 52(1): 7–51.

Ríos, Merarys, Fabián Romero, and Roberto Ramírez. 2014. "Race Reporting among Hispanics: 2010." Population Division Working Paper No. 102. Washington: U.S. Census Bureau. http://www.census.gov/population/www/documentation/twps0102/twps0102.pdf.

Rivera-Salgado, Gaspar. 2003. "Transnational Political Strategies: The Case of Mexican Indigenous Migrants." In *Immigration Research for a New Century: Multidisciplinary Perspectives*, edited by N. Foner, R. Rumbaut, and S. J. Gold, pp. 134–55. New York: Russell Sage Foundation.

Rivero, Yeidy M. 2002. "Erasing Blackness: The Media Construction of 'Race' in Mi Familia, the First Puerto Rican Situation Comedy with a Black Family." *Media Culture Society* 24(4): 481–97.

Rockquemore, Kerry Ann. 2002. "Negotiating The Color Line: The Gendered Process of Racial Identity Construction among Black/White Biracial Women." *Gender and Society* 16(4): 485–503.

Rockquemore, Kerry Ann, and Patricia Arend. 2002. "Opting for White: Choice, Fluidity and Racial Identity Construction in Post Civil-Rights America." *Race and Society* 5: 49–64.

Rodriguez, Clara. 2000. *Changing Race: Latinos, the Census and the History of Ethnicity*. New York: New York University Press.

Roediger, David R. 2005. *Working Toward Whiteness: How America's Immigrants Became White: The Strange Journey from Ellis Island to the Suburbs*. New York: Basic Books.

Rogers, Reuel. 2001. ""Black Like Who?" Afro-Caribbean Immigrants, African Americans and the Politics of Group Identity." In *Islands in the City: West Indian Migration to New York*, edited by N. Foner. Berkeley: University of California Press.

———. 2004. "Race-Based Coalitions among Minority Groups Afro-Caribbean Immigrants and African-Americans in New York City." *Urban Affairs Review* 39(3): 283–317.

Romero, Simon. 2011. "Foreigners Follow Money to Booming Brazil, Land of $35 Martini." *New York Times*, August 13.

Roth, Wendy. 2012. *Race Migrations: Latinos and the Cultural Transformation of Race*. Palo Alto, Calif.: Stanford University Press.

Rohter, Larry. 2005. "Brazilians Streaming into United States through Mexican Border." *New York Times*, June 30.

Rutherford, Paul. 2004. *Weapons of Mass Persuasion: Marketing the War against Iraq*. Toronto: University of Toronto Press.

Sakamoto, Arthur, Hyeyoung Woo, and Chang Hwan Kim. 2010. "Does an Immigrant Background Ameliorate Racial Disadvantage? The Socioeconomic Attainments of Second-Generation African Americans." *Sociological Forum* 25(1): 123–46.

Sales, Teresa. 1999. *Brasileiros Longe De Casa*. São Paulo: Cortez Editora Ltda.

Sansone, Livio. 2003. *Negritude sem Ethnicidade: O Local e O Global Nas Relações Raciais e Na Produção Cultural Negra do Brasil.* Salvador/Rio de Janeiro: Edufba/Pallas.

Santos, Gevanilda, and Maria Palmira da Silva, eds. 2005. *Racismo no Brasil: Percepções da Discriminação e do Preconceito Racial no Século XXI.* São Paulo: Editora Fundação Perseu Abramo.

Sasaki, Elisa Massae. 1999. "Movimento Dekassegui: A Experiência Migratória e Identitária dos Brasileiros Descendentes de Japoneses no Japão." In *Cenas do Brasil Migrante,* edited by R. Reis and T. Sales. São Paulo: Boitempo Editoral.

Schildkraut, Deborah. 2005. "The Rise and Fall of Political Engagement among Latinos: The Role of Identity and Perceptions of Discrimination." *Political Behavior* 27(3): 285–312.

Schlegel, Alice. 1998. "A Cross-Cultural Approach to Adolescence." In *Adolescent Behavior and Society: A Book of Readings,* vol. 5, edited by R. E. Muus and H. D. Porton. Boston: McGraw-Hill College.

Schuman, Howard, Charlotte Steeh, Lawrence D. Bobo, and Maria Krysan. 1997. *Racial Attitudes in American: Trends and Interpretations.* Cambridge, Mass.: Harvard University Press.

Schwalbe, Michael L. and David L. Morgan. 1990. "Mind and Self in Society: Linking Social Structure and Social Cognition." *Social Psychology Quarterly* 53(2): 148–64.

Schwarcz, Lilia Moritz. 1999. *The Spectacle of Races: Scientists, Institutions, and the Race Question in Brazil,1870–1930.* Translated by L. Guyer. New York: Hill and Wang.

Schwartzman, Luisa Farah. 2007. "Does Money Whiten? Intergenerational Changes in Racial Classification in Brazil." *American Sociological Review* 72(6): 940–63.

Segatto, Cristiane, and Suzane Frutuoso. 2006. "Beleza Brasileira: Como O Brasil Se Tornou Referência Mundial Na Área de Cirugia Plástica—E O Que Isso Significa." *Revista Época* 440: 70–77.

Segura, Gary, and Shaun Bowler. 2011. *The Future Is Ours: Minority Politics, Political Behavior, and the Multiracial Era of American Politics.* Washington, D.C.: CQ Press College.

Sellers, Robert M., Mia A. Smith, J. Nicole Shelton, Stephanie A. J. Rowley, and Tabbye M. Chavous. 1998. "Multidimensional Model of Racial Identity: A Reconceptualization of African American Racial Identity." *Personality and Social Psychology Review* 2(1): 18–39.

Shannon, Thomas Jr.. 2012. "Brazil's Strategic Leap Forward." *Americas Quarterly* (Fall). Available at http://www.americasquarterly.org/Brazils-Strategic-Leap-Forward.

Shapiro, Thomas M. 2004. *The Hidden Cost of Being African American: How Wealth Perpetuates Inequality.* New York: Oxford University Press.

Sharman, Russell Leigh. 2001. "The Caribbean Carretera: Race, Space, and Social Liminality in Costa Rica." *Bulletin of Latin American Research* 20(1): 46–62.

Sheriff, Robin. 2001. *Dreaming Equality: Color, Race, and Racism in Urban Brazil.* New Brunswick, N.J.: Rutgers University Press.

Silva, Denise Ferreira da. 1996. "Morenidade: Modo de Usar." *Estudos Afro-Asiaticos* 30: 79–98.

Silva, Graziella Morães D. 2012. "Folk Conceptualizations of Racism and Antiracism in Brazil and South Africa." *Ethnic and Racial Studies* 35(3): 506–22.

Silva, Graziella Morães D., and Elisa P. Reis. 2012. "The Multiple Dimensions of Racial Mixture in Rio de Janeiro, Brazil: From Whitening to Brazilian Negritude." *Ethnic and Racial Studies* 35(3): 382–99.

Siqueira, Carlos Eduardo, and Tiago Jansen. 2008. "Updating Demographic, Geographic, and Occupational Data on Brazilians in Massachusetts." In *Becoming Brazuca: Bra-zilian Immigration to the United States*, edited by C. Jouet-Pastre and L. J. Braga, pp. 105–24. Cambridge, Mass.: Harvard University.

Siqueira, Sueli. 2008. "Emigrants from Governador Valadares: Projects of Return and In-vestment." In *Becoming Brazuca: Brazilian Immigration to the United States*, edited by C. Jouet-Pastre and L. J. Braga, pp. 175–94. Cambridge, Mass.: Harvard University.

———. 2009a. "A Crise Econômica nos EUA e o Retorno à Terra Natal." Paper pre-sented at annual meeting of the Latin American Studies Association, Rio de Janeiro, Brazil, June 11–14.

———. 2009b. *Sonhos, Successo, e Frustações na Emigração de Retorno: Brasil/ Estados Uni-dos*. Belo Horizonte, Brazil: Argvmentvm Editora.

Siqueira, Sueli, Emerson César DeCampos, and Gláucia de Oliveira Assis. 2010. "Do Local para Global: Configuração de Laços Transnacionais entre Brasil e os EUA." Paper presented at annual meeting of the Latin American Studies Association, To-ronto, October 8.

Skidmore, Thomas. 1990. "Racial Ideas and Social Policy in Brazil, 1870–1940." In *The Idea of Race in Latin America 1870–1940*, edited by R. Graham, pp. 7–36. Austin: Uni-versity of Texas Press.

———. 1993. *Black into White: Race and Nationality in Brazilian Thought*. Durham, N.C.: Duke University Press.

———. 2003. "Racial Mixture and Affirmative Action: The Cases of Brazil and the United States." *American Historical Review* 108(5): 1391–96.

Snipp, C. Matthew. 2003. "Racial Measurement in the American Census: Past Practices and Implications for the Future." *Annual Review of Sociology* 29: 563–88.

Soares, Weber. 2002. "Da Metáfora à Substáncia: Redes Sociais, Redes Migratórias eMi-gração Nacional e Internacional em Valadares e Ipatinga." PhD diss., Universidade Federal de Minas Gerais, CEDEPLAR, Belo Horizonte, Brazil.

Souza, Jessé. 2005. "Raça ou Classe? Sobre a Desigualdade Brasileira." *Lua Nova* 65: 43–69.

Stevenson, Howard C. 1995. "Relationship of Adolescent Perceptions of Racial Socializa-tion to Racial Identity." *Journal of Black Psychology* 21(1): 49–70.

Stryker, Sheldon, and Richard T. Serpe. 1994. "Identity Salience and Psychological Cen-trality: Equivalent, Overlapping, or Complementary Concepts?" *Social Psychology Quarterly* 57(1): 16–35.

Suarez-Orozco, Carola, and Irina Todorova. 2003. "The Social Worlds of Immigrant Youth." *New Directions for Youth Development* 100: 15–24.

Takenaka, Ayumi. 2000. "Transnational Community and Its Ethnic Consequences: The Return Migration and the Transformation of Ethnicity of Japanese Peruvians." In *Im-migration Research for a New Century: Multidisciplinary Perspectives*, edited by Nancy Foner, Ruben G. Rumbaut, and Steven J. Gold, pp. 442–57. New York: Russell Sage Foundation.

Tannenbaum, Frank. 1947. *Slave and Citizen: The Negro in the Americas*. New York: Vin-tage Books.

Telles, Edward E. 2002. "Racial Ambiguity among the Brazilian Population." *Ethnic and Racial Studies* 25(3): 415–41.

———. 2004. *Race in Another America: The Significance of Skin Color in Brazil*. Princ-eton, N.J.: Princeton University Press.

Telles, Edward E., and Stanley R. Bailey. 2013. "Understanding Latin American Beliefs about Racial Inequality." *American Journal of Sociology* 118(6): 1559–95.

Telles, Edward E., and Project on Ethnicity and Race in Latin America (PERLA). 2014. *Pigmentocracies: Ethnicity, Race, and Color in Latin America.* Chapel Hill: University of North Carolina Press.

Tomlinson, John. 1999. *Globalization and Culture.* Chicago: University of Chicago Press.

Travassos, Claudia and David Williams. 2004. "O Conceito e Mensuração de Raça em Relação à Saúde Pública no Brasil e nos Estados Unidos." *Caderno de Saúde Pública* 20(3): 660–78.

Treitler, Vilna Bashi. 2013. *The Ethnic Project: Transforming Racial Fiction into Ethnic Factions.* Palo Alto, Calif: Stanford University Press.

Tsuda, Takeyuki. 2009a. *Diasporic Homecomings: Ethnic Return Migration in Comparative Perspective.* Palo Alto, Calif: Stanford University Press.

———. 2009b. "Global Inequities and Diasporic Return: Japanese Americans and Brazilian Encounters with the Ethnic Homeland." In *Diasporic Homecomings: Ethnic Relations in Comparative Perspective,* edited by T. Tsuda, pp. 227–59. Palo Alto, Calif: Stanford University Press.

Tufte, Thomas. 2000. *Living with the Rubbish Queen.* Luton, U.K.: University of Luton Press.

Turner, John C., Penelope J. Oakes, S. Alexander Haslam, and Craig McGarty. 1994. "Self and Collective: Cognition and Social Context." *Personality and Social Psychology Bulletin* 20(5): 454–63.

Trivellato, Ugo. 1999. "Issues in the Design and Analysis of Panel Studies: A Cursory Review." *Quality and Quantity* 33(3): 339–52.

Twine, France Winddance 1998. *Racism in a Racial Democracy: The Maintenance of White Supremacy in Brazil.* New Brunswick, N.J.: Rutgers University.

Ungar, Sheldon. 2008. "Ignorance as an Under-Identified Social Problem." *British Journal of Sociology* 59(2): 301–26.

Van den Berghe, Pierre. 1978. *Race and Racism: A Comparative Perspective.* New York: Wiley.

Verba, Sidney, Kay Lehman Schlozman, and Norman H. Nie. 1993. "Race, Ethnicity and Political Resources: Participation in the United States." *British Journal of Political Science* 23(4): 453–97.

Vickerman, Milton. 1994. "The Response of West Indians to African Americans: Distancing and Identification." In *Research in Race and Ethnic Relations,* edited by R. Dennis, pp.83–128. Greenwich, Conn.: JAI Press.

———. 1999. *Crosscurrents: West Indian Immigrants and Race.* New York: Oxford University Press.

———. 2007. "Recent Immigration and Race: Continuity and Change." *Du Bois Review* 4(1): 141–65.

Vidal-Ortiz, Salvador. 2004. "On Being a White Person of Color: Using Autoethnography to Understand Puerto Ricans' Racialization." *Qualitative Sociology* 27(2): 179–203.

Wade, Peter. 1996. *Race and Ethnicity in Latin America.* London: Pluto Press.

Wagley, Charles. 1952. "Race Relations in an Amazon Community." In *Race and Class in Rural Brazil,* edited by C. Wagley, Chapter 7. Paris: UNESCO.

Wang, Hongyu, and Grace Kao. 2007. "Does Higher Socioeconomic Status Increase

Contact between Minorities and Whites? An Examination of Interracial Relationships among Adolescents." *Social Science Quarterly* 88(1): 146–64.

Waters, Mary. 1999. *Black Identities: West-Indian Immigrant Dreams and American Realities.* New York: Russell Sage Foundation.

Wellman, Barry. 2007. "Challenges in Collecting Personal Network Data: The Nature of
Personal Network Analysis." *Field Methods* 19(2): 111–15.

Whitefield, Mimi. 2012. "Day When Brazilians Can Travel to the United States without a
Visa May Be Getting Closer." *Miami Herald,* July 20.

Williams, David R., James S. Jackson, Hector M. González, Harold Neighbors, Randolph
Nesse, Jamie M. Abelson, and Julie Sweetman. 2007. "Prevalence and Distribution of
Major Depressive Disorder in African Americans, Caribbean Blacks, and Non-His-
panic Whites." *Archives of General Psychiatry* 64(3): 305–15.

Wise, Tim. 2013. *Colorblind: The Rise of Post-Racial Politics and the Retreat from Racial Eq-
uity.* San Francisco, Calif.: City Lights Books.

Wolcott, Harry F. 1994. *Transforming Qualitative Data: Description, Analysis, and Interpretation.* Thousand Oaks, Calif.: Sage.

Xavier, Elton, and Solange Xavier. 2009. "Políticas de Ação Afirmativa e Relações Raciais
no Brasil e nos Estados Unidos." *Desenvolvimento em Questão* 7(14): 43–87.

Zamora, Sylvia. 2014. "Transnational Racialization: How Migration Shapes Mexicans'
Conceptions of Race in Home and Host Societies." PhD diss., University of California at Los Angeles.

INDEX

Locators in italics indicate pages with figures, maps, photos, or tables.

Stanford Studies in
COMPARATIVE RACE AND ETHNICITY

Published in collaboration with the Center for Comparative Studies in Race and Ethnicity, Stanford University

SERIES EDITORS
>Hazel Rose Markus
>Paula M.L. Moya

EDITORIAL BOARD
>H. Samy Alim
>Gordon Chang
>Gary Segura
>C. Matthew Snipp

This series publishes outstanding scholarship that focuses centrally on comparative studies of race and ethnicity. Rather than exploring the experiences and conditions of a single racial or ethnic group, this series looks across racial and ethnic groups to take a more complex, dynamic, and interactive approach to understanding these social categories.

The Ethnic Project: Transforming Racial Fiction into Racial Factions
Vilna Bashi Treitler
2013

On Making Sense: Queer Race Narratives of Intelligibility
Ernesto Javier Martínez
2012